De

Authors of Books for Young People

by

Martha E. Ward
and
Dorothy A. Marquardt

The Scarecrow Press, Inc.
New York & London 1964

L. C. Card no. 64-21970

Preface

Authors of Books for Young People includes 1030 biographies. The following factors were considered in determining the authors to be included:

(1) This book has been based on biographical information compiled in the Children's Department of the Free Public Library, Quincy, Illinois. Frequently the decision to include an author was based on the number of times that this particular biography was requested by a student. Although the "author file" was used by students of all ages, the majority of requests came from boys and girls who were between the ages of twelve to fourteen.

(2) Any contemporary author whose biography proved difficult to locate was given preference for inclusion over a well-known author whose biographical information was more readily available.

(3) All recipients of the Newbery (1922-1964) and Caldecott (1938-1964) Medals have been included. The Newbery Medal is given "to the author of the most distinguished contribution to American literature for children." The Caldecott Medal is awarded "to the artist of the most distinguished American picture book for children."

The symbols which follow the biographies refer to volumes in which additional author information can be found.

Key to Symbols:

CA 1-6	Contemporary Authors, Vols. 1-6. James M. Ethridge, ed. (c. 1963) Gale Research Company

JBA-1	Junior Book of Authors, The. Stanley J. Kunitz and Howard Haycraft, eds. (c. 1934) The H. W. Wilson Company
JBA-2	Junior Book of Authors, The. Stanley J. Kunitz and Howard Haycraft, eds. (2nd ed., rev., 1951) The H. W. Wilson Company
MJA	More Junior Authors. Muriel Fuller, ed. (c. 1963) The H. W. Wilson Company

We are grateful to the many children's book editors who supplied additional information upon our request.

Martha E. Ward
Dorothy A. Marquardt

Authors of Books for Young People

ADLER, Irving 1913- and Ruth
Known for books of science and mathematics. Both have taught at Bennington College. Dr. Adler has been a mathematics instructor at Columbia University and former head of mathematics of a high school in New York. Ruth Adler taught art and science in the New York school system. She illustrated Electronics, How Life Began, Magic House of Numbers. Mr. and Mrs. Adler lived in the country near Bennington, Vermont. They have written: The Earth's Crust, Insects and Plants, Oceans.

AGLE, Nan Hayden 1905-
Author and teacher, born in Catonsville, Maryland. Many of her books have had historical backgrounds since Mrs. Agle has always been interested in history. She has taught art in Baltimore at the Friends School. Mrs. Agle wrote Makon and the Dauphin. Also, she has co-authored Three Boys and a Helicopter, Three Boys and a Lighthouse, Three Boys and Space, etc. CA-4

ALDIS, Dorothy (Keeley) 1896-
Born in Chicago, Illinois, the daughter of newspaperman James Keeley. She married Graham Aldis, and has lived in Lake Forest, Illinois. She has been on the staff of a Chicago newspaper, and has written many books and volumes of verse for young people. Children have enjoyed Mrs. Aldis' poems because they are about familiar situations, things, and places. Juvenile titles include: All Together; A Child's Treasury of Verse, Boy Who Cared, Everything and Anything, Hello Day, Jane's Father, Lucky Year. CA-3, JBA-2.

ALEXANDER, Anne
Born in Shanghai, China, Mrs. Alexander became an American citizen and lived in Burlingame, California. As a teacher at the College of San Mateo and Menlo High, she has contributed children's stories to magazines. Among her books are: ABC of Cars, Boats and Ships from A to Z, I Want to Whistle.

ALLAN, Mabel Esther
Ardent traveler and full-time author. Many of her books include some of her actual travel experiences. Born and educated in England, Miss Allan traveled extensively in Great Britain, Europe, and has made two trips to the United States enjoying its warmth and beauty. Her works include: Black Forest Summer, Catrin in Wales, Strangers in Skye.

ALLEN, Merritt P. 1892-1954
Born July 2, 1892, he lived in Bristol, Vermont and died December 26, 1954. Enthusiastic research into his country's past, enabled Mr. Allen to write books of adventure with warmth and understanding. Among books contributed to the young reader are: Battle Lanterns, Green Cockade, Johnny Reb, Blow, Bugles, Blow. JBA-2

ALTSHELER, Joseph A. 1862-1919
Born in Kentucky, he attended Liberty College in Glasgow, Kentucky, and Vanderbilt University in Nashville, Tennessee. He was a reporter, newspaper correspondent, and an editor of the magazine edition of the New York World. He married Sarah Boles, and they lived in New York City until his death in 1919. Juvenile contributions include: Apache Gold; A Story of the Strange Southwest, The Guns of Bull Run; A Story of the Civil War's Eve, Horseman of the Plains; A Story of the Great Cheyenne War, Hunters of the Hills; A Story of the Great French and Indian Wars. JBA-1

ANCKARSVARD, Karin 1918-
Psychologist and writer, Mrs. Anckarsvard was a na-

tive of Stockholm. Educated in Sweden, she also attended Oxford for a year. When she married, her schooling came to an end, but she continued her storytelling and writing which include: Aunt Vinnie's Invasion, Bonifacius the Green, Madcap Mystery.

ANDERSEN, Hans Christian 1805-1875
This master storyteller was born in the fishing village of Odense, near the coast of Denmark. When he was fourteen years old, he traveled to Copenhagen where he later met Chancellor Jonas Collin, a director of the Royal Theater. Through Mr. Collin's efforts, Hans Andersen attended school, and at the age of twenty-three, he passed the entrance examinations to Copenhagen University. The village of Odense has been illuminated in his honor, and the house where he was born has become a museum. Juvenile contributions include: Andersen's Fairy Tales, The Little Mermaid, Snow Queen. JBA-1, JBA-2.

ANDERSON, Clarence W. 1891-
A native of Nebraska, Mr. Anderson studied in Chicago and New York. He predominated the etching and lithograph field and is a member of the American Society of Etchers. As author and illustrator his works have been displayed in most sections of this country. Fortunate collectors prize his works as great assets. He has written and illustrated books for young children as well as other ages who have a great interest in horses. Included in his works are: Billy and Blaze, Blaze and the Forest Fire, Deep Through the Heart. JBA-2.

ANDREWS, Roy Chapman 1884-
Explorer, author, scientist. He was born in Beloit, Wisconsin. He has been Director of the American Museum of Natural History in New York. Dr. Andrews has traveled throughout the world on scientific expeditions, and has been the recipient of many awards given by scientific societies. His books for young people include: All About Dinosaurs, All About Strange Beasts of the Past, In the Days of the

Dinosaurs, Quest in the Desert.

ANGELO, Valenti 1897-
He was born in Italy. When he was eight years old, he came with his family to America. He started working at an early age, and held various jobs including the position of confectioner and pastry maker in a San Francisco hotel. This experience was put to good use in writing his book, The Candy Basket. He has illustrated books for other authors (including the 1937 Newbery Medal winner, Roller Skates, by Ruth Sawyer), and has written and illustrated: Acorn Tree, Angelino and the Barefoot Saint, Marble Fountain. JBA-2

ANGLUND, Joan Walsh
Born in Hinsdale, Illinois, the daughter of artists. She studied at the Art Institute of Chicago and at the American Academy of Art. She has done advertising illustrations, but in 1947 illustrated her first book for children. Since that time, she has written and illustrated many books, including: Brave Cowboy, Christmas Is a Time of Giving, Cowboy and His Friend, Cowboy's Secret Life, Spring is a New Beginning.

ARBUTHNOT, May Hill 1884-
She received her M.A. degree from Columbia University, and her Ph.D. degree from the University of Chicago. When she taught at Western Reserve University, she founded the University Nursery School. May Hill Arbuthnot has written many articles which have been published in Elementary English Review, Childhood Education, National Education Association Journal, and Parents' Magazine. She wrote Children and Books, and compiled The Arbuthnot Anthology of Children's Literature.

ARCHIBALD, Joe 1898-
Author, lecturer, and cartoonist. He was a staff member of Flying Aces and United Features Syndicate and graduated from Chicago Academy of Fine Arts. He began his career at an early age and at

fifteen won a prize for his drawings in the Boston Post. Active in civic affairs, Mr. Archibald lived in Port Chester, New York. A free-lancer he has written many articles and stories for boys on adventure, aviation, and sports. Juvenile contributions include: Backfield Twins, Falcons to the Flight, Touchdown Glory, Windmill Pilot.

ARMER, Laura Adams 1874-
Artist-author, born in Sacramento, California. She grew up in San Francisco. She attended the California School of Design in San Francisco, where she met and married art student Sidney Armer. Laura Armer has painted canvases inspired by visits to a Navaho Reservation and produced a motion picture of a Navaho ceremonial entitled "The Mountain Chant." In 1932, she was awarded the Newbery Medal for her book, Waterless Mountain, illustrated by the author and her husband. Laura Armer has also written: Dark Circle of Branches, The Forest Pool, The Trader's Children. JBA-1, JBA-2

ARNOV, Boris Jr. 1926-
Native of Los Angeles, California, the author has lived in Hawaii and Florida. He now resides in Boca Raton. He attended Rollins College, Yale University and the Chicago School of Medicine. He wrote a weekly column on fishing and has an active interest in boats, fishing and books. He is the author of Wonders of the Ocean Zoo. CA-4

ASIMOV, Isaac 1920-
A graduate of Columbia University, has been Associate Professor of Biochemistry at Boston University School of Medicine. He is married and has two children. His zest in his work and daily living are obvious in his writing. Dr. Asimov is the author of many books among which are: David Starr, Space Ranger, The Double Planet, Inside the Atom, Realm of Numbers. CA-2

ATWATER, Montgomery Meigs 1904-
Born in Oregon, he attended schools in the East, and

has lived in the Midwest. During World War II, he served in the 87th Cavalry Reconnaissance Troop. Following the war, Mr. Atwater has served in the United States Forest Service. He has specialized in avalanche and snow problems. Juvenile contributions include: Avalanche Patrol, Cattle Dog, Government Hunter, The Ski Lodge Mystery. MJA

AUSTIN, Margot
Author-illustrator, born in Portland, Oregon. She received her education at St. Mary's Academy, University of Oregon Extension, the National Academy of Design, and the Grand Central Art School. Mrs. Austin's painter-husband has worked with the Perts Galleries of Paris, New York and Hollywood. Some of the books written by Margot Austin are: Archie Angel, Brave John Henry, Gabriel Churchkitten, Growl Bear, Peter Churchmouse, Poppet, The Three Silly Kittens, Trumpet, William's Shadow. MJA

AVERILL, Esther
Avid interest in the production of books for children led to the opening of the Domino Press of Paris. Through this media Miss Averill was the first to print Daniel Boone by Rojankovsky. She has contributed to The Horn Book and The Colophon, and has worked in the young people's branch of the New York Public Library but is devoting her entire time to writing and illustrating. Included are these: The Fire Cat, Jenny Goes to Sea, Jenny's Moonlight Adventure. JBA-2

AYRE, Robert Hugh 1900-
Author of a weekly art column, he has also been biographer, lecturer, and supervisor of the visual redesign for the Canadian National Railways. He enjoys the theater, concerts, and reading. His book Sketco, the Raven, centers around his experiences while hiking through the mountains. CA-4

B

BACON, Paul 1913-
Born in Maryland in 1913, Paul Bacon received his degree from Columbia University. The Near East was his home for many years, but his is now located in New York and California. Medical and biological articles and books have reaped the rewards of his research and editing. Mr. Bacon wrote Creating New and Better Plants: Luther Burbank.

BAILEY, Bernadine Freeman 1901-
Born in Mattoon, Illinois, graduate of Wellesley College, she received her M.A. degree from the University of Chicago. Editor and writer, she wrote about "things that did, or could, really and truly happen." She has written numerous articles for the Reader's Digest, Coronet, New York Times, Ford Times and others. Her extensive travels have provided her with a rich background for her writing. She has been a member of many organizations including the Society of Midland Authors, the National Woman's Book Association, and the Children's Reading Round Table. Included in her books are: Abraham Lincoln: Man of Courage, Carol Carson: Books Across the Border, Famous Latin-American Liberators, Forest and Fiords, Our Nation's Capital, Washington, D.C., Picture Book of Alaska. CA-5/6

BAILEY, Carolyn Sherwin 1875-
Lived in Temple, New Hampshire, graduate of Teachers College, Columbia University. She has been author, editor, story-teller, teacher. Young readers are captivated by her ability to relate a good story. Juvenile books include: Children of the Handcrafts, Enchanted Village, Finnegan II; His Nine Lives, Flickertail, Little Red Schoolhouse, Merry Christmas Book, Miss Hickory (winner of the 1947 Newbery Medal). JBA-2

BAILEY, Flora
Intensive interest in the Navaho Indians led to much research at the University of New Mexico's Field School for Miss Bailey. Teaching and activities with children urged her to transplant this knowledge of In-

dian life to the young reader. She shares actual experiences and creates interest and understanding of the Navaho in her books: Between the Four Mountains and Summer at Yellow Singer's.

BAIN, Edward Ustick
Graduate of the University of Missouri and member of the American Helicopter Society. Actual experience with aircraft and the delivery of mail by helicopter (a special project) inspired this author to tell boys and girls about helicopters. He wrote: S-O-S Helicopter.

BAKELESS, Colonel John Edwin 1894-
A veteran of thirty-five years of army service, active and reserve, and recipient of three university degrees including a Ph.D. from Harvard. He was assistant military attaché to Turkey, and was Chief of the Military Section of the American Delegation of the Allied Control Commission in Bulgaria. He is the author of The Adventures of Lewis and Clark and with Katherine Bakeless wrote Spies of the Revolution. CA-5/6

BAKER, Charlotte 1910-
Artist, teacher, and wife of Roger Montgomery, she lived in Texas and was a member of the Texas Institute of Letters. Miss Baker has traveled extensively throughout the United States, and at one time was on the staff of the Portland Art Museum. Juvenile books: ABC of Dog Care for Young Owners, The Green Poodles, The House on the River, Little Brother, Sunrise Island, Thomas, the Ship's Cat.

BAKER, Margaret Joyce 1918-
An English author born in 1918 at Reading, Berkshire, she has lived in Marlowe, a small town on the Thames near the part of the river made famous by Kenneth Grahame in The Wind in the Willows. After taking journalism at London University, and driving a mobile canteen for troops during the war, she has written adult short stories and numerous articles about children's writers for the Junior Book-

shelf. Juvenile contributions: Anna Sewell and Black Beauty, Bright High Flyer, Four Farthings and a Thimble, Homer Goes to Stratford, Homer the Tortoise. MJA

BAKER, Nina Brown 1888-1957
Born in Galena, Kansas and in 1957 died in her home in Brooklyn Heights, New York. She has taught in Colorado where she traveled to and from the school on horseback. Mrs. Baker always believed that the most interesting way to learn about a country was through the lives of its famous men. Juvenile contributions: Amerigo Vespucci, Big Catalogue: the Life of Aaron Montgomery Ward, He Wouldn't Be King; the Story of Simon Bolivar, Henry Hudson, Juan Ponce de León, Jaurez, Hero of Mexico, Nickels and Dimes; the Story of F. W. Woolworth, Pike of Pike's Peak, Sir Walter Raleigh, Story of Abraham Lincoln, Story of Christopher Columbus, Ten American Cities. JBA-2

BAKER, Rachel Mininberg 1903-
After studying at the University of Minnesota and living in Europe, Rachel Baker began her present writing career. She is one of the outstanding writers of biography in the teen age field. She attributes this interest in biography to an incident which happened when she was fourteen in Dickinson, North Dakota. She interviewed a man who was writing a book about Theodore Roosevelt. "He told me he was a biographer, and I decided that someday I would be one too." She wrote: America's First Trained Nurse, Linda Richards, and First Woman Doctor; the Story of Elizabeth Blackwell, M. D. CA-5/6, MJA.

BALCH, Glenn 1902-
A Texan, who has always loved horses. While very young he learned to ride, and later joined in roundups in West Texas and Idaho, and on cavalry drill fields. During World War II he rode on jungle trails in Burma. After his marriage he made his home in Idaho, where much of the actual background has been described in his books. His books include:

Brave Riders, Christmas Horse, Horse in Danger, Indian Fur, Lost Horse, Spotted Horse, Squaw Boy, The Stallion King, Tiger Roan, White Ruff, Wild Horse Tamer. CA-3, MJA

BALDWIN, Arthur
This author's interests are writing, sailing, and scouting. He grew up in East Orange, New Jersey and spent his summers on Long Island. He was a radio operator with the Navy in the World War and returned to live in Vermont. Juvenile books include: Junior Skipper's Handbook; A Guide to Sailing for Boys and Girls (which he also illustrated), and Sou'wester Goes North.

BALDWIN, James 1841-1925
He grew up in Indiana where he became a teacher and later, was superintendent of the Indiana elementary schools. De Pauw University conferred an honorary degree of doctor of philosophy upon him. James Baldwin served on the staff of large publishing houses for many years. He lived in South Orange, New Jersey, before his death at the age of eighty-three. Juvenile books include: John Bunyan's Dream Story; Pilgrim's Progress retold for children and adapted to school reading by James Baldwin, Hero Tales Told in School, Old Greek Stories, The Story of Roland, Story of Siegfried. JBA-1, JBA-2

BALET, Jan B. 1913-
Author-illustrator. Born in Germany, he received his education at the Arts and Crafts School in Munich and Berlin. Arriving in America after the Hitler regime arose in Germany, he acquired his American citizenship. Mr. Balet has contributed work to such magazines as Madamoiselle, Seventeen, and Vogue. He has done advertising for Macy and Saks Fifth Avenue. He has written and illustrated Amos and the Moon and What Makes An Orchestra.

BALL, Zachary 1897-
His real name is Kelly Ray Masters. He grew up along the Verdigris River in southeastern Kansas where

he devoted much time to boating, rafting, and camping. "I was still a boy when I first met Old Man River, and I got to know him well. Probably that's why a goodly portion of all my writing has had the big river for its setting." He has been an actor and musician, and has contributed many short stories to magazines. Juvenile books: Bristle Face, Kep, Wilderness Teacher, Young Mike Fink. CA-3

BANNON, Laura May ? -d. 1963
Author-illustrator. Children and adults have benefited from her books. She has done painting and sketching in the Orient, North and South America. Also, she has been director of the Junior Department at the Art Institute of Chicago. Experiences from her travels enabled Miss Bannon to write and illustrate numerous award winning books. She died December 14, 1963, in Roswell, New Mexico. Included in her children's books are: The Best House in the World, Big Brother, Burro Boy and His Big Trouble, The Famous Baby Sitter, Horse on a Houseboat, Jo-Jo, the Talking Crow, The Little Sister Doll, Red Mittens, When the Moon is New; a Seminole Indian Story. CA-3, MJA

BARBOUR, Ralph Henry 1870-1944
Known for his books on athletics. He began his career in journalism and became reporter, literary editor, columnist, cartoonist, and city editor. He was a native of Cambridge, Massachusetts. He continued to maintain an active interest in all athletics, and the men associated with them until his death in 1944. Juvenile titles include: Barclay Back, Crimson Sweater, Fighting Guard, Football Plays for Boys; With Rules and Strategies of Touch Football (with La Mar Sarra), For Safety, Goal to Go, Good Manners for Boys, How to Play Better Basketball, Mystery of the Bayou. JBA-1, JBA-2

BARNOUW, Adriaan Jacob 1877-
Born in Amsterdam, Holland, the author studied at Leiden University and Berlin University, receiving a Ph.D. in 1902. He was a teacher and lecturer at

The Hague and Leiden University. Mr. Barnouw traveled extensively and came to America in 1919. He became the associate editor of The Weekly Review. Later, he taught at Columbia University and became Emeritus Professor in 1948. He has had his portraits, landscapes, and still lifes exhibited in The Hague, New York, and Washington. He wrote: The Land and People of Holland, Land of William of Orange.

BARNUM, Jay Hyde

Born in Geneva, Ohio. He attended Cleveland Art School and later joined the Newspaper Enterprise Association's art department. He has lived in Chicago where he made fashion posters and advertising drawings for Marshall Field and attended the Art Institute at night. Also, Mr. Barnum has illustrated stories for magazines. After moving to Hastings-on-Hudson, New York, he lived near the headquarters of a volunteer fire company which location inspired him to write The New Fire Engine. He also wrote: Little Old Truck, Motorcycle Dog.

BARR, Jene 1900-

A graduate of Chicago Teachers College who has studied at Northwestern University and the University of Chicago, Jene Barr often relies on her teaching experience in the Chicago schools to furnish material and inspiration for stories. She has contributed to the Chicago Schools Journal, Junior Magazine, and Highlights for Children. Juvenile titles include: Ben's Busy Service Station, Big Wheels! Little Wheels! Dan, the Weatherman, Fast Trains! Busy Trains! Good Morning, Teacher, Miss Terry at the Library. CA-5/6

BARROWS, Marjorie

Compiler and editor, Marjorie Barrows has written a poetry anthology which ranked high among the best-sellers of the past fifty years. She was former editor of Child Life and won the Chicago Foundation for Literature award "in recognition of her notable contribution to the literary heritage of Chicago through her many years of devotion to and influence upon young readers." She wrote Read-Aloud Poems Every Young Child Should Know.

BARRY, Katharina
Born in Germany and educated in Europe. At the Kunstgewerbeschule in Zurich, Switzerland, she studied scientific drawing, typography, and lettering and met her husband, American artist, Robert Barry. The Barrys lived at one time in San Juan, Puerto Rico. It was this location which led to Mrs. Barry's writing A is For Anything. She had found some old wooden type in a printing shop which provided ideas for the book. A Is For Anything; an ABC Book of Pictures and Rhymes.

BARRY, Robert Everett 1931-
Author-artist, born in Newport, Rhode Island. He has studied in Zurich at the Kunstgewerbeschule. He has been a partner in Pava Prints which had an office in San Juan, Puerto Rico. Mr. Barry's book, This Is the Story of Faint George Who Wanted To Be a Knight, was selected by the New York Times as one of the "Ten Best Illustrated Books of the Year." He wrote: Mr. Willowby's Christmas Tree, Boo, Next Please. CA-5/6

BEACH, Stewart
A graduate of the University of Michigan, he has been writer, editor, and teacher. From 1934 to 1939 he was managing editor of House Beautiful. He has lived in New York and Boston. He has written short stories and a Broadway play, and is the author of Racing Start.

BEALS, Carleton 1893-
Born in Medicine Lodge, Kansas, he graduated from the University of California and received an M.A. from Columbia University. He has traveled extensively and lived with the Indians of Guatemala, the Amazon, and the Andes. At one time Mr. Beals was asked why he wrote about John Eliot, and he re-

plied, "I felt that Eliot was one of the few great men of early colonial times, and his interest in the Indians coincided with my own interest in the Indian peoples of North and South America...In John Eliot I saw a kindred spirit." He wrote John Eliot: the Man who Loved the Indians (July 31, 1604-May 20, 1690). CA-4

BEATTY, Hetty Burlingame 1907-
Sculptor, writer and illustrator. Born in New Canaan, Connecticut, she attended the Goodyear-Burlingame school in Syracuse, New York, the Boston Museum School, and studied drawing with George Demetrios. Her works have been exhibited at the Worcester Art Museum and in New York. The American Federation of Arts has included some of her illustrations in their traveling exhibitions. Mrs. Beatty wrote: Blitz, Bucking Horse, Droopy, Moorland Pony, Saint Francis and the Wolf, Voyage of the Sea Wind. CA-4, MJA

BEATY, John Yocum 1884-
Born and educated in Iowa, he has been editor of a farm paper and professor of agricultural journalism at the University of Wisconsin. In the preparation of an autobiography of Luther Burbank, he visited the Burbank farms in California. From this observation, he wrote Luther Burbank, Plant Magician. Other titles include: Baby Whale, Sharp Ears, Mountain Book, The River Book, Story Pictures of Farm Foods, Story Pictures of Transportation and Communication, What We See in the City.

BEECROFT, John 1902-
Born in Superior, Wisconsin. Graduated from Columbia University and has studied in Europe. Mr. Beecroft was Editor-in-Chief of the Literary Guild, the Book League of America, Doubleday Dollar Book Club, The Family Reading Club, and the Mystery Guild. He has also compiled anthologies. The Beecroft's summer home near Old Deerfield, Massachusetts, was the background for his book Rocco Came In. CA-5/6

BEELER, Nelson Frederick 1910-
Born in Adams, Massachusetts, he graduated from the University of Massachusetts and Columbia University. He has taught at Potsdam (New York) State Teachers' College and at Clarkson College. Also, he has been a high school science teacher. He and Franklyn M. Branley have been co-editors of the science page of Young America. They wrote: Experiments in Chemistry, Experiments in Optical Illusion, Experiments in Science, Experiments With a Microscope. Mr. Beeler wrote Experiments in Sound. MJA

BEIM, Jerrold 1910-1957
Married and the father of twin sons, the author was born in Newark, New Jersey, and lived in Westport, Connecticut. He attended New York University. Mr. Beim wrote advertising copy for various department stores and became interested in writing as a career. He especially showed great interest in children. "I think children's books need more realism; children need it, want it, like it when they find it in their literature." His own books include these important factors. Juvenile contributions: Across the Bridge, The Boy on Lincoln's Lap, Country Fireman, Country School, Eric On the Desert, Flood Waters, Kid Brother, Shoeshine Boy, Swimming Hole. JBA-2

BEISER, Arthur and Germaine
Husband-wife team. Graduate of the Massachusetts Institute of Technology and recipient of a master's degree in physics from New York University, Germaine Beiser has collaborated with her husband in cosmic-ray balloon research. Arthur Beiser received his Ph. D. from New York University, has been a Scientific Director, Associate Professor of Physics at the New York University, a Senior Research Scientist, and vice-president of Nuclear Research Associates, Inc. The Beisers have written: Physics for Everybody, The Story of Cosmic Rays.

BEITLER, Stanley 1924-
He is a New Yorker who began his career as a copy

boy for the New York Post. He received his B.A. degree from New York University, and upon graduation was a research assistant in journalism at Iowa State University. He has held several positions with magazines; i.e., production manager of Home Craftsman, associate editor of Popular Science Monthly, and associate editor of Astronautics, a publication of the American Rocket Society. He wrote Rockets and Your Future. CA-5/6

BELDEN, Shirley
Attended the University of Connecticut and the American Academy of Dramatic Arts in New York. Miss Belden has been employed in book departments of stores in Hartford, Connecticut, and on the staff of the Hartford Public Library. Her main interests centered around cooking, photography, and surf casting. She wrote: Sand in My Castle, Star Dust.

BELL, Joseph N.
Avid sports enthusiast, Mr. Bell has been an assistant publicity man for the St. Louis Cardinals baseball team. Born in Indiana, he attended the School of Journalism at the University of Missouri and served as a pilot in the Navy Air Corps in World War II. After the war he returned to college and received his degree. He has worked in public relations and advertising for commercial companies but in 1956 decided to become a full time free-lance writer. Several of his articles have appeared in the Reader's Digest and The Saturday Evening Post. He wrote: World Series Thrills.

BELL, Kensil 1907-
Born in Camden, New Jersey, the author worked as a copywriter, entered into the advertising field and later became a free-lance writer. He did book reviews for the Philadelphia Inquirer and contributed articles to periodicals. As a Lieutenant in the Coast Guard in World War II he acted as a traveling historian. He served as an observer aboard ships and planes. His home address has been Chester Springs, Pennsylvania near Valley Forge. His story Jersey

Rebel received honorable mention in the Boys' Life - Dodd, Mead Competition.

BELL, Margaret Elizabeth 1898-
Born in Alaska, and lived in Loring, Alaska which is on an island twenty-five miles north of Ketchikan. Miss Bell attended school at the Annie Wright Seminary in Tacoma and the University of Washington in Seattle. She has lived in Portland, Oregon and San Francisco, California. As a Red Cross worker during World War II, she spent more than a year in the Aleutian Islands. Juvenile contributions include: Danger On Old Baldy, Daughter of Wolf House, Enemies in Icy Strait, Kit Carson, Mountain Man, Ride Out The Storm, Touched With Fire, Alaska's George William Steller, Watch for a Tall White Sail. CA-2, MJA

BELPRÉ, Pura
She lives in New York City but was born and educated in Puerto Rico. As a student in Library School in New York, she wrote Perez and Martina as part of an assignment for a storytelling course taught by the late Mary Gould Davis. She has given puppet shows and told stories derived from her rich Puerto Rican heritage. It is her hope that all children may be come better acquainted with the cultural backgroun of her native land.

BELTING, Natalia Maree 1915-
As a history professor at the University of Illinois, she has lived in Urbana in a house shared by several dogs and fifteen cats. Miss Belting not only likes cats but enjoys collecting folklore about them. Also, she has enjoyed such diversions as textile painting, baking bread, and translating a manuscript written in the Illinois Indian language. She has written a textbook on High School Curriculum and Cat Tales, Elves and Ellefolk, Indy and Mr. Lincoln, Long-tailed Bear and Other Indian Legends, Three Apples Fell From Heaven. CA-1

BEMELMANS, Ludwig 1898-1962
Born in Meran (then part of Austria), the son of a Belgian painter. After working and learning about hotels with the help of an uncle, he arrived in the United States at the age of sixteen. He worked in several New York hotels, and studied painting. His first children's book was Hansi. Many of the incidents for his "Madeline" books were provided during the author's stay in France. In 1954, he was awarded the Caldecott Medal for his book, Madeline's Rescue. Juvenile titles include: The High World, Marina, Parsley. MJA

BENARY-ISBERT, Margot
Born in Saarbrucken, Germany. She had her first short story published when she was nineteen. She has been a secretary in the Museum of Ethnology in Frankfurt. After her marriage, Mrs. Benary lived in Erfurt, Germany. When this section of her country was taken over by the Russians, her family moved to the farm of a friend in whose honor, Mrs. Benary wrote The Ark. Later, the Benarys became residents of the United States. Her books which have been translated from the German by Richard and Clara Winston include: Blue Mystery, Castle On the Border, Long Way Home, Rowan Farm, Shooting Star. MJA

BENNETT, Eve
Born in Neligh, Nebraska, she later lived in Yankton, South Dakota where her father was mayor and editor of a newspaper. She graduated from Yankton College, and took courses in writing at Colorado University and the University of Southern California. It was in a writing class that she met her husband, Carl. In Denver she has been a writer for the Rocky Mountain News. A champion of young people she once said: "... Young people of my day and age didn't discuss world affairs with the interest and grasp that most of the young people today have." Juvenile titles include: I, Judy, April Wedding, Little Bit.

BENTEL, Pearl Bucklen
Born in Beaver County, Pennsylvania. She began writing in high school, and later wrote pageants and plays for charity and civic organizations. During World War II she worked in an advertising agency and radio station. Drawing upon her experiences in radio, she wrote Program for Christine.

BERGAUST, Erik
Born in Norway, Erik Bergaust became an American citizen. With a background in chemistry and journalism, he has been editor of the magazine Missiles and Rockets, and president of the National Rocket Club. Also, he has contributed to the Voice of America program and one entitled Washington Radio Features. Juvenile contributions include: Birth of a Rocket, First Men in Space, Our New Navy, Rockets Around the World, Rockets of the Air Force, Rockets of the Navy, Rockets to the Moon, Rockets to the Planets, Satellites and Space Probes, Saturn Story.

BERNSTEIN, Ralph 1921-
Born in Philadelphia, Pennsylvania, and graduated from Temple University where he majored in business administration and accounting. After serving with the Coast Artillery during World War II, Mr. Bernstein has been a writer for both the United Press and the Associated Press. Also, he has contributed articles to Collier's and Sport. Although he has written all types of news stories, his specialty was sports. He has been president of the Philadelphia Basketball Writers Association. He wrote Story of Bobby Shantz.

BERRILL, Jacquelyn
Born in Kentucky, she graduated from the University of Toledo in Ohio, and married Dr. N. J. Berrill, Professor of Zoology at McGill University, Montreal. She enjoyed photography and crafts which included the cutting of lino blocks and hand-blocking drapes and bed spreads. Juvenile contributions include: Albert Schweitzer: Man of Mercy, Wonders of the Antarctic,

Wonders of the Fields and Ponds at Night, Wonders of the Seashore, Wonders of the Woodland Animals, Wonders of the Woods and Desert at Night.

BERRY, Erick 1892-
Author cards in libraries refer to her as Mrs. Allena (Champlin) Best. She was born in New Bedford, Massachusetts and is married to Herbert Best. As an artist, she has had two one-man shows and illustrated many books. She has traveled widely, and has collaborated many times with her husband in writing books. Her juvenile titles include: Green Door to the Sea, Harvest of the Hudson, Hay-foot, Straw-foot, Honey of the Nile, The King's Jewel, Land and People of Finland, Land and People of Iceland, Men, Moss, and Reindeer, Valiant Captive. JBA-1, JBA-2

BETHERS, Ray 1902-
Born in Corvallis, Oregon, he studied at the University of Oregon, art at the California School of Fine Arts in San Francisco, and later in Paris, France. He has depicted Mexico, Tahiti, and South America through his paintings, photographs, and wood-engravings. His wood-engraving entitled "Still Life with Flowers" won the Pennell Purchase Prize of the Library of Congress. Juvenile titles include: Can You Name Them? The Magic of Oil, Nature Invents; Science Applies, Perhaps I'll Be a Railroad Man, Story of Rivers.

BETTINA 1903-
In libraries author cards are listed as Ehrlich, Bettina. Married to sculptor George Ehrlich, Bettina is known as the creator of the Cocolo books for children. Also, she has achieved distinction in the designing and printing of textiles. In 1937 she won the Silver Medal at the International Exhibition for Arts and Industries in Paris. Juvenile contributions include: Castle in the Sand, Cocolo's Home, Piccolo, Trovato. Also, she illustrated Virginia Haviland's Favorite Fairy Tales Told in England. MJA

BETZ, Betty 1920-
Born in Chicago, Illinois, she attended Sarah Lawrence College. She was quite instrumental in helping to establish teen-age recreation centers in various cities. She has written a newspaper column, contributed drawings and articles to magazines, and has made frequent guest appearances on radio programs. Her titles include: Betty Betz Career Book; the Teen-Age Guide to a Successful Future, Betty Betz Party Book, Your Manners are Showing; the Handbook of Teen-Age Know-How; With Verses by Anne Clark. CA-4, MJA

BEVANS, Michael H.
Born in New York City. His summers were spent in the Watchung Mountains of New Jersey. At an early age he became interested in zoology. At one time he accompanied Carl Kauffeld, Curator of the Staten Island Zoo, to Florida in order to collect reptiles. Mr. Bevans has done biological pictures, writing for textbooks and magazines. He wrote and illustrated Book of Reptiles and Amphibians, The Book of Sea Shells.

BICE, Clare
Artist, illustrator, author. Graduated from the University of Western Ontario, he was a student at the Art Student's League and the Grand Central School of Art in New York. Mr. Bice has been an Associate of the Royal Canadian Academy and member of the Ontario Society of Artists. Mr. Bice is best known for his landscapes and portraits. Books he has written in the juvenile field are: Across Canada; Stories of Canadian Children, A Dog For Davie's Hill, Jory's Cove; A Story of Nova Scotia.

BISCHOFF, Ilse 1903-
A native New Yorker, she attended Horace Mann School, and studied art in New York City, Paris and Munich. After enrolling in the Juvenile Workshop at Columbia University, she wrote the story of Timothy and Gilbert Stuart. Also, painting and wood engraving have been her interests. Some of her prints were

purchased by the Baltimore, Metropolitan, and Boston Museums and one of her books has been chosen for the Fifty Books of the Year. Painter's Coach is one of her books for children.

BISHOP, Claire (Huchet)
Born in France, but now an American citizen. She founded the first French children's public library L'Heure Joyeuse, in Paris. She has been the recipient of several prizes. Pancakes-Paris was a prize-winner in the 1948 New York Herald Tribune Spring Book Festival. All-Alone was selected as the best-liked book by the Boys' Club of America. In 1952 the Child Study Association of America selected Twenty and Ten as the story that "offers young readers an affirmative answer to today's living question: 'Am I my brother's keeper?'" She has contributed articles to many magazines and has been children's book editor for The Commonweal. Her books include: Blue Spring Farm, Five Chinese Brothers. JBA-2

BISHOP, Curtis Kent 1912-
As a student at the University of Texas, he was editor of The Texas Ranger, the college magazine. He has worked in oil fields, newspapers, and as an announcer for rodeos. During World War II he served in the Foreign Broadcast Intelligence Service. His first book was published in 1947, and it was in 1953 that he became interested in baseball for boys and the organization of the Little League. Juvenile books include: Larry of Little League, Little League Heroes, Little Leaguer, Lone Star Leader: Sam Houston, Playmaker.

BLACK, Irma Simonton 1906-
Graduate of Barnard College, Psychology student at New York University, Director of Publications and the Writers' Laboratory at Bank Street College of Education, New York City. She was born in Paterson, New Jersey. She wrote articles for the Saturday Review and Art in America. Juvenile contributions are: Big Puppy and Little Puppy, Castle,

Abbey and Town, Hamlet, A Cocker Spaniel, Maggie, A Mischievous Magpie, This Is the Bread That Betsy Ate. CA-4

BLOCH, Marie Halun 1910-
She grew up in Cleveland, Ohio, but has lived in Denver, Colorado. She married Don Bloch who has collected and sold books in Denver. Although Mr. Bloch's specialty has been Americana, Mrs. Bloch has written books on a variety of subjects. Juvenile titles include: Dinosaurs, The Dollhouse Story, Marya, Mountains on the Move, Tunnels. CA-4

BLYTON, Enid
Teacher, writer, mother of two daughters. Children searching for good adventure stories find enjoyment reading books by Enid Blyton. Most famous of her stories are the series of the same "five" characters. Included are: Castle of Adventure, Circus of Adventure, Five Go Adventuring Again, Five Go Down to the Sea, Five Go to Mystery Moor, Five Go to Smuggler's Top, Five On Treasure Island, Mountain of Adventure, The Sea of Adventure.

BOLTON, Ivy May 1879-
Born in England, the daughter of a famous historian, Reginald Pelham Bolton. She graduated from Saint Mary's School in Peekskill, and has taken special courses in English at the University of Chicago. Miss Bolton has been both librarian and teacher as she was Mistress of Studies at Saint Mary's School for Mountain Girls in Sewanee, Tennessee. Her interest in Tennessee and the subsequent study of its history provided the background for her book Wayfaring Lad. Also, she wrote Father Junipero Serra.

BONNER, Mary Graham 1890-
Spent her childhood in Halifax, Nova Scotia, where she grew to know and love the outdoors. She has visited Canada, America, Honolulu, Paris, Belgium, England, and Scotland. Her interests varied from swimming to baseball, hockey, music, and reading. Miss Bonner began her career writing for magazines

and while still in her teens was the author of two books of collected stories for children. She obtained information for her books during the day, then she would write until late at night. Juvenile books include: The Base-Stealer, Dugout Mystery, Mysterious Caboose, Spray Hitter, Wait and See, Wonders Around the Sun, Wonders of Inventions.

BONTEMPS, Arna Wendell 1902-
Born in Alexandria, Louisiana. He received his B.A. degree from Union Pacific College, Napa County, California and his M.A. from the University of Chicago. Mr. Bontemps has been a teacher in high schools and junior colleges, and Chief Librarian at Fisk University, Nashville, Tennessee. He has written poetry and prose, and has been the recipient of several fellowships and prizes. Juvenile titles include: Frederick Douglass: Slave-Fighter-Freeman, Golden Slippers; An Anthology of Negro Poetry for Young Readers, Lonesome Boy, Story of George Washington Carver, Story of the Negro, You Can't Pet a Possum. CA-1, JBA-2

BONZON, Paul-Jacques 1908-
Born in Sainte Marie, France. Mr. Bonzon has taught school in Valence, France, and has written several books for young readers. Three of his books have won awards in France. His two children usually read his material first and offer their criticisms. An award winner, The Orphans of Simitra, is among his juvenile contributions.

BORTEN, Helen Jacobson 1930-
Author-illustrator, she attended the Philadelphia Museum School of Art. Mrs. Borten feels "that a rich cultural background in art and music is one of the most valuable gifts we can give a child." It was this idea that moved her to write Do You See What I See? This book was chosen by the New York Times Children's Book Section as one of the hundred best books for young readers. She also wrote: Copycat, Do You Move As I Do? CA-5/6

BOTHWELL, Jean

Nebraskan, who has lived in New York. Publication of her poems, short stories, articles, and plays, have appeared in America and India. She believed that childhood's world, regardless of language or location, is "one world." In 1945, her first book Little Boat Boy was published. Following this was The Thirteenth Stone, which won an award in the New York Herald Tribune Spring Book Contest. Other books are: The Borrowed Monkey, Cal's Birthday Present, The Emerald Clue, Empty Tower, The Hidden Treasure, Little Flute Player, Promise of the Rose, The Red Scarf, River Boy of Kashmir, and others. CA-2, JBA-2

BOYLSTON, Helen (Dore) 1895-

Nurse, author. During World War I, she served in France with the Harvard Unit. Following the war, she did relief work in Italy, Poland, Russia, Germany, and the Balkans. After her return to America, she continued her work in hospitals. Later, she devoted all of her time to writing. Young people have enjoyed her many books, including: Carol Goes Backstage, Clara Barton; Founder of the American Red Cross, Sue Barton; Neighborhood Nurse. JBA-2

BRADDY, Nella 1894-

Born in Georgia, she attended Converse College in South Carolina, and has done graduate work at Columbia University. Nelle Braddy has edited and compiled numerous books including The Standard Book of British and American Verse and Facts, the New Concise Pictorial Encyclopedia. Also, she has written articles and book reviews for magazines; however, her main interest was biography and autobiography. In this field she has written Rudyard Kipling; Son of Empire. In private life she is the wife of Keith Henney, editor and author.

BRADY, Rita G.

A graduate of Brooklyn College who continued her studies at New York University and Hunter College. She has taught in a New York City high school and a course in Children's Literature at Russell Sage College in Troy, New York. At one time her husband was a judge in the Occupation Courts in Bavaria, Germany. She wrote: Jane Cameron, Schoolmarm, Lois Thornton, Librarian, Christine Bennet, Chemist, Vida Prescott, Attorney.

BRAGDON, Lillian Jacot
Free-lance writer, editor, and editorial consultant. Born in New Jersey, she attended German private and public schools. Mrs. Bragdon studied at the University of Lausanne in Switzerland and traveled in France and Italy. She has lectured on children's books, and also, has written book reviews for newspapers and magazines. Her books for young readers include: It's Fun to Speak French, The Land and People of France, The Land and People of Switzerland, Words On Wings; the Story of Communication.

BRANLEY, Franklyn Mansfield 1915-
Born in New Rochelle, New York, he graduated from New York and Columbia Universities. He has taught science at the Horace Mann School in New York, and has been an instructor at Troy (Alabama) State Teachers College and at Columbia University. He and Nelson F. Beeler have collaborated on many books. Mr. Branley wrote: Air Is All Around You, The Big Dipper, A Book of Astronauts for You, Exploring by Astronaut: The Story of Project Mercury. MJA

BRANN, Esther
Artist-author, born in New York City; she attended school in Mount Vernon and studied art in New York City and at the Fontainbleau School in France. During a trip abroad, she visited a village in Brittany named Plougastel-Daonlas, where she became friends with nuns. They introduced her to a convent school in Spain where she met "Lupe," the heroine of her book Lupe Goes to School. Her books include: Book for Baby, Yann and His Island. JBA-1, JBA-2

BRATTON, Karl H. 1906-
Singer, choral conductor, music director. He re-

ceived his B.M. degree in music from Kansas University, and his M.A. degree from Teachers' College, Columbia University. A recipient of music scholarships and awards, he studied in Holland with Willem van Giesen. Mr. Bratton has been Music Adviser of the Tacoma Municipal Recreation Association, a member of the Board of Trustees of the Tacoma Philharmonic Association, and Associate Editor of Journal of Musicology. He has contributed articles on music and recreation to educational and music journals. He has written Tales of the Magic Mirror.

BRAUN, Wernher von 1912-
Born in Wirsitz, Germany, he came to the United States in 1945, and became an American citizen. He has lived in Huntsville, Alabama, where he has been Director of the Army's Guided Missile Development Division at Redstone Arsenal. He has written a great deal on space exploration, including First Men to the Moon.

BRICK, John
Born in Newburgh, New York, he graduated from New York and Columbia Universities. He has served as managing editor of Export Trade Magazine and as secretary to the Chairman of the Academic Board of the United States Military Academy at West Point. He was very interested in working with public education of the state of New York. Other activities included fly fishing and hunting with bow and arrow. He wrote Yankees on the Run.

BRIDGES, William 1901-
Born in Indiana, he graduated from Franklin College. He wrote articles about animals in the Bronx Zoo for the New York Sun. He went on a trip to British Guiana and Trinidad and wrote about the expedition for his paper. Later he was appointed Curator of Publications for the zoo. At one time Mr. Bridges took 10,000 live earthworms to Panama in order to feed three duckbilled platypuses which were being sent to the zoo. He is the author of: True Zoo Stories,

Wild Animal World; Behind the Scenes at the Zoo, Zoo Babies, Zoo Doctor.

BRIER, Howard Maxwell 1903-

Author, teacher, public-school administrator. He has been on the faculty of the University of Washington and a director of the Pacific Slope School Press. Also, Mr. Brier has done public-relations work for the State Division of Forestry. While in high school and college he wrote sport stories; later, he was a newspaper sports reporter. Several of his short stories may be found in anthologies and magazines. Mr. Brier enjoys young people and because of this factor he has found little trouble in gathering material that will delight and hold the interest of his young readers. Among his titles are: Cinder Cyclone, Phantom Backfield, Shortstop Shadow, Smoke Eater. MJA

BRIGGS, Barbara

Author-illustrator. She received her B.A. degree in Art and Philosophy from the University of California at Berkeley and attended the Los Angeles Art School. After her marriage to Dex Briggs, an advertising art director, they lived in Chicago where she furthered her studies at the Chicago Art Institute. The Briggs family later moved to the San Francisco Bay area. The author's interests center around rock hunting and gardening, but she enjoys visiting zoos much more where she can sketch its occupants. She has written and illustrated: The Otter Twins; or, Narrow Escape at Beaver Dam.

BRINK, Carol Ryrie 1895-

Author of numerous short stories published in popular children's magazines. St. Paul, Minnesota, has been the home of Mrs. Brink and her husband. Her book, Caddie Woodlawn, won the Newbery Medal in 1936. Concerning this, she wrote: "Almost everything in the book, except for a few incidents which I have painted up for the sake of plot, is drawn from the childhood of my grandmother." Other titles include: All Over Town, Anything Can Happen on the River, Family Grandstand, Family Sabbatical, Mademoiselle Misfortune, Magical Melons; More Stories About Caddie Woodlawn, Pink Motel. CA-2, JBA-2

BROCK, Emma Lillian 1886-
Born at Fort Shaw, Montana. She graduated from the University of Minnesota, and studied figure drawing and design at the Minneapolis School of Art. She has been on the staff of the Minneapolis and New York Public Libraries. While employed at the New York Public Library, Miss Brock worked in the children's rooms of the different branches. Following this, she returned to Minneapolis to write and illustrate children's books. Her titles include: Come On-Along, Fish! Drusilla, The Greedy Goat, Mary's Camera, One Little Indian Boy, Pancakes and the Merry-Go-Round, Too Many Turtles. CA-5/6, JBA-1, JBA-2

BRONSON, Wilfrid Swancourt 1894-
Studied at the Chicago Art Institute. When he was assistant to mural painter Ezra Winter, he helped in the decoration of the Eastman School of Music in Rochester, the Cunard Building in New York, and the Washington, D.C. Chamber of Commerce. His book Fingerfins, the Tale of a Sargasso Fish was written following a marine expedition, and Pinto's Journey was created while he was living in New Mexico. His titles include: Cats, Children of the Sea, The Chisel-Tooth Tribe, Coyotes (kiýotes or ki-yo'tays), Freedom and Plenty: Ours to Save, Goats, Turtles. JBA-1

BROWN, Eleanor Frances 1908-
Born in Spokane, Washington. She graduated from the University of Washington, and has been a teacher and librarian. She taught English in Nevada, Michigan, New York, Oregon, and Washington. She was librarian at the Deschutes County Library in Bend, Oregon. Her interests have been: horses, books, and photography (and she claims "in that order"). Her book A Horse for Peter was runner-up in the

Ford Foundation Award Contest. She has contributed articles to the American Horseman and Popular Horseman. Juvenile titles include: A Horse for Peter, Wendy Wanted a Pony.

BROWN, Lloyd Arnold

Outstanding cartographer. He has been Librarian at Peabody Institute in Baltimore, and curator of maps at the William L. Clements Library at the University of Michigan. In addition to his writing for young people, he wrote an adult book entitled The Story of Maps which was praised by Jacob Skop of the Army Map Service. Mr. Skop said that the book was an authoritative reference source. Also, Mr. Brown has written articles on maps and surveys concerning American history and geography. He wrote Map Making; the Art That Became a Science for young people.

BROWN, Marcia Joan 1918-

Born in Rochester, New York. She studied at the State College for Teachers in Albany, the Woodstock School of Painting, and painting at the New School for Social Research. Especially valuable was her experience working with children in the New York Public Library. After telling the story of Stone Soup to the children, she decided to create a picture book of it. She won the Caldecott Medal in 1955 for Cinderella and again in 1962 for her book Once a Mouse. Other titles include: Little Carousel, Tamarindo, Dick Whittington and His Cat; Told and Cut in Linoleum, Felice, Henry-Fisherman; a Story of the Virgin Islands, Skipper John's Cook. MJA

BROWN, Margaret Wise 1910-1952

Golden MacDonald is her pseudonym. Born in New York City, Miss Brown attended Hollins College and Columbia University. She died at the age of forty-two while on a vacation in Nice, France. In 1947, her book, Little Island, won the Caldecott Medal. She wrote many books including: A Child's Good Morning, Christmas in the Barn, Country Noisy Book, Dead Bird, The Diggers, Four Fur Feet, The

Golden Egg Book, Goodnight Moon. JBA-2

BROWN, Marion Marsh 1908-
Nebraskan who graduated from State Teachers College and received her M.A. from the University of Nebraska. She began writing at the age of six when she was awarded a book due to a letter which she sent to a newspaper. She has been an active worker in the city of Omaha, Nebraska, maintaining such offices as president of the Omaha chapter of the American Association of University Women. Also, she has taught night school at the University of Omaha. She wrote Young Nathan. CA-4

BROWN, Pamela Beatrice 1924-
Noted English author, actress, and producer. She acted under the name of Mela Brown and has produced plays for the B.B.C. Children's Television. She has had homes in London and Kent. Her books include: As Far As Singapore, Back-Stage Portrait, The Bridesmaids, Louisa, Understudy.

BROWN, Paul 1893-
Author-illustrator, born in Mapleton, Minnesota. While very young his family moved East, and he obtained his education in New York City. His drawings have been in demand by many sporting magazines. His book Spills and Thrills published in a limited edition was sold out in one night. Mr. Brown and his family lived on Long Island, and he found enjoyment in having children and animals around him. He has written and illustrated many books including: Circus School, Crazy Quilt, Daffy Taffy, Insignia of the Services, No Trouble At All, Piper's Pony; the Story of Patchwork, Pony Farm, Silver Heels. JBA-2

BROWN, Vinson 1912-
Explorer-naturalist. He graduated from Stanford University, and organized the Naturegraph Company which produced pamphlets and records on nature for the schools and scout groups. He has been camp counselor and farmer in Santa Clara County, California. Juvenile contributions include: How to Ex-

plore the Secret Worlds of Nature, How to Make a Home Nature Museum, How to Make a Miniature Zoo, How to Understand Animal Talk. CA-4

BRUNHOFF, Jean de 1899-1937
French painter and author. He studied painting, and had his first exhibition in Paris. In order to entertain their children, he and his wife told stories about a gay little elephant, and from these stories Mr. de Brunhoff created his book, The Story of Babar, the Little Elephant, in 1932. At the age of thirty-eight, he died in Switzerland. Juvenile titles include: Babar and Father Christmas; Translated from the French by Merle Haas, Babar the King; Translated from the French by Merle Haas. JBA-2

BRUNHOFF, Laurent de 1925-
French author and painter. His father was the late Jean de Brunhoff who created The Story of Babar, and Laurent de Brunhoff has continued this popular series about the little elephant named Babar. He studied to be a painter, and his studio was located in the Montparnasse district of Paris. Juvenile titles include: Anatole and His Donkey; Translated from the French by Richard Howard, Babar and the Professor; Translated from the French by Merle Haas, Babar's Castle; Translated from the French by Merle Haas, Captain Serafina. MJA

BRYAN, Joseph 1904-
Born in Richmond, Virginia. He studied at Princeton University and has been associate editor of The Saturday Evening Post. He has been a member of the United States Air Force Reserve. At one time, he spent a month each year traveling with the circus. Consequently, he has often contributed articles on the circus to The Saturday Evening Post, Collier's, and Life. He wrote World's Greatest Showman; the Life of P. T. Barnum for young people.

BUCK, Pearl (Sydenstricker) 1892-
Distinguished novelist, born in West Virginia, the daughter of missionaries. She attended Randolph-

Macon College, and received her master's degree from Cornell. The second book which she wrote, The Good Earth, was awarded the Pulitzer Prize. This was not her only honor, as she has been the recipient of many, including the Nobel Price for Literature in 1938. Her husband was the late Richard J. Walsh, and she has lived in Pennsylvania. Her books for young people include: The Beech Tree, Big Wave, The Christmas Ghost, Christmas Miniature, Johnny Jack and His Beginnings, Man Who Changed China; The Story of Sun Yat-Sen. CA-2

BUDD, Lillian (Peterson) 1897-
Born in Chicago, Illinois. She lived in New Jersey, New York, Pennsylvania, Virginia, Washington, D. C., and California before returning to Illinois to live. Her story grew out of an attempt to explain to her own grandchildren how America was when she was a little girl. Miss Budd said: "It was different then. The picturesque wagons and carts and vendors have disappeared forever from the city streets. And so I feel that my story introduces children to a bit of Americana." Her stories include: The Pie Wagon, Tekla's Easter. CA-2

BUEHR, Walter Franklin 1897-
Chicagoan who has studied art in New York, Philadelphia, and Europe. In addition to writing stories for young people, Mr. Buehr has been a time-and-study man in an automobile plant. He has been interested in ships and the sea, and has spent many summers living on his 43-foot cutter. Juvenile contributions include: The Birth of a Liner, Bread; the Staff of Life, Cargoes in the Sky, Chivalry and the Mailed Knight, The Crusaders, The First Book of Machines, Genie and the Word; Electricity and Communication. CA-5/6

BUFF, Mary 1890- and Conrad 1886-
Author and artist team. Mary Marsh Buff graduated from Bethany College, Kansas. After teaching art in Montana and Idaho, she became assistant art curator of the Los Angeles Museum where she met her

husband, artist Conrad Buff. Mr. Buff was from Switzerland where he studied in a school of applied art. After arriving in America, he enjoyed painting western landscapes. His painting and lithographs can be found in permanent collections of many museums. Their juvenile contributions include: The Apple and the Arrow, Big Tree, Dancing Cloud; the Navajo Boy, Dash and Dart, Elf Owl, Hah-Nee of the Cliff Dwellers, Hurry, Skurry, & Flurry, Magic Maize. JBA-2

BUGBEE, Emma
Born in Shippensburg, Pennsylvania. She attended Barnard College, Columbia University, and in her senior year wrote about campus activities for The New York Tribune. Later she joined the staff of this paper and wrote about many topics including murders, beauty contests, and political conventions. Due to her writing about women in politics, Miss Bugbee was assigned to cover Mrs. Franklin D. Roosevelt in 1933. At one time, she was one of the women reporters who were presented to Their Majesties King George and Queen Elizabeth at the White House. She wrote Peggy Goes Overseas for young people.

BULLA, Clyde Robert 1914-
He was born near King City, Missouri. Clyde Bulla has worked on a newspaper and has written short stories. He has traveled in Europe, Hawaii, Mexico, and the United States. Also, Mr. Bulla has lived in Los Angeles where he has composed songs. Juvenile books include: Down the Mississippi, Eagle Feather, Ghost Town Treasure, Old Charlie, Poppy Seeds, Riding the Pony Express, Song of St. Francis, Star of Wild Horse Canyon, Sword in the Tree. MJA

BUNCE, William Harvey
Born in Stillwater, New York. Mr. Bunce studied at Columbia University and the New York School of Design. He has been illustrator, writer, and in 1936-37 was supervising draftsman on the TVA-WPA

archeological survey of Chickamauga Basin. His adult books, Tennessee, A Guide to the Volunteer State, and Alabama, A Guide to the Deep South, were written for the National Writers' Program. He wrote War Belts of Pontiac for young people.

BURGOYNE, Leon E. 1916-
Graduated from Western Michigan College, and has a M.A. degree from the University of Michigan. He has coached the basketball team of St. Joseph High School in Michigan. During World War II he served with the Navy in the South Pacific. He wrote Jack Davis, Forward, State Champs.

BURKE, Lynn
Swimmer who attended St. John's University in New York. She won two Gold Medals in the 1960 Olympic Games, and held five world records. She has coached many children in swimming in the New York area. She wrote The Young Sportsman's Guide to Swimming.

BURNETT, Frances (Hodgson) 1849-1924
Born in England but became an American citizen. While she was in her teens, two of her stories were published in an American magazine. She married a Washington doctor, and lived in Long Island and Bermuda. For some time she lived in Kent, England, at Maytham Hall. There were brick-walled gardens at Maytham Hall, and this gave her the inspiration to write The Secret Garden which her family called her most "artistic" book. Her titles include: Little Lord Fauntleroy, A Little Princess, Being the Whole Story of Sara Crewe, Racketty-Packetty House, as Told by Queen Crosspatch, Sara Crewe; or What Happened at Miss Minchen's. JBA-1

BURNFORD, Sheila 1918-
Born in Scotland and attended St. Georges and Harrogate College. She has contributed articles to Punch, Canadian Poetry, the Glasgow Herald, and Blackwoods. During the war she served in Royal Naval Hospitals, and later, as an ambulance driver.

Her interests have included flying (she has a pilot's license) and shooting. Her first book was The Incredible Journey. CA-2

BURT, Olive (Woolley) 1894-
Graduated from the University of Utah. She has been a teacher in Utah and Wyoming and an editor on the Salt Lake Tribune and The Deseret News. Miss Burt said: "Through my teaching and my work I have had a great deal to do with schools and libraries and the young people of the West. Naturally when I began to write books, I chose the West as the background." Her titles include: Brigham Young, First Woman Editor: Sarah J. Hale, John Wanamaker; Boy Merchant, Luther Burbank, Boy Wizard, The Oak's Long Shadow.

BURTON, Virginia Lee 1909-
Born in Newton Centre, Massachusetts. She studied art and dancing at the California School of Fine Arts. She has taught dancing and contributed sketches to the Boston Transcript. She won the Caldecott Medal in 1942 for her book The Little House. Juvenile titles include: Calico, the Wonder-Horse; Or, The Saga of Stewy Stinker, Choo Choo; the Story of a Little Engine Who Ran Away, Katy and the Big Snow, Life Story, Maybelle, the Cable Car, Mike Mulligan and His Steam Shovel. JBA-2

BUSBY, Edith
Born in Terre Haute, Indiana. She attended Baylor University, and the Institute of Musical Art, Juilliard School of Music in New York. After spending a summer working in the New York Public Library, she decided to make a career of librarianship. She has been a children's librarian in the New York Public Library, and Supervisor of Book Ordering in the Brooklyn Public Library. Also, she has taught courses in library science at both Pratt Institute and Columbia University. She wrote: Behind the Scenes at the Library, What Does A Librarian Do?

BUSONI, Rafaello 1900-
Artist and author, born in Berlin, the son of a famous Italian musician. He spent several years in Spain gathering material on the life of Miguel Cervantes and later wrote The Man Who Was Don Quixote. His father was a "Quixote" collector, and at one time he was known to have had fifty-six different editions of this book. Juvenile titles include: Australia, Italy, Mexico and the Inca Lands, Somi Builds a Church, Stanley's Africa. JBA-2

BUTLER, Beverly Kathleen 1932-
Born in Fond du Lac, Wisconsin. She graduated from Mount Mary College in Milwaukee, and received an M.A. degree from Marquette University. She has lived in Milwaukee with her family and guide dog named Heidi, spending part of her time teaching writing courses at Mount Mary College and the rest of the time writing books for young people. She wrote: The Lion and the Otter, The Fur Lodge, The Silver Key. CA-2

C

CALDWELL, John Cope 1913-
Born in the Orient, Mr. Caldwell received his education there before coming to the United States. During World War II he served fifteen months on the coast of China. He held numerous positions with the Department of State after the war. Obtaining material for his books, Mr. Caldwell has often traveled in Asia, Africa, and South America. He has written: Let's Visit Argentina, Let's Visit Brazil, Let's Visit Ceylon, Let's Visit China, Let's Visit Japan, Let's Visit the South Pacific, Our Neighbors in Peru.

CALHOUN, Mary Huiskamp 1926-
Born in Keokuk, Iowa. She was a newspaper reporter before she married Frank Calhoun, a member of the staff of The Californian in Bakersfield, California. Making the Mississippi Shout was her first book. One hot day in summer she returned to Keokuk,

Iowa, and gave a delightful talk about her books in the Keokuk Public Library. Her books for boys and girls include: *Cowboy Cal and the Outlaw*, *Houn' Dog*, *Hungry Leprechaun*, *Katie John*, *The Nine Lives of Homer C. Cat*, *Wobble the Witch Cat*. CA-5/6

CAMERON, Polly
Attended Phoenix College and the University of California at Santa Barbara. In 1951 she left for Europe where she was a draftsman in French Morocco, and later painted in Paris. Following this, she lived in New York with her Briard dog named Stilt (the heroine of her book). She has been an illustrator, designer, writer, and sculptor. Her books include: *Boy Who Drew Birds*, *The Cat Who Couldn't Purr*, *Dog Who Grew Too Much*.

CAMPBELL, Wanda Jay
Texan, newspaper woman, author, and the mother of four children. *The Museum Mystery* was her first book. It had the Palo Duro Canyon for its background. She has lived in Pampa, Texas. Juvenile titles include: *Mystery of McClelland Creek*, *Ten Cousins*.

CAMPION, Nardi Reeder, 1917-
Graduated from Wellesley College. She is the sister of Colonel Red Reeder, and collaborated with him to write the book, *The West Point Story*. One of her books, *Bringing Up the Brass* was made into the movie called *The Long Gray Line*. She has contributed articles to *Collier's*, *Sports Illustrated*, and the *New York Times Magazine*. She wrote *Patrick Henry, Firebrand of the Revolution*. CA-4

CANDY, Robert 1920-
Born in Milton, Massachusetts. He attended the Massachusetts Institute of Technology, the Massachusetts School of Art, and the Rhode Island School of Design. During World War II he served as a B-25 pilot in the Aleutians and Burma. He has always enjoyed nature; later, sharing this enthusiasm with his son, he decided "to compile a nature notebook

for all children and their parents." The book was called Nature Notebook.

CARDEN, Priscilla
Born in Boston, Massachusetts. She graduated from the University of Chicago, and has been a children's librarian. She believes that "children's books meet high-powered competition nowadays in the form of radio shows, comic books, and TV shows. I think books can meet that competition, and offer other values as well." She wrote Young Brave Algonquin for young people.

CARLSON, Bernice Wells 1910-
Graduated from Rippon College in Wisconsin. She married Dr. Carl W. Carlson and lived in New Jersey. She has been active in Scout groups both as a Den Mother and a Brownie Scout Leader. These experiences and her own children taught her "what kinds of things children really like to make and to do most." Her titles include: Act It Out, Do It Yourself! Tricks, Stunts, and Skits, Fun For One-Or Two, Junior Party Book. CA-5/6

CARLSON, Esther Elisabeth 1920-
Born in Belmont, Massachusetts. She has worked in the Probation Office at the Cambridge Courthouse and has been secretary to the Superintendent of Schools in Belmont. She has been interested in writing, dancing, and traveling including a visit to the native land of her parents, Sweden. Her books include: Milestone, Sixes and Sevens. CA-5/6

CARLSON, Natalie Savage 1906-
Born in Winchester, Virginia. She has lived in the Pacific Northwest and in Newport, Rhode Island, where her husband was on the Naval War College Staff. Mrs. Carlson's books include: Alphonse, That Bearded One, A Brother for the Orphelines, Carnival in Paris, Family Under the Bridge, Happy Orpheline, Sashes Red and Blue, Wings Against the Wind and many others. CA-4, MJA

CARMER, Carl Lamson 1893-
Born in Cortland, New York. Tall tales and folk music were a part of Carl Carmer's boyhood. He became a distinguished American folklorist. Windfall Fiddle contained his own experiences as a boy, and he said: "Writing it was a labor of love." Also, he has written: Eagle in the Wind, A Flag for the Fort, Henry Hudson, Captain of Ice-Bound Seas, The Hudson River, Pets at the White House.

CARR, Mary Jane 1899-
Born in Portland, Oregon. She attended St. Mary's College for Women (later called Marylhurst College) in Oswego, Oregon. She has worked on a newspaper, and has written plays, verses, and stories for children. She once said: "I suppose that it was then, when I was in the seventh or eighth grade, that I really wrote my first historical romance. I liked to write, even in those young days, and I dreamed of writing books, but I had not the faintest idea that I should turn to that most distasteful, difficult subject, history for material for my books." She wrote: Children of the Covered Wagon, Young Mac of Fort Vancouver. JBA-2

CAUDILL, Rebecca 1899-
Born in Harlan County, Kentucky. She received her education at Wesleyan College in Macon, Georgia and a M.A. degree from Vanderbilt University in Nashville. At one time she taught English at Collegio Bennett in Rio de Janeiro. She received a certificate for "distinguished achievement" from Wesleyan College. Her juvenile contributions include: The Best-Loved Doll, Happy Little Family, Higgins and the Great Big Scare, House of the Fifers, Saturday Cousins, Schoolhouse in the Woods. CA-5/6, MJA

CAVANAH, Frances 1899-
Born in Princeton, Indiana. She graduated from DePauw University. Miss Cavanah has been associate editor of Child Life and book review editor of a religious magazine. She received a citation for "distinction as writer and editor of books for young

people" at the DePauw Inaugural Convocation. Juvenile contributions include: Abe Lincoln Gets His Chance, Adventure in Courage; the Story of Theodore Roosevelt, Benjy of Boston, Boyhood Adventures of Our Presidents, Children of America, Children of the White House. MJA

CAVANNA, Betty 1909-
Author, art director. Journalism was her major at the New Jersey College for Women. Her realistic characterizations and her understanding of young people and their problems have contributed to the popularity of her books. Juvenile contributions include: Accent on April, Almost Like Sisters, Angel on Skis, Catchpenny Street, Fancy Free, Going on Sixteen, Paintbox Summer, Scarlet Sail, Spring Comes Riding, A Time for Tenderness. MJA

CERF, Bennett Alfred 1898-
President of Random House, columnist, lecturer, panelist on television program, What's My Line. He has written numerous books of humor for children and adults alike. Included in his juvenile books are: Bennett Cerf's Book of Riddles, Bennett Cerf's Book of Laughs, Bennett Cerf's Houseful of Laughter, More Riddles.

CHAFETZ, Henry 1916-
He wrote The Lost Dream when his little boy was awakened and couldn't go back to sleep because he had lost the dream which he was dreaming. He has been a navigator in the Air Force during World War II. Mr. Chafetz has served with the New York City Board of Child Welfare and operated a second-hand bookstore on Fourth Avenue in New York City. He wrote The Lost Dream. CA-1

CHALMERS, Audrey 1899-
Born in Canada. She graduated from Havergal College in Toronto, and studied kindergarten work in New York. Her first book for older boys and girls was High Smoke. It was based on a real house which belonged to her sister-in-law. Juvenile titles

include: Birthday of Obash, Hundred and Hundreds of Pancakes, The Lovely Time, Mr. Topple's Wish.

CHANDLER, Ruth Forbes 1894-
Born in New Bedford, Massachusetts. She graduated from Teachers College in Bridgewater, Massachusetts. She has been a teacher and principal. In addition to teaching and writing, she has been very interested in music and has studied the mandolin, violin, and piano. Her books for young people include: The Happy Answer, Middle Island Mystery, Too Many Promises. CA-4

CHAPMAN, Mary Ilsley and John Stanton
For many years this team wrote stories under the pseudonym of Maristan Chapman. Mrs. Chapman has been a missionary, lecturer, and engineering technician. Mr. Chapman was born in London and has been an aeronautical engineer. He has served in the Air Service of the British Army Reserve. Maristan Chapman's books include: Mountain Mystery, Mystery of the Hectic Holidays, by Jane Selkirk, pseudonym.

CHARLIP, Remy
Writer-illustrator, and graduate of the Fine Arts Department at Cooper Union. Mr. Charlip has designed textiles, posters, book jackets, fabrics, wallpaper, costumes, and sets. Leaving the art field, Mr. Charlip turned his attention to dancing and became a member of Merce Cunningham's professional Dance Company. Writing and illustrating then claimed his attention with several children's books added to his credit. He has written and illustrated for children Dress Up and Let's Have a Party.

CHILDS, John Farnsworth
He graduated from Trinity College and received a M.B.A. from Harvard Graduate Business School. He has been a security analyst for an investment firm on Wall Street, and has been commissioned in the Naval Reserve. He wrote Navy Gun Crew.

CHRISMAN, Arthur Bowie 1889-
Born near White Post, Virginia, he grew up listening to good stories, and later, bewitched young listeners with his own stories. Arthur Chrisman was a patient not a prolific writer, but his stories have been among the best written for boys and girls. In 1926, his book, Shen of the Sea, won the Newbery Medal. He also wrote Treasures Long Hidden, and The Wind That Wouldn't Blow. JBA-1, JBA-2

CHRISTIE, Agatha
Born in Torquay, England. During World War I, she served as a V.A.D. in France. It has been said that her "masterpiece" was The Murder of Roger Ackroyd. This book was dramatized, and Charles Laughton portrayed Poirot, the detective, on the London stage. She wrote 13 for Luck! A Selection of Mystery Stories for Young Readers.

CHRYSTIE, Frances Nicholson 1904-
New Yorker who graduated from the School of Journalism, Columbia University. She has been manager of the book department of F.A.O. Schwarz. Juvenile titles include: First Book of Jokes and Funny Things, First Book of Surprising Facts.

CHUTE, Marchette Gaylord 1909-
Author, illustrator. Born at Wayzata, Minnesota, she graduated from the University of Minnesota. Since the publication of her first book in 1932, Miss Chute has been ranked among the most esteemed American authorities in the history of English literature. In 1950 she won the Author-Meets-The-Critics Award for the best in the field of non-fiction; also, the Secondary Education Board and Poetry Chap-Book Awards, both in 1954. Juvenile contributions include: Around and About; Rhymes, Innocent Wayfaring, Jesus of Israel, Rhymes About the City, Rhymes About the Country, Stories From Shakespeare. CA-4, MJA

CIARDI, John 1916-
Teacher and lecturer. He has translated The Inferno

and has contributed several volumes of poetry to the adult field. He has been Poetry Editor of the Saturday Review. Many of his verses for boys and girls have appeared in periodicals. Mr. Ciardi has taught at Rutgers University in New Brunswick, New Jersey. His books include: I Met a Man, The Man Who Sang the Sillies, Reason for the Pelican, Scrappy the Pup, You Read to Me, I'll Read to You.

CLARK, Ann (Nolan) 1898-
Native of New Mexico, she has studied, understood, and written about the Indians in America. At one time, the government gave her permission to live with a tribe in order to study and help them. Her book, In My Mother's House, was a result of this study. In 1953, she was awarded the Newbery Medal for her book, Secret of the Andes. Juvenile contributions include: Blue Canyon Horse, The Desert People, Little Navajo Bluebird, Medicine Man's Daughter. CA-5/6, JBA-2

CLARK, Denis d. 1950?
He has traveled in the Far East and became the head of a plantation in Ceylon. He lived closely with the natives while on his many explorations, learning their customs and ways of life. Actual experiences of Mr. Clark included a bear attack and an episode with a leopard. After his marriage in England, he later lived in Corsica. During World War II he served in the Royal Air Force. Ceylon was the setting for his juvenile book Black Lightning; the Story of a Leopard, and Australia for Boomer; the Life of a Kangaroo.

CLARK, Ronald William
Soldier, statesman, in World War II was a war correspondent with Field Marshall Montgomery's armies in Europe. Mr. Clark wrote for magazines and periodicals, and has written several biographies of famous people of today. Juvenile books include: Great Moments in Battle, Sir Winston Churchill.

CLARKE, Arthur Charles 1917-
Born in Somerset, England, attended King's College

and the University of London, where he received his B. S. degree. Lieutenant Clarke was a radar specialist in World War II. He has been a science editor, television and radio writer, and also, has written numerous short stories and articles. Mr. Clarke has been a Fellow of the Royal Astronomical Society, and chairman of the British Interplanetary Society, and belonged to the Underwater Explorers Club. Among his books are: The Challenge of the Sea, Dolphin Island; a Story of the People of the Sea, Indian Ocean Adventure, Islands in the Sky. CA-4

CLEARY, Beverly Bunn 1916-
Born in McMinnville, Oregon, she attended Chaffee Junior College in Ontario, California, the University of California at Berkeley, and the School of Librarianship at the University of Washington in Seattle. She was a children's librarian in Yakima, Washington until her marriage to Clarence T. Cleary. The Clearys have lived in Berkeley, California. Juvenile titles include: Beezus and Ramona, Ellen Tebbits, Fifteen (in 1958, it was awarded the Dorothy Canfield Fisher Children's Book Award), Henry and Beezus, Jean and Johnny. CA-1, MJA

CLEMENS, Samuel Langhorne 1835-1910
This popular author is known by the name of Mark Twain. Born in Florida, Missouri, he spent his boyhood in the river town of Hannibal, Missouri. He has been a printer, reporter, lecturer, and a Mississippi river pilot. His books have been enjoyed by boys and girls throughout the world. Juvenile titles include: Adventures of Huckleberry Finn, Adventures of Tom Sawyer, Connecticut Yankee in King Arthur's Court, Prince and the Pauper. JBA-1

CLYMER, Eleanor Lowenton 1906-
Born in New York City. She attended Barnard College, the University of Wisconsin, and studied writing at New York University. She has worked in camps, playgrounds, and offices. Mrs. Clymer always enjoyed writing, and while in high school she contributed much to her school magazine. Juvenile

books include: Country Kittens, Latch Key Club, Mr. Piper's Bus, Modern American Career Women, Treasure at First Base, Trolley Car Family.

COATSWORTH, Elizabeth Jane 1893-
Born in Buffalo, New York, she attended Vassar, and received her Master's degree from Columbia University. After graduation from college, she traveled throughout the Orient. In 1931, she was awarded the Newbery Medal for her book, The Cat Who Went to Heaven. She has written poetry, and there is a poetic quality apparent in her books. She married author, Henry Beston. Her juvenile titles include: Captain's Daughter, Hide and Seek, House of the Swan, Poems, Wishing Pear. JBA-1, JBA-2

COGGINS, Jack 1911-
He was born in London, England and came to the United States at the age of twelve. He attended art school. During World War II, Jack Coggins' battle pictures appeared in magazines such as Life. Also, he illustrated Fighting Ships of the United States Navy. He and his wife have lived on a farm in Pennsylvania, where he has been interested in collecting old guns and weapons. He wrote Illustrated Book of Knights and collaborated with the late Fletcher Pratt to write: By Space Ship to the Moon, Rockets, Jets, Guided Missiles and Space Ships, Rockets, Sattellites and Space Travel, edited by Willy Ley. MJA

COIT, Margaret Louise 1922-
Born in Norwich, Connecticut, graduate of Woman's College, in Greensboro, North Carolina. An assistant professor of English and history at Fairleigh Dickinson University, Miss Coit resided in Rutherford, New Jersey. Enthusiasm in biography and American history resulted in the beginning of her writing career. In the adult field, John C. Calhoun: American Portrait, received the Pulitzer Prize. She wrote The Fight for the Union, her first book for young people. CA-1

COLBY, Carroll Burleigh 1904-
Born in Claremount, New Hampshire, and graduated from the School of Practical Art in Boston, Massachusetts. He has been aviation editor of Popular Science Monthly, and during World War II, was a war correspondent in Labrador and Newfoundland. Juvenile contributions include: Arms of Our Fighting Men, Jets of the World, Colby's Nature Adventures, Night People, Strangely Enough. CA-4, MJA

COLEMAN, Pauline (Hodgkinson)
A native Californian, her interests have consisted of books, travel, people. She was a librarian in San Mateo. She has contributed book reviews and columns to the local newspaper. She said, "I like to write about teen-agers and for teen-agers. It is the happiest, most miserable, mixed-up, exciting, disturbing and glamorous period in a girl's life." Juvenile contributions include: Beau Collector, The Different One, Preposterous Voyage.

COLLIER, Edmund
Descendant of New England churchmen, he contributed articles about cowboys and life in the west to magazines. Later, Mr. Collier was made editor of West magazine. He served in the army and the Forestry Service. From his stock of western knowledge he was able to create The Story of Buffalo Bill. He also wrote for young people The Story of Annie Oakley.

COLLINGS, Ellsworth
Author of professional books, Dean of the School of Education at the University of Oklahoma. His life as a rancher provided him with the necessary background in order to write informative and entertaining books for boys and girls. Adventures on a Dude Ranch was judged by young people who acted as "critics" to be one of the best western books.

COLUM, Padraic 1881-
Author, critic, dramatist, poet, and storyteller. Born in Ireland, he has lived in America since 1914.

At the age of twenty, Mr. Colum had his first play produced; his second, The Land, proved to be the Irish Theatre's first success. His translation of an Irish folk story published in the New York Tribune started him on a writing career for boys and girls. Juvenile books include: The Children of Odin, The Children Who Followed the Piper, Forge in the Forest, The King of Ireland's Son. JBA-1, JBA-2.

COLVER, Alice Mary (Ross) 1892-
Graduated from Wellesley College, and shortly after that finished her first book. She has enjoyed extensive traveling which included an exciting experience of encountering a gale while aboard ship on her way to the West Indies. She has lived in Tenafly, New Jersey and in Stockbridge, Massachusetts. Mrs. Colver's interests have been: "rockgardens, swimming, traveling, the theatre, hills, trees, sincerity, courage--and young people." Her titles include: Joan Foster, Bride, Joan Foster in Europe, Joan Foster, Junior, Joan Foster, Senior, Joan, Free Lance Writer.

COLVER, Anne 1908-
The wife of S. Stewart Graff. They lived in Irvington-on-Hudson. She has been keenly interested in history. She said, "I am always charmed to discover that people--especially children--of other generations are so exactly like myself and my own family." Included in her books for young people are: Abraham Lincoln: For the People, Borrowed Treasure, Florence Nightingale: War Nurse, Lucky Four, Nobody's Birthday, Old Bet, Secret Castle.

COMMAGER, Henry Steele 1902-
Author, editor, and historian. Mr. Commager has been a history professor at Columbia University. Also, he has lectured on American history at universities here and abroad. He was editor of the St. Nicholas Anthology, and has written for young people: Chestnut Squirrel, Crusaders For Freedom, First Book of American History, The Great Constitution; a Book for Young Americans, The Great Proclama-

tion; a Book for Young Americans.

CONE, Molly Lamken 1918-
Editor of her high school paper, and active worker on the campus newspaper while a student at the University of Washington, Molly Cone came from Tacoma, Washington. Her hobbies have been listed as: "skiing, fishing, clam-digging, and the collecting of driftwood." Juvenile titles include: Mishmash, Only Jane. CA-4

CONKLING, Fleur
She studied at Newburg Academy. She has written songs, and many of her stories and poems for adults have been published in magazines. Fleur Conkling has worked for the Dill Publishing Company as a staff writer and in the editorial office of Walt Disney. She has always enjoyed children and has written many books for them. She collaborated with Vardine Moore to write Billy Between.

CONWAY, Helene
Born in Roxbury, Massachusetts, she graduated from Manhattanville College of the Sacred Heart in New York City. She has worked for the Russell Sage Foundation, McCall Publishing Company, and the Welfare Council of New York City. Her aunt is writer and journalist Katherine E. Conway. She wrote A Year to Grow.

COOK, Fred J.
Newspaperman who has been reporter, editor, rewriteman, and feature writer. Mr. Cook has been recipient of several awards including ones presented by the Newspaper Guild of New York, best reporting of 1958, and awards of 1959 and 1960 for magazine articles. In February, 1960, The American History Publication Society selected his book, What Manner of Men, Forgotten Heroes of the American Revolution as their choice. His titles for young people include: Rallying a Free People: Theodore Roosevelt, Golden Book of the American Revolution; adapted for young readers, by Fred Cook from the American Heritage

Book of the Revolution.

COOK, Olive Rambo
Grew up on a farm in Missouri, and graduated from college in Chillicothe. While in high school, she and a cousin built a boat which they used on a trip from Chillicothe to Brunswick on the Grand River, then on a trip down the Missouri River to Glasgow. She has been interested in swimming, photography, sketching, and horseback riding. She wrote Coon Holler.

COOKE, Barbara
Born in Shanghai, China, she has been a columnist, teacher of writing for young people, and free-lance writer. The enjoyment experienced by her children and grandchildren in taking trips provided the inspiration for her book, My Daddy and I.

COOKE, Donald E. 1916-
He has served as assistant illustration instructor under American artist Henry C. Pitz at the Philadelphia Museum School of Art. After intensive study of the pre-Revolutionary attack made on Fort Bedford, Mr. Cooke had this to say: "The research was worth-while, because I think I've brought to light a remarkable patriot, James Smith... a real American Robin Hood... He used commando tactics nearly two hundred years before professional military men practiced them." Juvenile contributions include: The Firebird, Men of Sherwood; New Tales of Robin Hood's Merry Band, Silver Horn of Robin Hood, Valley of Rebellion. CA-4

COOLIDGE, Olivia 1908-
Daughter of R. C. K. Ensor, English newspaperman and historian, the author was born in London and graduated from Oxford University where she studied the classics. She has taught in Germany and England. Mrs. Coolidge came to the United States and settled in Connecticut. "We always live as far out in the country as is practicable, and try to own a very large dog. I read a good deal, but only a

small proportion of current books, mostly history and biography." Juvenile titles include: Caesar's Gallic War, Men of Athens, Trojan War, Winston Churchill, and the Story of Two World Wars. CA-5/6, MJA

COOMBS, Charles Ira 1914-
Graduate of the University of California at Los Angeles. Since he had been active in athletics while in school, his writing started with sports fiction. He has been interested in aviation, and has enjoyed flights in several types of aircraft. This has resulted in his writing Skyrocketing Into the Unknown in 1954, and later Survival in the Sky. Juvenile contributions include: B-70, Monarch of the Skies, Gateway to Space, Lift-off; the Story of Rocket Power, Project Mercury. CA-5/6

COONEY, Barbara 1917-
Born in Brooklyn, New York. She graduated from Smith College, and has lived in New York, Iowa, Illinois, and Massachusetts. In 1959 she won the Caldecott Medal for her book Chanticleer and the Fox. For this book she utilized the services of chickens loaned by a neighbor, and the local Grange supplied a pen so that the chickens could be kept in her studio. Also, she adapted The Little Juggler from an old French legend and illustrated many books including an edition of Walter De La Mare's Peacock Pie. CA-5/6, MJA

COPELAND, Frances Virginia
Taught three years in the American Community School at Beirut, returned to the United States to obtain an M.A. degree in library science, then became librarian and elementary school supervisor in Beirut until 1956. She has been very interested in the Middle East and its young people. Also, she has been elementary school librarian of the Bellevue Public Schools of Bellevue, Washington. She wrote Land Between: the Middle East.

CORMACK, Maribelle 1902-
Native of Buffalo, New York and graduate of Cornell University. She has collected material abroad for several of her books and did graduate work at the University of Vienna, Austria, and at the Alpine Botanical Station of the University of Geneva. She received a M.A. degree from Brown University. She has been associated with the Park Museum at Providence, Rhode Island. Her books include: First Book of Stones, First Book of Trees, Road to Down Under, Timber Jack, Wind of the Vikings; a Tale of the Orkney Isles. JBA-2

COY, Harold 1902-
Born in California. He has been a radio newswriter, newspaper reporter, and free-lance writer. Mr. Coy has been interested in American history. Juvenile titles include: First Book of Congress, First Book of Presidents, The First Book of the Supreme Court, Real Book About Rivers.

CREDLE, Ellis 1902-
Author, illustrator, teacher. She was born and grew up in Hyde County, North Carolina. She attended Louisburg College and studied interior decoration in New York. Ellis Credle has been a teacher in the Blue Ridge Mountains. She was selected to paint the murals for the Brooklyn Children's Museum. She married photographer Charles de Kay Townsend, and they have lived in Mexico. Included in her children's books are: Big Doin's On Razorback Ridge (a Junior Literary Guild selection), Down, Down the Mountain, Here Comes the Showboat, Johnny and His Mule. JBA-2

CRESPI, Pachita
Born in Costa Rica. Although she has lived in New York, she has often returned to Central America to paint. The book, Mystery of the Mayan Jewels, which was written in collaboration with Jessica Lee was based on an actual jewel robbery in her family. Other titles she wrote were: Cabiya's Rancho, Wings Over Central America.

CRISS, Mildred 1890-
Born in Orange, New Jersey. She has studied in Switzerland and France. In Paris she became acquainted with Abbé Ernest Dimnet and Madame Charles Mercier. As she traveled with Madame Mercier and her children, the author obtained the information upon which she based her story, Red Caravan. Also, she wrote: Book of Saints, Jefferson's Daughter.

CROSBY, Alexander L.
He was born in Maryland, but grew up in California. Mr. Crosby has been a newspaperman, book editor, and free-lance writer. He married author Nancy Larrick, and they have lived in New York City. They collaborated on Rockets Into Space, and Mr. Crosby wrote The Colorado, Mover of Mountains.

CROUSE, William Harry 1907-
Scientist, author, editor. He has been a member of the Society of Automotive Engineers and the American Society for Engineering Education. At one time, Mr. Crouse was Service Engineer and Director of Field Service Education for the Delco-Remy Division of the General Motors Corporation. He has written more than a dozen scientific books including: Science Marvels of Tomorrow, Understanding Science.

CUNNINGHAM, Julia
Born in Spokane, Washington. She attended art school in Charlottesville, Virginia. She lived for two years in France, and this led to the writing of her first book, The Vision of François the Fox. She has lived in Santa Barbara, California, and has been associated with a bookstore there. Her juvenile titles include: Dear Rat, Macaroon.

CUNNINGHAM, Virginia 1909-
Born in Dayton, Ohio. She graduated from Ohio State University, and received her Master's degree from Northwestern University. She has been a

teacher and has edited children's books. At one time, she searched for information on Dayton's Paul Laurence Dunbar, and this search continued for over five years. She wrote Paul Laurence Dunbar and His Song.

D

DALGLIESH, Alice 1893-
She was born on Trinidad in the West Indies, and received kindergarten training at Pratt Institute, and graduated from Columbia University. She has been a teacher, and an editor of children's books at Charles Scribner's Sons. Juvenile contributions include: Adam and the Golden Cock, America Begins; the Story of the Finding of the New World, Bears on Hemlock Mountain, Choosing Book, Columbus Story. JBA-2

DALY, Maureen 1921-
Author, reporter, editor. County Tyrone, Northern Ireland, was her birthplace but she grew up in Fond du Lac, Wisconsin. She attended Rosary College, and later, wrote a book about the summer when she was seventeen. It was Seventeenth Summer, winner of the Dodd, Mead Intercollegiate Literary Fellowship contest. She has been an Associate Editor of the Ladies' Home Journal, and a reporter for the Chicago Tribune where Maureen Daly wrote a teen-age column, "On the Solid Side." Also, she has edited an anthology for teen-agers. She married William McGivern. For young people she has written: Moroccan Roundabout, Patrick Takes a Trip, Patrick Visits the Library, Sixteen and Other Stories, Spanish Roundabout. MJA

DANIELS, Jonathan 1902-
Southern author, born in North Carolina. He received a Guggenheim Fellowship in creative writing and studied for a year in Europe. He has been Assistant Director of Civilian Defense, and was President Roosevelt's press secretary. Also, he has been editor of Raleigh's The News and Observer.

Juvenile titles include: Mosby, Gray Ghost of the Confederacy, Stonewall Jackson.

DARBY, Ada Claire 1883-
She was born in St. Joseph, Missouri. Miss Darby had such illustrious ancestors as an early Governor of Massachusetts Bay Colony, one was President of Harvard College, and another was chaplain to George Washington. Miss Darby has been a lecturer and has written historical stories for children. Juvenile titles include: Columbine Susan, Gay Soeurette, Island Girl, Jump Lively, Jeff!, Pull Away Boatman.

DAUGHERTY, James Henry 1889-
James Daugherty attended evening classes at the Corcoran Art School. Also, he has studied at the Philadelphia Art Academy, and in London. His book, Daniel Boone, was the winner of the 1940 Newbery Medal. James Daugherty and his author-wife (Sonia V. Daugherty) have lived near Westport, Connecticut. Other juvenile titles include: Abraham Lincoln, Andy and the Lion, Poor Richard, William Blake. JBA-1, JBA-2

D'AULAIRE, Ingri (Mortenson) 1904- Edgar Parin 1898-
Husband-wife team. Ingri Mortenson was born in Norway, and Edgar who was the son of an Italian portrait painter was born in Switzerland. They met when both were studying art in Paris. After their marriage, they arrived in the United States. They have achieved distinction in their early picture books by drawing directly on lithograph stone. They have lived on a farm in Wilton, Connecticut. The Caldecott Medal was awarded to their book, Abraham Lincoln, in 1940. They wrote: Animals Everywhere, Benjamin Franklin, Ingri and Edgar Parin D'Aulaire's Book of Greek Myths, Buffalo Bill, Ola. JBA-1, JBA-2

DAVIS, Burke 1913-
Born in Durham, North Carolina. He attended Duke University and the University of North Carolina. He

has been a newspaper reporter, and married a former foreign correspondent, Evangeline McLennan. They have lived in Williamsburg, Virginia and also, spent some time living in a restored log cabin located near the site of the Battle of Guilford Courthouse in North Carolina. He has been very interested in the history of the Civil War. He wrote Appomattox; Closing Struggle of the Civil War; edited by Walter Lord. CA-1

DAVIS, Lavinia (Riker) 1909-
Author, editor, born in New York. She grew up in Red Bank, New Jersey. She has been interested in horses and writing. Prior to being an author, Mrs. Davis has been a research editor for Fortune magazine. She has lived on a farm in the Still River Valley in Connecticut. Juvenile books include: Danny's Luck, Donkey Detectives (a Junior Literary Guild selection), Fish Hook Island Mystery, Melody, Mutton Bone, and Sam, Sandy's Spurs, The Secret of Donkey Island. JBA-2

DAVIS, Reda
Born in San Francisco, California. She graduated from the University of California at Berkeley, and the University of Chicago Library School. She has been a children's librarian in California. She wrote Martin's Dinosaur.

DE ANGELI, Marguerite (Lofft) 1889-
Born in Lapeer, Michigan. At one time, she had considered becoming a singer, but she married John de Angeli instead. In spite of the many activities involved in raising a family of five children, she studied drawing, and later, began illustrating stories which she had written. Many of Mrs. de Angeli's stories preceded the work being done for civil rights in the 1960's. She often wrote good stories about minority groups, (Bright April). In 1950 her book, The Door in the Wall, was awarded the Newbery Medal. Juvenile titles include: Black Fox of Lorne, Henner's Lydia, Jared's Island, Yonie Wondernose. CA-5/6, JBA-2

DECKER, Duane Walter 1910-
Graduated from Colgate. He has contributed articles to Collier's, Cosmopolitan, American Legion Magazine, New Republic, and Esquire. During World War II, he served in the United States Marine Corps and was combat correspondent for their publication, Leatherneck. His first book on sports was Good Field, No Hit which was published in 1947. His books include: Big Stretch, Catcher From Double-A, Hit and Run, Rebel in Right Field.

DE JONG, Dola 1911-
A native of Holland, she came to New York and obtained her American citizenship. The background she received while growing up in Holland provided her with the knowledge she needed in writing some of her stories. She has written several books for children and also, was the author of an adult book entitled And the Field Is the World. Juvenile contributions include: The House on Charlton Street, The Level Land, Picture Story of Holland, Return to the Level Land. CA-5/6, MJA.

DE JONG, Meindert 1906-
Born in the village of Wierum in the Netherlands. Arriving in America in 1918, he settled in Grand Rapids, Michigan. He obtained an A. B. degree at John Calvin College, and was a student at the University of Chicago. He has been college professor, mason, tinner, gravedigger, and farmer. Mr. DeJong has written: Along Came a Dog, Bible Days, Dirk's Dog Bello, Good Luck Duck, House of Sixty Fathers, The Little Cow and the Turtle, Nobody Plays With a Cabbage, Shadrack, The Singing Hill, The Tower By the Sea, Wheel On the School (winner of the 1955 Newbery Medal). MJA

DE LA MARE, Walter John 1873-1956
Poet and author, born in Kent, England. He attended St. Paul's Cathedral Choir School in London where he started the school paper, Choristers' Journal. Mr. De La Mare was a statistician with the Anglo-American Oil Company. In 1953, he was a-

warded the Order of Merit by Queen Elizabeth II. Juvenile titles include: Come Hither; a Collection of Rhymes and Poems for the Young of All Ages (ed. by the author), Down-Adown-Derry; a Book of Fairy Poems, Mr. Bumps and His Monkey, Peacock Pie, A Penny a Day, ... Poems for Children, Stories From the Bible. JBA-1, JBA-2

DE LA TORRE, Lillian 1902-
Native of New York City. She received her education at Radcliffe and Columbia University. She has been an English teacher, playwright, and actress. Alfred Hitchcock produced her play The Older Sister on a television program. Her husband has been Professor of English at Colorado College. She wrote: The Actress; Being the Story of Sarah Siddons. CA-2

DE LEEUW, Adèle Louise 1899-
Born in Ohio, she has lived in Plainfield, New Jersey. Adèle DeLeeuw conducted story hours for children when she was assistant librarian at the Plainfield Public Library. Also, she was secretary to her father who was a consulting engineer in New York. In 1958, she and her sister, Cateau DeLeeuw, were honored for their high standards of writing by the Library Association of Ohio. She has enjoyed photography, cooking, and ceramics. Juvenile books include: Blue Ribbon For Meg, Career For Jennifer, Clay Fingers, Curtain Call, Doll Cottage, The Goat Who Ate Flowers, Hawthorne House, Patchwork Quilt, Rugged Dozen. CA-4, JBA-2

DE LEEUW, Cateau 1903-
She has lived in Plainfield, New Jersey and in Ohio. She attended the Metropolitan School of Art and the Art Students' League in New York. Cateau DeLeeuw's career in writing began when she wrote magazine stories with her sister, author Adèle DeLeeuw. In 1958, the DeLeeuw sisters received a joint citation for their high standards of writing from the Library Association of Ohio. Cateau DeLeeuw has written: Determined to Be Free, Fear

In the Forest, Give Me Your Hand (a Junior Literary Guild selection), The Proving Years, The Turn In the Road. CA-4, JBA-2

DEL REY, Lester 1915-
Born in Saratoga, Minnesota, and attended George Washington University in Washington, D. C. He has done bibliographical and editorial work. In writing for young people Mr. Del Rey feels "that giving young readers a better knowledge of the world--its past as well as the possibilities of its future--is the most important job an author can undertake." His juvenile contributions include: Cave of Spears, Moon of Mutiny, Outpost of Jupiter, Rockets Through Space; the Story of Man's Preparations to Explore the Universe, Step to the Stars.

DEMING, Dorothy 1893-
Nurse and author. She graduated from Vassar College, and the School of Nursing of the Presbyterian Hospital in New York City. Dorothy Deming has been associated with Public Health Nursing and the Red Cross; also, she has been a staff nurse and supervisor at the Henry Street Settlement Nursing Service. Actual experiences of nurses in public health have formed the basis for Dorothy Deming's books, which include: Nurse's Dilemma In the Private Corridor, Penny Marsh, R. N. Director of Nurses, Strange Disappearance From Ward 2, Sue Morris: Sky Nurse, Trudy Wells, R. N. Pediatric Nurse.

DENISON, Carol
Has traveled extensively in the United States and Europe. She has been employed in a Massachusetts art museum, taught school, and has written and produced classroom films. Her books include: What Every Young Rabbit Should Know, Where Any Young Cat Might Be.

DE REGNIERS, Beatrice (Schenk) 1914-
She was born in LaFayette, Indiana, but grew up in Crawfordsville. She attended the University of Illi-

nois, graduated from the University of Chicago, and obtained her master's degree from Winnetka Graduate Teachers College. Mrs. DeRegniers has been Educational Materials Director for the American Heart Association, and has lived in Manhattan. Juvenile books include: Cats, Cats, Cats, Cats, Cats, Child's Book of Dreams, Giant Story, Little House of Your Own, The Shadow Book, Snow Party, Was It a Good Trade? MJA

DESMOND, Alice (Curtis) 1897-
Received an honorary degree of Doctor of Letters from Russell Sage College in 1946, and during that same year the Rochester Museum of Arts and Sciences made her an honorary Fellow. Her husband was former New York State Senator Thomas C. Desmond. Both Senator and Mrs. Desmond have traveled extensively throughout the world. Juvenile contributions include: George Washington's Mother, Jorge's Journey; a Story of the Coffee Country of Brazil, Lucky Llama, Sea Cats, Your Flag and Mine. CA-4

DICK, Trella Lamson
Nebraskan who has been a teacher, mother of four children, and writer. She wrote Tornado Jones, winner of the Charles W. Follett Award in 1953. Mrs. Dick once said that "travelers often remark that Nebraska is only a place to go through, but really it is rich in lore of one of the most interesting periods in American history--the era of the pioneer." Her titles include: The Island On the Border; a Civil War Story, Tornado Jones, Tornado Jones on Sentinel Mountain, Tornado's Big Year.

DICKSON, Marguerite (Stockman) 1873-1953
Born in Portland, Maine. She has been a teacher, and also, has been secretary and registrar in a dance studio in Massachusetts. She wrote a book (Lightning Strikes Twice) about a girl who wanted to be a dancer. Other titles include: Only Child, Turn in the Road. MJA

DILLER, Angela
Author, lecturer, inventor of the Diller Keyboard, and in 1920 with Elizabeth Quaile, founded the Diller-Quaile School of Music in New York City. She was the first winner of the Mosenthal Fellowship in Composition at Columbia University. She wrote The Splendor of Music.

DITMARS, Raymond Lee 1876-1942
An outstanding authority on reptiles, born in Newark, New Jersey. He has been assistant curator of entomology at the American Museum of Natural History, curator of reptiles and head of the department of mammals of the New York Zoological Park. Mr. Ditmars is the subject of a biography written by Laura N. Wood. He wrote: The Book of Insect Oddities; Where the Strange Insects of the World Are Found, Book of Living Reptiles, Wild Animal World; Behind the Scenes at the Zoo. JBA-1, JBA-2

DIXON, Marjorie 1887-
Was secretary to the Foreign Editor of The London Times. During the last months of World War I, she was "reader of the foreign press" at the British War Office. After a trip to Ireland with her husband, she began to write about this country. Later, Mrs. Dixon lived on a farm in Surrey, England. She wrote The Forbidden Island.

DOANE, Pelagie 1906-
Author-illustrator, native of Philadelphia, Pennsylvania. She studied interior decorating and art. She has designed greeting cards and illustrated many children's books. She married Warren Hoffner, and they have lived in New Jersey. Juvenile book titles include: The Big Trip, Book of Nature, The Boy Jesus, First Day, God Made the World, One Rainy Night, A Small Child's Bible, Story of Moses, Understanding Kim. CA-4, MJA

DODGE, Mary (Mapes) 1831-1905
Editor, author, born in New York City. For thirty years she was the editor of that distinguished maga-

zine for young people, St. Nicholas. When her family moved to a farm in New Jersey, she and her father managed the farm and contributed articles for their magazine, The Working Farmer. She married William Dodge. Generations of children will always remember her as the author of the book, Hans Brinker; or, The Silver Skates. JBA-1

DODGSON, Charles Lutwidge 1832-1898
His pseudonym is Lewis Carroll. He was born in Daresbury, England, the son of a parson. He attended Christ Church College, Oxford, graduated with high honors, and later, was a professor of mathematics there. His book, Alice's Adventures in Wonderland, began with a story which he told to three small girls who were enjoying a boat ride with him on the river. Also, he wrote Through the Looking-Glass and What Alice Found There. JBA-1

DOHERTY, John Stephen
Graduated from Syracuse Uniersity, and did graduate work at Yale University. He has served in the Field Artillery, and during the war in Korea was an Intelligence Officer. He has been editor of Saga magazine. He has been interested in boats, and has owned a 24-foot sloop. He wrote The Mystery of Hidden Harbor for young people.

DOLBIER, Maurice 1912-
Born in Skowhegan, Maine. He studied at the Whitehouse Academy of Dramatic Arts in Boston. He has been a columnist for the New York Herald Tribune. His titles include: The Magic Bus, Magic Shop, Paul Bunyan, Torten's Christmas Secret. MJA

DONAHEY, William and Mary Dickerson
Author of the "Teenie Weenie" books, he was born in Ohio and attended the Cleveland School of Art. He wrote articles for children for the Cleveland Plain Dealer, and later, joined the staff of the Chicago Tribune where he created the "Teenie Weenies." Mr. Donahey married author Mary Dickerson, and

they have lived in Chicago. Mrs. Donahey graduated from St. Mary's School in New York. She selected their summer cottage near Lake Superior as the place to write Apple Pie Inn. He wrote: Teenie Weenie Days, Teenie Weenie Land, Teenie Weenie Town.

DORIAN, Marguerite
She has lived in Providence, Rhode Island, and has written poetry and short stories. One of her stories A Ride On the Milky Way appeared in the New Yorker magazine. Her first book for boys and girls was When the Snow Is Blue. Also, she wrote The Alligator's Toothache.

DOUGLAS, Emily (Taft) 1899-
Native Chicagoan, daughter of famed sculptor, Lorado Taft. She married Paul Douglas who was a professor of economics at the University of Chicago, and has been a Senator from Illinois. Mrs. Douglas, interested in civic affairs, at one time was a congresswoman-at-large from Illinois. Appleseed Farm was her first book for boys and girls.

DU BOIS, William Pène 1916-
Author-illustrator. He was born in Nutley, New Jersey, the son of painter and art critic, Guy Pène Du Bois. Mr. Du Bois attended school in France from the time he was eight until he was fourteen years old. He felt that this experience enabled him to develop as an artist. He was only twenty when he wrote and illustrated The Three Policemen. He was awarded the Newbery Medal in 1947 for his book, The Twenty-One Balloons. Juvenile titles include: Bear Party, The Giant, Great Geppy, Lion, Otto At Sea; the Adventures of Otto. CA-5/6, JBA-2

DU JARDIN, Rosamond (Neal) 1902-1963
Popular author for teen-agers, she died March 27, 1963. She has contributed stories to Cosmopolitan and Good Housekeeping magazines. Her first novel for young people was Practically Seventeen which

was published in 1949. It has been published in Sweden, Japan, and in braille. Her daughter, Judy, also, wrote. Mrs. DuJardin believed that "...the majority of teen-agers are interesting, normal and basically dependable people." Her books for young people include: Double Wedding, A Man for Marcy, One of the Crowd. CA-3, MJA

DUKERT, Joseph Michael 1929-
Scientist, author. He won a four year scholarship to Notre Dame University where he graduated magna cum laude. In the Korean war, he was an Air Force psychological warfare officer. He has been Director of Public Relations for the Nuclear division of the Martin Company. Mr. Dukert has contributed articles to Space Aeronautics, Labor Law Journal, and Catholic Digest. He wrote Atompower. CA-5/6

DUNLOP, Agnes Mary Robertson
Elisabeth Kyle is her pseudonym. Born in Ayr, Scotland, she studied journalism in Glasgow. She was a correspondent for the Manchester Guardian and was assigned to Central Europe. She has been interested in collecting antiques, music, and in traveling (although Ayr has remained her home). She wrote many books for young people including: The Captain's House, Carolina House; A Mystery, Maid of Orleans, the Story of Joan of Arc.

DURANT, John 1902-
Outdoor man, author. As a member of the Yale University track squad, he competed in England against the Oxford-Cambridge team. He has enjoyed hunting in Canada, and on one occasion he and his wife undertook a ten-day canoe trip (the only other inhabitants of the area were twenty-six moose). Mr. Durant has contributed articles to Saturday Evening Post, Sports Illustrated, American Heritage, and Outdoor Life. Juvenile contributions include: The Heavyweight Champions, Highlights of the Olympics; From Ancient Times to the Present, Highlights of the World Series.

DURLACHER, Ed
Freeport, Long Island, has been his home, but he has taught square dancing throughout America. Also, he has been in charge of the square dances held in New York's city parks. Mr. Durlacher believed that "square dancing should be fun above all, and that in communities where all ages join in to have a good time, the future of the square dance is assured." He compiled the book, Honor Your Partner; 81 American Square, Circle, and Contra Dances, With Complete Instructions for Doing Them.

DUVOISIN, Roger Antoine 1904-
Author-illustrator. Born in Switzerland. He received his education in Switzerland and France. Mr. Duvoisin has worked in design in Geneva, Lyons, and Paris. Upon his arrival in America, he has done outstanding work in the fields of painting, design and illustration. He has combined imagination and humor which created a demand for his books. His titles include: A For the Ark, And There Was America, Christmas Whale, Easter Treat, The Happy Hunter, House of Four Seasons, I Saw the Sea Come In, Lonely Veronica, Petunia, Spring Snow. Also, he illustrated Alvin Tresselt's White Snow, Bright Snow which won the Caldecott Medal in 1948. JBA-2

E

EAGER, Edward McMaken
Born in Toledo, Ohio. He attended Harvard University, and has written for radio and stage. Mr. Eager once said: "...As time went on I developed the idea of writing a book humanizing animal characters without going either coy or slapstick in the process." All boys and girls who love magic certainly enjoy this author's books. They include: Half Magic, Knight's Castle, Magic By the Lake, Magic Or Not? Mouse Manor. MJA

EAMES, Genevieve Torrey

Born in Pasadena, California, she has lived in most of the states of New England, London, and in Paris. She has always enjoyed animals, and has raised and exhibited collies and cocker spaniels. Her articles have appeared in Story Parade and in Adventure Trails. She wrote: Flying Roundup, Ghost Town Cowboy, Good Luck Colt, Handy of the Triple S, Pat Rides the Trail.

EASTMAN, P.D.

Author and illustrator of books for the beginning reader containing only a primary vocabulary. Also, known for his work in the animated motion picture field and author of scripts for visual education films. Juvenile contributions include: Are You My Mother? Go, Dog, Go!

EBERLE, Irmengarde 1898-

Former textile designer and staff writer on Brooklyn Daily Eagle. She was a graduate of Texas State Women's College and a contributor of short stories to national magazines. Former Texan transplanted to New York. Juvenile titles include: Apple Orchard, Bands Play On, Come Be My Friend, Evie and Cookie, Family to Raise. CA-4, JBA-2

EBERSTADT, Isabel 1934?- and Frederick

Frederick Eberstadt, a graduate of Phillips Exeter and Princeton, was a professional photographer. His wife is the daughter of Ogden Nash and author of a novel, The Banquet Vanishes. This team has written: What Is For My Birthday? Who Is At The Door?

EBY, Lois Christine 1908-

Her pseudonym is Patrick Lawson. She has loved horses since she was a little girl who lived on a California orange ranch. Her childhood friends often permitted her to ride their fine Arabian horses. She once said, "All Arabian horse owners are so versed in facts about their animals that it is impossible to be around them without becoming infected with a measure of wonder and enthusiasm for this fascinating breed of horses." Her book, Star-Crossed Stallion, was a winner in the Boys' Life-Dodd, Mead Prize Competition. She wrote Star-Crossed Stallion's Big Chance.

EDELMAN, Lily
A Californian who holds degrees from Hunter College, Columbia, and a professional diploma in adult education from Teachers College of Columbia University. As a person concerned in cementing ties between East and West, she has served as educational director of Pearl Buck's East and West Association and has worked in the U. S. Department of State's Overseas Information Program. She has been associated with the Department of Adult Education of B'nai B'rith. Juvenile contributions: Hawaii, U. S. A., Israel; New People In An Old Land.

EDMONDS, Richard W.
Columnist and author. He had planned to become an engineer, but decided upon writing as a career. He has also written a column. Mr. Edmonds read about Captain Joshua Barney during a train trip, and became so enthusiastic that he decided to write about him. His book, Young Captain Barney, was the result of his research.

EDMONDS, Walter Dumaux 1903-
Born in Boonville, New York, he attended St. Paul's School at Concord, New Hampshire, Choate at Wallingford, Connecticut and received his A. B. at Harvard. Many of his short stories were published in Scribner's Magazine, The Atlantic Monthly, The Saturday Evening Post. His life around the Black River and Mohawk Valley gave him the background for his children's book, The Matchlock Gun (winner of the 1942 Newbery Medal). Other contributions include: Cadmus Henry, Corporal Bess, Wilderness Clearing. MJA

EDWARDS, Cecile Pepin 1916-
While attending Wheelock College, Boston, Mrs.

Edwards realized she wanted to write for children. A teaching background and the exploration of New England enabled her to write such books as: Champlain, Father of New France, Roger Williams, Defender of Freedom. CA-5/6

EIFERT, Virginia S. 1911-
As a native of the "Land of Lincoln" country she has used this background in writing historical fiction about Lincoln; however, non-fiction is her main field. As a free-lance writer she has demonstrated her abilities in nature illustrations, photographs and short articles in many publications. Mrs. Eifert is married and has a son. Family efforts are combined in gathering material for her books which include: Delta Queen; the Story of a Steamboat, Mississippi Calling, New Birth of Freedom; Abraham Lincoln in the White House. CA-1

EISENBERG, Azriel Louis 1903-
Editor, director, and authority on books for young people. Dr. Eisenberg received degrees from New York University, Columbia and studied at the Teacher's Institute of the Jewish Theological Seminary, graduating with honors. He has written Great Discovery for young people.

ELKIN, Benjamin 1911-
Graduate of Lewis Institute and Northwestern University. As principal of Rogers School in Chicago he has encouraged the art of storytelling. Also, a lecturer in education at Roosevelt College, Dr. Elkin has written: Al and the Magic Lamp, Gillespie and the Guards, Loudest Noise in the World, Six Foolish Fishermen. CA-4

ELLSBERG, Commander Edward 1891-
Honor graduate in the class of 1910 at the United States Naval Academy and recipient of a Master of Science degree in Naval Architecture from the Massachusetts Institute of Technology. He was born in New Haven but moved to Colorado while very young. Commander Ellsberg was a specialist in engineering

and diving and was recruited as a Salvage Officer. He received the Distinguished Service Medal while in that service. He is the author of: I Have Just Begun to Fight, Spanish Ingots, and Thirty Fathoms Deep. JBA-1, JBA-2

EMBERLEY, Ed 1931-
A graduate of the Massachusetts School of Art with illustrating and painting as his interests. After serving in the army as a mechanic, Mr. Emberley entered the Rhode Island School of Design. He was a free-lance artist, is married, has two children and lived in Millis, Massachusetts. With the use of design, he shows children that they can see many things if they really want to. Juvenile contributions are: The Big Dipper, The Parade Book, The Wing On a Flea. CA-5/6

EMERSON, Caroline D. 1891-
Born at Amherst, Massachusetts, she has lived in Holland, Massachusetts. She received her education at Evanston, Illinois, Amherst and Northampton, Massachusetts, receiving her B.S. from Teachers College, Columbia University. Miss Emerson was a teacher for many years in New York City. In her writing she attempted to stimulate the young reader with an idea that would inspire and enrich his mind. Included in her books are: New York City, Old and New, Old New York for Young New Yorkers, Pioneer Children of America.

EMERY, Anne 1907-
Author, teacher, traveler, born in Fargo, North Dakota. She received her B.A. degree from Northwestern University, and studied at the University of Grenoble in France. After her marriage to John Emery she devoted her entire time to raising a family and to writing for teen-age girls. Popular titles of Anne Emery include: Campus Melody, Dinny Gordon, Sophomore, First Love, True Love, First Orchid for Pat, Hickory Hill, High Note, Low Note, Senior Year, Sorority Girl, Sweet Sixteen, Vagabond Summer. CA-3, MJA

EMERY, Russell Guy 1908-

Graduate of West Point, University of Virginia Law School and teacher of law at West Point. Married and the father of two children, Colonel Emery wrote numerous magazine articles on sports and is the author of such juvenile books as: Adventure North, Gray Line and Gold, High Inside, Robert E. Lee, and Warren of West Point.

ENRIGHT, Elizabeth 1909-

Author-illustrator, born in Chicago, daughter of artists. She attended the Art Students League in New York, and continued her studies in Paris. She married Robert Gillman. She illustrated many books for other authors before she decided to write and illustrate her own book, which was Kintu: A Congo Adventure. This was followed by Thimble Summer, winner of the 1939 Newbery Medal. Other titles include: Gone-Away Lake, The Saturdays, Tatsinda. JBA-2

EPSTEIN, Samuel 1909- Epstein, Beryl (Williams) 1910-

Husband-wife team. They have written under the names of Douglas Coe and Martin Colt. In addition to writing for boys and girls, they have written many adult magazine articles. She was born in Columbus, Ohio, and he was born in Boston. She graduated from New Jersey College for Women (now called Douglass College). He graduated from Rutgers University. When Mr. Epstein served in the Army during World War II, Beryl wrote and did research alone (Fashion Is Our Business). They wrote: All About Prehistoric Cave Men, All About the Desert, First Book of Codes and Ciphers, Real Book About Spies. MJA

ERDMAN, Loula Grace

A Missourian by birth she later "adopted" Texas as her permanent home and was a teacher of creative writing in the West Texas State College. She received her education at Warrensburg, Central Missouri State Teachers College, and received her Master's degree at Columbia University. At a later date she furthered her studies at the University of Wisconsin and Southern California. Writing for her began as a hobby, and her contributions include: Good Land, Room to Grow, The Wide Horizon, The Wind Blows Free. MJA

ERICKSON, Phoebe 1907-
Of Swedish descent, the author was born in Wisconsin and was the twelfth child in a family of thirteen. In private life she is Mrs. Arthur Blair of Connecticut. During her childhood while listening to stories told by her father, she "covered yards of brown paper or birchbark with drawings of strange looking horses and even stranger looking people." This was the beginning of her career as an artist and illustrator. She studied at the Chicago Art Institute and many of her paintings have been displayed at the Metropolitan Museum and the Art Institute in Chicago. Her books include: Baby Animal Stories, Black Penny, Just Follow Me, Nature Almanac, Sea Shells. CA-1

ERLICH, Lillian 1910-
Born in Johnstown, Pennsylvania, she attended Cornell University where she met her husband. A musical background was her inheritance as her mother was a piano teacher and her father sang; an uncle was a jazz pianist. Mrs. Erlich was a newspaperwoman and magazine writer before beginning her career as an author. What Jazz Is All About is one of her contributions to the young reader. CA-4

ERNEST, Brother, C. S. C.
Born in Elyria, Ohio. Brother Ernest graudated and later taught at the University of Notre Dame, Catholic University of America, and the University of Portland. Brother Ernest has been writing books for young people since 1923. His titles include: A Story of Saint Agatha, A Story of Saint Benedict the Negro, A Story of Saint Hyacinth, A Story of Saint Paschal Baylon.

ESTES, Eleanor 1906-
Born in West Haven, Connecticut. After working in the New Haven Free Public Library as a children's librarian, she was awarded the Caroline M. Hewins scholarship and studied at the Pratt Institute Library School. She married Rice Estes who has been both student and professor at Pratt Institute. Mrs. Estes' sincere and warm personality can be detected in her writing. The Newbery Medal was awarded to Mrs. Estes in 1952 for her book Ginger Pye. Juvenile titles include: Hundred Dresses, A Little Oven, Middle Moffat. CA-2, JBA-2

ETS, Marie Hall 1895-
Born in Wisconsin, she studied at the University of Chicago, the Art Institute, and Columbia University. At one time, she did social work, and lived for a year in Czechoslovakia. She married Harold Ets who was on the staff of Loyola University School of Medicine. In 1960, she was awarded the Caldecott Medal for her illustrations in Nine Days to Christmas (by Marie Hall Ets and Aurora Labastida). Juvenile titles include: Another Day, Beasts and Nonsense, Gilberto and the Wind, Mister Penny, Play With Me. CA-3, JBA-2

EVANS, Edna (Hoffman) 1913-
Teacher, author, editor. She graduated from Florida State University. Miss Evans has been on the staff of the Times in St. Petersburg, Florida, and has taught a course in children's literature at Phoenix College in Arizona. She began to be interested in brands when she moved to Arizona in 1948, and has collected branding irons from Mexico, Canada, the Southwest, and Florida. She has been a photography editor for Nature Magazine. She wrote: Bill and the Bird Bander, Written With Fire; the Story of Cattle Brands.

EVANS, Eva (Knox) 1905-
She was born in Roanoke, Virginia, the daughter of a minister. After graduation from college, she taught school in many states including rural Alabama

and Mississippi, and in schools where children of migrant workers attended in Florida and Texas. She married Boris Witte, and they have resided in New Hampshire. Her titles for young people include: The Adventure Book of Archaeology, Araminta, Home Is a Very Special Place, People are Important, Why We Live Where We Live. MJA

EVANS, Katherine 1901-
Author-illustrator, founder of the Artists' Market, now known as the Evanston Art Center at Evanston, Illinois. She attended the Art Institute of Chicago, the Art Colony in Provincetown, Massachusetts and studied in Paris. Mrs. Evans has exhibited her work in Ethiopia. She has written and illustrated: Big Jump, A Bundle of Sticks, A Camel in the Tent, Little Bear Bumble. CA-5/6

EVERS, Alf 1905-
Author of picture books for small children, and has written for older groups of boys and girls. Mr. Evers and his family lived in Woodstock, New York. His wife, Helen, combined her talents with his and together they wrote Copy-Kitten and The Happy Hen, followed by others. He also was an authority on folklore in New York State and did writing and lecturing on the subject. Juvenile contributions include: Abner's Cabin, Baldhead Mountain Expedition, Bobby's Happy Day, In the Beginning, There's No Such Animal, Three Kings of Saba.

F

FABER, Doris
Newspaper reporter, author, native New Yorker. She attended Goucher College, Baltimore, Maryland, and New York University. She was a campus correspondent for the New York Times at N.Y.U., and later, joined its staff. She married the reporter who worked nearby; his name was Harold Faber. She wrote Printer's Devil to Publisher; Adolph S. Ochs of The New York Times.

FARGO, Lucile Foster 1880-
Born in Wisconsin. She attended Yankton College, Whitman College in Walla Walla, Washington, and completed library training at the New York State Library School. Her activities in the library profession have been outstanding. She has been associated with the American Library Association in Chicago, the library school of the George Peabody College for Teachers in Nashville, Tennessee, Columbia University, and the School of Library Science at Western Reserve University in Cleveland. Juvenile titles include: Come, Colors, Come, Marian-Martha, Prairie Chautauqua.

FARJEON, Eleanor 1881-
Born in London, daughter of B. L. Farjeon, the novelist, and granddaughter of Joseph Jefferson, the actor. At an early age she was writing and also, became an opera librettist at the age of sixteen. Her work has included fiction, poems, music, games, adult fiction, and plays. Eleanor Farjeon received many honors and awards for her writing for children, namely the Carnegie Medal presented by the English Library Association, the Regina Medal from the Catholic Library Association, and the Hans Christian Andersen Award. Young readers have enjoyed such books as: Cherrystones, Children's Bells; a Selection of Poems, Glass Slipper, Italian Peepshow, Kaleidoscope, Kings and Queens, Martin Pippin in the Apple Orchard, and others. JBA-1, JBA-2.

FARLEY, Walter 1915-
Born in Syracuse, New York, attended school in Pennsylvania and Columbia University. He has written for radio and newspapers. After serving in World War II, Mr. Farley returned to Pennsylvania and fulfilled his desire to own his own farm and stock it with horses. He has visited in South America, Central America, and Mexico, collecting material to write about in his books. Juvenile books include: Big Black Horse, Adapted from The Black Stallion, The Black Stallion, The Black Stallion and

Satan, Black Stallion Mystery, Black Stallion Revolts, Blood Bay Colt, The Horse-Tamer, Island Stallion, Little Black, a Pony, Man o' War. JBA-2

FARMER, Penelope 1939-
Born in Westerham, Kent, England. She studied at St. Anne's College, Oxford, and did graduate work in social studies at Bedford College, London University. In England she has had a play produced on television plus a book of adult stories, but The Summer Birds was her first book which was published in America.

FARRINGTON, S. Kip, Jr.
Interested in railroads and fishing. After writing about the Republic of Chile, Mr. Farrington received a decoration from that country. He has been a member of the committee which designed emergency fishing equipment used by the armed forces of the United States. He wrote Giants of the Rails.

FAST, Howard Melvin 1914-
Librarian and author. He has advocated the idea of "seeing America first," and has traveled throughout the United States. He has worked in the Everglades, and has lived on an Indian reservation in Oklahoma. He has been interested in the colonial period of American history and has written books which have this background. Juvenile titles include: Goethals and the Panama Canal, Haym Salomon, Son of Liberty, Lord Baden-Powell of the Boy Scouts, Tall Hunter. CA-2

FAULKNER, Nancy 1906-
Teacher, editor, author, born in Lynchburg, Virginia. She graduated from Wellesley, and received her M. A. degree from Cornell. She has been a history teacher at Sweet Briar and an editor of Recreation Magazine. Miss Faulkner (with Gloria Chandler) has done radio and television work and children's recordings. Juvenile titles include: Mystery At Long Barrow House, Pirate Quest, The Sacred Jewel, Side Saddle for Dandy, A Stage for

Rom, Tomahawk Shadow, The Traitor Queen (all Junior Literary Guild selections), and Undecided Heart. CA-4

FELLOWS, Muriel

Author, illustrator, teacher. She has done research in anthropology at the University of Pennsylvania. Also, she has taught at the Shady Hill Country Day School, Junior Department of the Stevens School in Philadelphia. She has been a teacher who believed in bringing both reality and creativity into the classroom. She has written and illustrated: The Land of Little Rain; a Story of Hopi Indian Children, Little Magic Painter, a Story of the Stone Age.

FELSEN, Henry Gregor 1916-

Born in Brooklyn, New York. He attended Iowa State University. During World War II, he served as a drill instructor in the Marine Corps and as an editor for Leatherneck magazine. One of his stories was selected for publication in the Best American Short Stories of 1949. His books for young people include: Anyone for Cub Scouts? Boy Gets Car, Hot Rod, Street Rod. CA-4, JBA-2

FENNER, Phyllis Reid 1899-

Librarian, teacher, author. She was librarian at Plandome Road School in Manhasset, Long Island, and was a teacher in the Library School at St. John's University. Also, she has reviewed books for the New York Times and the Elementary English Review. She wrote Proof of the Pudding: What Children Read, and compiled many books including: Adventure, Rare and Magical, Crack of the Bat, Fools and Funny Fellows; More "Time to Laugh" Tales, Giggle Box. CA-5/6

FENTON, Carroll Lane 1900- and Mildred Adams 1899-

Husband-wife team. Authors, illustrators. They met at a Geological Society dinner. Both graduated from the University of Chicago and have been associated with the University of Cincinnati, and Rutgers.

New Jersey was their home, and they helped to bring in new industries by contributing geological information about their state. Devoting their entire time to writing, Mr. and Mrs. Fenton's juvenile books include: In Prehistoric Seas, Land We Live On, Our Changing Weather, Riches From the Earth, Rocks and Their Stories, Worlds in the Sky. CA-1, MJA

FERAVOLO, Rocco V. 1922-
Graduate of Montclair State College, did post graduate work at Rutgers University. He has written science books, has been an elementary school principal, science instructor, and fencing coach at Drew University in Madison, New Jersey. Mr. Feravolo received the Science Teacher Achievement Recognition Award. Juvenile books include: Junior Science Book of Light, Junior Science Book of Weather Experiments, Wonders of Sound. CA-1

FERMI, Laura Capon 1907-
After her marriage to the late physicist, Enrico Fermi, she lived in close association with the scientific world. She said: "After I married, the only true vacation from physics that I ever had was the wartime period of secrecy. At the end of the war, the vacation was over." She has been associated with the Physical Science Study Committee and was present at the First International Conference on the Peaceful Uses of Atomic Energy in 1955. Her work Atoms for the World was the result of this meeting. Mrs. Fermi wrote The Story of Atomic Energy for young readers. CA-2

FERRIS, Helen Josephine 1890-
Author, editor. Born in Nebraska, the daughter of a clergyman, she has lived in Wisconsin, New Jersey, and Pennsylvania, and located near Croton Falls, New York, after her marriage to Albert B. Tibbets. Graduate of Vassar College, she accomplished many "firsts." Helen Ferris was the first editor of the Girl Scout magazine, The American Girl, and the first editor of the children's book review department

of The Atlantic Monthly Bookshelf. She has been recreational director of girls' camps, and for many years was editor-in-chief of the Junior Literary Guild. Juvenile titles include: Girls Who Did; Stories of Real Girls and Their Careers, Girls, Girls, Girls; Stories of Love, Courage, and the Quest for Happiness; selected by Helen Ferris. JBA-1, JBA-2

FIELD, Rachel 1894-1942
Author, poet, she grew up in Stockbridge, Massachusetts. She attended Radcliffe and later worked in New York in an editorial capacity. Her verse, plays, and stories have endeared her to children of all ages. One of her most popular stories was Hitty: Her First Hundred Years, winner of the 1930 Newbery Medal. Other juvenile books include: Calico Bush, Patchwork Plays, Poems, Prayer for a Child (which won the Caldecott Medal in 1945 for Elizabeth Orton Jones' illustrations), Rachel Field Story Book. JBA-1, JBA-2

FINGER, Charles Joseph 1871-1941
Born in Willesden, England, he received his education in London at King's College, and in Germany at Frankfort-on-the-Main. Charles Finger has been shipwrecked, hunted gold, and found adventure in Africa, Alaska, Canada, and Mexico. After he decided to write at the age of fifty, Arkansas has been his home. In 1925, he was awarded the Newbery Medal for Tales From Silver Lands. Other children's books include: Courageous Companions, A Dog at His Heel. JBA-1

FITCH, Florence Mary 1875-1959
Born in Stratford, Connecticut, graduate of Oberlin, and received her Ph. D. in philosophy from the University of Berlin. She did graduate work at Union Theological Seminary and the University of Chicago Divinity School. She has lived in Egypt, India, China, and Japan where she studied religious customs. Miss Fitch has been Dean of Women and on the faculty of Oberlin College. Juvenile books in-

clude: Book About God, Child Jesus, One God; the Ways We Worship Him, Their Search for God; Ways of Worship in the Orient. MJA

FLACK, Marjorie 1897-1958
Author-illustrator. Born in Greenport, Long Island. She studied at the Art Students League in New York. Several of her books have been written about experiences which she shared with her daughter, Hilma. She once said that she particularly enjoyed writing Tim Tadpole and the Great Bullfrog because it grew out of visits to the Museum of Natural History and walks in the woods. The death of Marjorie Flack in 1958 was a great loss to children's literature. Her books include: Angus and the Cat, Angus and the Ducks, Ask Mr. Bear, New Pet, The Story About Ping, Topsy, Wag-Tail Bess, Wait for William, Walter the Lazy Mouse. JBA-1, JBA-2

FLETCHER, Beale
Attended the University of North Carolina, also was active in the Carolina Playmakers. Later, he taught dancing and organized his own dance act. After his marriage, he and his wife operated their own dance studio, the Fletcher School of Dancing, which grew into one of the largest dancing schools in the South. For young people he wrote: How to Improve Your Tap Dancing; For the Beginning, Intermediate, and Professional Dancer.

FLOETHE, Louise Lee
Author, dramatic teacher. She has lived in Sarasota, Florida, with her illustrator-husband, Richard Floethe. Daughter of an artist, she has been an actress and a director of children's plays. Her interests have centered around sailing and horsemanship. The Winning Colt was written by Mrs. Floethe and illustrated by Mr. Floethe, and based upon a true story. She has written, and her husband has illustrated: Blueberry Pie, The Fisherman and His Boat, Sea of Grass. CA-1

FLOHERTY, John Joseph 1882-
Author, photographer, reporter, artist. His factual books have been based on his own observations and experiences. He has witnessed a hurricane aboard a Coast Guard cutter, flown on transport planes, and has served with city and state police in order to write authoritative books for young people. He has studied at the Art Students League in New York, and has been in charge of a Photographic Illustration Studio. Juvenile titles include: Aviation From the Ground Up, Behind the Microphone, Behind the Silver Shield, Deep Down Under, Inside the F.B.I., Sons of the Hurricane. JBA-2

FORBES, Esther 1894-
She was born in Westborough, Massachusetts, and studied at the University of Wisconsin. She has been the recipient of honorary degrees from colleges and of awards for her books. In 1943 her book, Paul Revere and the World He Lived In, won the Pulitzer Prize, and in 1944 she was awarded the Newbery Medal for her book, Johnny Tremain. She wrote America's Paul Revere for young people. MJA

FORRESTER, Frank H.
A native of New York. He has lived in Jacksonville, Florida, with his family, and was weather expert over TV station WMBR. He was a meteorologist, a member of the American Meteorological Society, and the New York Academy of Sciences. Mr. Forrester has worked in New York's Hayden Planetarium where he served as "deputy manager" which included teaching, special programming, and promotion work. In the juvenile field he wrote Real Book About the Weather.

FORSYTH, Gloria
Graduate of Bennett Junior College, New York. She received her A.B. degree from Stanford University in Social Sciences. She has been a reporter for the Santa Barbara News-Press, and helped her husband edit This Week in Santa Barbara. Also, she has

worked in radio. She has attended the Writers' Conference at the University of Connecticut, where she studied children's literature, taught by author Elizabeth Yates. She wrote Pelican Prill for young readers.

FOX, Mary Virginia
She began writing at the age of ten. She became interested in painting and majored in art at Northwestern University. After her marriage, she returned to writing, and many of her short stories were published. A trip to New York included a visit to the Statue of Liberty which inspired her to write Apprentice to Liberty. She also wrote Ambush at Fort Dearborn.

FOX, William W. 1909-
Graduate of the University of California, with a degree in Paleontology. He has worked for the United States Department of Agriculture, Soil Conservation Service, and has worked in water-shed planning in California. He lived in Berkeley with his librarian-wife who interested him in writing books on conservation for young readers. He wrote Rocks and Rain and the Rays of the Sun, which was the recipient of an Award of Merit by the Soil Conservation Society of America. He has also written Careers in Biological Sciences for young people. CA-4

FRASCONI, Antonio 1919-
Born in Montevideo, Uruguay. In 1945 he came to the United States when he received a scholarship to the Art Students League in New York. He has received many awards for his work, and in 1954 was given a grant by the National Institute of Arts and Letters. Mr. Frasconi has had many one-man shows, and his work can be seen in many museums. He wrote: House That Jack Built; la maison que Jacques a batie, See and Say, guarda e parla, mira y habla, regarde et parle, The Snow and the Sun; la nieve y el sol. CA-1

FRASER, Beatrice and Ferrin
Husband and wife team who met in high school at Lockport, New York. Beatrice Fraser attended Eastman School of Music at the University of Rochester, and Ferrin went to Columbia University in New York. After their marriage in Paris, France, they returned to America where Beatrice started a Music School, and Ferrin continued writing and publishing. They wrote: A Song Is Born; a Story of Music for Beginners, and Ferrin Fraser was the joint author of On Jungle Trails, by Frank Buck.

FRAZIER, Neta (Lohnes) 1890-
Born in Owosso, Michigan. She graduated from Whitman College in Walla Walla, Washington. She taught school before her marriage to Earl C. Frazier. Also, she has been on the staff of a newspaper. From this experience, she wrote By-Line Dennie. Her books for young people include: The Magic Ring, Young Bill Fargo. CA-2

FREEMAN, Godfrey
Born in Oxfordshire, England. He attended St. Edward's, Oxford. During World War II, he was an army glider pilot and captured by the Germans at Arnhem. He has lived in Iran, and has been a schoolmaster in England. He wrote about Till Eulenspiegel, the legendary figure of Germany, in his book The Owl and the Mirror.

FREEMAN, Ira Maximilian 1905-
Scientist-author. He has been a professor of physics at Rutgers University in New Jersey. Also, he has been a consultant to UNESCO, and to Coronet Instructional Films. Dr. Freeman served on the Physics Committee of the Educational Testing Service. Juvenile contributions include: All About Electricity, All About Sound and Ultrasonics, All About the Wonders of Chemistry. Dr. Freeman and his wife, Mae Blacker Freeman, have written many books including: You Will Go to the Moon, Your Wonderful World of Science.

FRITZ, Jean Guttery 1915-
Born in China, the daughter of missionaries. She has been a textbook editor. The year 1952 marked the appearance of her first book for children. Many of her stories have appeared in magazines. Juvenile titles include: Brady, The Cabin Faced West, How to Read a Rabbit, Late Spring, San Francisco. CA-4

G

GÁG, Flavia 1907-
Illustrator-author, born in Minnesota. She was the youngest in a family of seven children. This included another author-illustrator of children's books, her sister Wanda who died in 1946. She has lived in New York City and has often visited New Jersey and Florida. Her juvenile contributions include: Chubby's First Year, Four Legs and a Tail, Fourth Floor Menagerie, Tweeter of Prairie Dog Town, A Wish for Mimi. MJA

GAGLIARDO, Ruth
Graduated from the University of Kansas. She has taught children's literature, and has been an active worker in the American Library Association and the National Parent-Teacher's Association. Mrs. Gagliardo once said, "... The excitement and enchantment of books and living were brought to my brother and me by our mother's bedtime reading. When our own children came along, their father and godmother and I shared with The Three our own joy in books..." She wrote Let's Read Aloud; Stories and Poems.

GALL, Alice (Crew)
Born in McConnelsville, Ohio. She and her brother, Fleming Crew, often took hikes together during their childhood, and later brought these delightful experiences to their books. Mrs. Gall once said: "My brother and I have often wished that every child could have the lively experience of spending at least part of its life in a little town surrounded by hills, at the edge of a lovely river." Juvenile titles in-

clude: Bushy Tail, In Peace and War; a Story of Human Service. Mrs. Gall and her brother have written many books which include: Flat Tail, Little Black Ant. JBA-2

GANNETT, Ruth Stiles 1923-
Her father was book critic, Lewis Gannett, of the New York Herald Tribune. She graduated from Vassar, and has served on the staff of the Children's Book Council. Her first book for boys and girls was My Father's Dragon, the illustrator was Mrs. Lewis Gannett (Ruth Chrisman Gannett). Also, she wrote: Dragons of Blueland, Elmer and the Dragon, Katie and the Sad Noise, Wonderful House-Boat-Train.

GARNETT, Eve
Born in the Midlands, England. She attended the Chelsea Polytechnic School of Art, the Royal Academy Schools where she was awarded the Cheswick Prize and Medal. The Carnegie Gold Medal was awarded to Miss Garnett for her first book, The Family From One End Street in 1937. Also, she has had paintings exhibited in London art galleries. Her juvenile titles include: Further Adventures of the Family From One End Street, Holiday at the Dew Drop Inn; a One End Street Story. CA-4

GARST, Doris (Shannon) 1899-
Teacher and author, she was born in Ironwood, Michigan. She received her education in Denver, Colorado, and in Oregon, where she was a teacher in a country school. Juvenile magazines have published her articles and short stories. She married an attorney and has lived in Wyoming. Gardening, photography, and stamp collecting have been her hobbies. This author has written many books for children, including: Amelia Earhart, Heroine of the Skies, Cowboy Boots, Custer, Fighter of the Plains, Jack London, Magnet for Adventure, James Bowie and His Famous Knife, Red Eagle (a Junior Literary Guild selection), Silver Spurs for Cowboy Boots, Will Rogers, Immortal Cowboy. CA-4, JBA-2

GARTHWAITE, Marion (Hook) 1893-
Born in Oakland, California. She graduated from the University of California, received library training at the Riverside Library School. She has been a librarian at El Centro High School, and children's librarian at the Madera County Library in California. Tomás was her first book, other titles include: Coarse Gold Gulch, Shaken Days. CA-5/6

GAUL, Albro T.
Entomologist-author, native of Brooklyn, New York. He has done special work for the New York City Department of Parks, and has worked in the United States Department of Agriculture. Mr. Gaul has been an officer of the Brooklyn Entomological Society. He wrote Picture Book of Insects.

GAULT, William Campbell
Born in Milwaukee, Wisconsin. He has been an aircraft assembler, manager of a hotel, mailman, instrument corporal, and has written many good books for young people. He wrote Drag Strip and said, "a drag strip in every town might help to build a vast reservoir of young men who are going to get interested in engineering." Juvenile titles include: Little Big Foot, Road-Race Rookie, Wheels of Fortune; Four Racing Stories.

GEISEL, Theodor Seuss 1904-
He is known as Dr. Seuss. Born in Springfield, Massachusetts, he graduated from Dartmouth, and did graduate work at Oxford, Vienna, and Paris. He had intended to become a history professor, but one of his cartoons was published in the Saturday Evening Post, and his plans were changed. In the 1930's he had a contract with "Flit," and his cartoons of "Quick Henry, the Flit!" became famous throughout the country. He married Helen Manon Palmer, a girl he met at Oxford. His books include: And to Think That I Saw It on Mulberry Street, Horton Hatches the Egg.

GEORGE, John Lothar 1916- and Jean Craighead 1919-

Husband-wife team, authors-illustrators. Mr. George attended the University of Wisconsin, received his B. S. in Wildlife Management in the School of Forestry and Conservation, and his M. S. degree in Zoology from the University of Michigan. He has been camp director and a Ranger Naturalist. Completing his service in the navy, he returned to graduate work at the University of Michigan. After their marriage in 1944, Jean George continued her work in art and writing. A graduate of Penn State, she was editor of the literary magazine. During the war, she was a reporter for the International News Service in Washington. Together John and Jean George have written for juvenile readers: Masked Prowler; the Story of a Raccoon, Vison, the Mink, Vulpes, the Red Fox. MJA

GILL, Richard

Born in Washington, D. C. Upon completing college, he worked in South America. Paralysis destined him to ultimately search for curare, a substance from South American trees, and return it for medical research. Mr. Gill wrote White Water and Black Magic for adults. In partnership with Helen Hoke he has written Paco Goes to the Fair and The Story of the Other America for children.

GIRVAN, Helen (Masterman) 1891-

She was born in Minneapolis, Minnesota. She has attended art school and has studied secretarial work at Columbia. Prior to her marriage to Coling Gemmill Girvan, Helen Girvan had been a secretary in the executive offices of the Condé Nast publications. She has been interested in art, the theater, cooking, and animals. The Girvans have lived in Connecticut. Juvenile contributions include: The Clue in the Antique Clock, The Frightened Whisper, Hidden Pond, Seventh Step; Mystery at Cedarhead. MJA

GOETZ, Delia 1898-

Born in Wesley, Iowa. A graduate of Iowa State

Teachers College, she has taught in the United States and in foreign countries. She has served as secretary to the Minister of Guatemala in Washington, D. C., has been on the staff of the Washington Bureau of the Foreign Policy Association, and on the staff of the United States Office of Education. Extensive travels, and the experiences derived from them, enabled Miss Goetz to write many juvenile books, including: Arctic Tundra, Deserts, Half a Hemisphere; the Story of Latin America, Let's Read About South America, Letters From Guatemala, Mountains, Swamps, Tropical Rain Forests.

GOLLOMB, Joseph 1881-1950
Teacher, author, reporter. He was born in Russia, but came to America at the age of ten. He attended the City College of New York and obtained his M.A. degree from Columbia University. Joseph Gollomb was a high school teacher and later, was a newspaper reporter and traveled abroad. Collier's, Cosmopolitan, The New Yorker, and The Atlantic Monthly have published his articles and stories. Juvenile books include: Albert Schweitzer: Genius In the Jungle, Tiger at City High, Tuning In at Lincoln High, Up at City High. JBA-1, JBA-2

GOTTLIEB, William P.
Author-photographer. His color photography has appeared in books and magazines. He has produced filmstrips on education and has been the head of a filmstrip company which has produced almost 500 filmstrips. During World War II, he was an aerial photographer. Juvenile contributions include: Jets and Rockets and How They Work, Real Book About Photography, Table Tennis, Photography With Basic Cameras.

GOUDEY, Alice E. 1898-
Born in Kansas. Mrs. Goudey has lived in New York where her husband has been Chairman of the Science Department of the Bronxville Public School. Her nature and animal stories have become well-known by young readers. Her books include: The

Day We Saw the Sun Come Up, Here Come the Bears, Here Come the Beavers, Here Come the Bees, Here Come the Dolphins, Houses From the Sea, Jupiter and the Cats, Sunnyvale Fair.

GOULD, Jean Rosalind 1909-
Born in Darke County, Ohio. She received her education at the University of Michigan and Toledo University. Miss Gould went to New York and began writing in Greenwich Village. She has enjoyed gardening, watercolor painting, and cooking. She wrote That Dunbar Boy; the Story of America's Famous Negro Poet, because she believed it "...might set an example for school children everywhere." Young Mariner Melville was another book she contributed to the juvenile field.

GRAHAM, Al 1897-
A native of Newburyport, Massachusetts, he has lived in Boston and New York City. His drawings, light verse, and informative material have appeared in several magazines including The Saturday Evening Post, The New Yorker, and The New York Times Magazine. His work has been featured in Franklin P. Adams famous newspaper column, "The Conning Tower." His children's books include: Songs For a Small Guitar; Verses by Al Graham, The Rhymes of Squire O'Squirrel, Timothy Turtle.

GRAHAM, Alberta (Powell)
Musician and composer, author, teacher. She was born in Harrington, Delaware, and grew up in Ottumwa, Iowa. She graduated from the American Conservatory in Chicago, and attended Columbia, Northwestern, and Cornell Universities. Music, poetry, education, and literature were studied by Mrs. Graham, and she obtained a great deal of special training in those fields. Also, history of the United States has been one of her main interests. Her books include: Christopher Columbus, Discoverer, Great Bands of America, Strike Up the Band, Bandleaders of Today, Thirty-Three Roads to the White House.

GRAHAM, Clarence Reginald 1907
Librarian of the Louisville Free Public Library. He has served as president of the American Library Association, the Southeastern Library Association, and the Kentucky Library Association. He has always been active in civic affairs. Articles on library science and educational films have been written by Mr. Graham. For the young reader he has written First Book of Public Libraries.

GRAHAME, Kenneth 1859-1932
Born in Edinburgh, Scotland. He spent a great part of his life at Cookham Dene on the Thames river which provided him with the setting for his book, The Wind in the Willows. This book began as stories told at bedtime to his small son Alastair. Mr. Grahame was associated with the Bank of England, first as a clerk and later, as secretary of the Bank. He wrote: Dream Days, The Golden Age. JBA-1

GRAMATKY, Hardie 1907-
Author-illustrator, born in Dallas, Texas, he grew up in Los Angeles, California. He attended Stanford University, Palo Alto, and the Chouinard Art School in Los Angeles. Mr. Gramatky has been a magazine illustrator, and had an art studio in New York with a view of the East River. It was here that he wrote and illustrated his children's classic, Little Toot. His work has been shown in the Chicago Art Institute, the Brooklyn Museum, and in the Toledo Museum of Fine Arts. Juvenile books include: Bolivar, Homer and the Circus Train, Loopy, Sparky, the Story of a Little Trolley Car. CA-2, JBA-2

GRANT, Bruce 1893-
Author, free-lance writer, war correspondent. Born in Wichita Falls, Texas. He attended private schools and studied at the University of Kentucky. As a newspaperman, he worked in Louisville, Kentucky, Chicago, and New York. During World War II, he was a war correspondent in Europe and was

the chief of the London foreign news bureau of his newspaper. Mr. Grant has been associated with naval and historical organizations. Interests and experiences in these activities helped to form the basis for some of his stories. Juvenile contributions include: American Indians, Yesterday and Today, Cyclone, Davy Crockett, American Hero, Leopard Horse Canyon, Pancho, a Dog of the Plains, The Star-Spangled Rooster. CA-1

GRAVES, Robert 1895-
Eminent poet, novelist, essayist, critic, and historian. Born in England, he studied at Oxford University. In World War I he was a captain with the Royal Welch Fusiliers. At the Royal University in Cairo, Egypt, Mr. Graves has occupied the Chair of English Literature. His main interest was poetry. He was awarded the gold medal of the National Poetry Society of America and the Foyle Award of England, for his work Collected Poems. Included in his works for children are: Greek Gods and Heroes, The Penny Fiddle; Poems for Children. CA-5/6

GRAY, Elizabeth Janet 1902-
Librarian, author. She studied at the Germantown Friends School and attended Bryn Mawr College. Also, she received a library science degree from the Drexel Institute. She has been a teacher, writer of short stories, and a librarian. After the death of her husband, Morgan Vining (who had been a faculty member of the University of North Carolina), she lived in Philadelphia. A very unusual opportunity was presented to Elizabeth Janet Gray when she was selected to teach English to the Crown Prince of Japan. Included in her books for children are: Adam of the Road (winner of the 1943 Newbery Medal), Cheerful Heart, Fair Adventure, Young Walter Scott. JBA-2

GREENE, Carla 1916-
Born in Minneapolis. At one time she worked in advertising. She has been interested in the theater,

ballet, concert music, child psychology, and education. Miss Greene has combined interesting material, delightful illustrations, and easy reading, to create a very popular book for the individual child. Also, she has written short stories, radio plays, and articles for adults. Juvenile contributions are many and include: Doctors and Nurses; What Do They Do?, I Want to Be a Ballet Dancer, I Want to Be a Carpenter, I Want to Be a Farmer, I Want to Be a Homemaker, I Want to Be a Librarian, I Want to Be a Teacher, A Trip On a Jet, A Trip On a Ship. CA-4

GRIFFIN, Gillett Good 1928-
Born in Brooklyn, New York, he has lived in Connecticut. A graduate of Deerfield Academy, he studied painting at the Yale School of Fine Arts. He wrote and illustrated A Mouse's Tale, a book for children, as an assignment in the Graphic Design Department at Yale. In 1952 it was selected as one of the Fifty Books of the Year. Design and typography were his interests but collecting children's books was his main hobby. Also, Mr. Griffin has been Curator of the Graphic Arts Foundation of Princeton University Library. He wrote A Mouse's Tale.

GRIMM, Jakob Ludwig Karl 1785-1863 and Wilhelm Karl 1786-1859
The Grimm Brothers attended the University of Marburg. They have been librarians in the library of Jerome Bonaparte and teachers at the University of Kassel and in Berlin. Their first volume of folk tales was published in 1812. The tales have been published in many languages, and have been loved by many generations of children. Their many titles include: Fairy Tales of the Grimm Brothers, Fisherman and His Wife, The Four Musicians, Hansel and Gretel, Rapunzel, The Seven Ravens.

GRONOWICZ, Antoni 1913-
A native of Poland, he was the recipient of an award from his government for literature. With the

money obtained from this award, Mr. Gronowicz came to America with the purpose of studying and writing about Americans with Polish backgrounds. Also, he has written for the English and Polish press, and has lectured in universities throughout the United States. His novels and poems have been published in France and Czechoslovakia, and his plays have been produced in several countries. Juvenile titles include: Chopin; Rendered in English by Jessie McEwen, Paderewski, Pianist and Patriot, Rendered in English by Jessie McEwen.

GRUENBERG, Sidonie (Matsner) 1881-
She has been Director and later, Special Consultant of the Child Study Association of America. Mrs. Gruenberg has been an authority on child development, and has traveled extensively in the United States in her work with parent education. She wrote Wonderful Story of How You Were Born, and edited: All Kinds of Courage, Favorite Stories Old and New, ...Let's Read a Story (a Junior Literary Guild selection).

GRUMBINE, E. Evalyn 1900-
Author and advertising authority. A native of Chicago, and graduate of the University of Illinois, this author's works will be found in libraries under her married name, McNally. Her husband Andrew McNally, Jr. was a Chicago doctor. She has served as secretary to the advertising manager of Child Life Magazine; later, became director of School and Camp advertising, advertising director, and assistant publisher. Together she and her husband have written for children This Is Mexico.

GUILLOT, René 1900-
Teacher, author, born in France. He graduated from the University of Bordeaux. After his marriage, René Guillot lived in Africa and taught mathematics in the high school of Dakar. During World War II, he received the Legion of Honor and the Bronze Star. Also, he has been a professor at the Lycée Condorcet in Paris. Mr. Guillot has been

the recipient of many literary awards, and in 1946 was awarded the Grand Prix du Roman d'Adventures. Included in his books for young people are: The King of the Cats; tr. by John Marshall, Mokokambo, the Lost Land; tr. by John Marshall, The 397th White Elephant; tr. by Gwen Marsh. MJA

GULLAHORN, Genevieve
Born in Lithuania. After her arrival in the United States at the age of eight, she has lived in Maryland, California, and Massachusetts. After her marriage she lived in Illinois. After learning English, Mrs. Gullahorn's interest turned to writing and at the age of twelve she sold her first children's story to the Baltimore Sunday Sun. She was editor of her high-school paper and also, was the women's editor of the paper at the University of Southern California, where she was awarded a scholarship in journalism. She worked for several newspapers after her graduation. For children she wrote Zigger, the Pet Chameleon, which was an actual account of family experiences with a chameleon.

GUTHRIE, Anne 1890-
Born in San Diego, California, she grew up in Denver, Colorado. A graduate of Stanford University, Guthrie House on the campus was named in her honor. An extensive traveler, she has served as Continental Secretary for the Y. W. C. A. 's of South America, acted as adviser to this organization in the Philippines, and was Y. W. C. A. Executive for India, Burma, and Ceylon. After her return from the Far East in 1947, Miss Guthrie has lived in New York City, where she has shown great interest in the United Nations. Her experiences created for her a background that enabled her to understand and to write her book, Madame Ambassador; the Life of Vijaya Lakshmi Pandit, for young readers.

H

HADER, Berta (Hoerner) Elmer 1889-
Husband-wife team, authors, illustrators. Born in

Mexico, Berta Hader studied journalism at the University of Washington, and attended the California School of Design. She married artist Elmer Hader. Born in Pajaro, California, Mr. Hader studied in Paris, France. After service in World War I, he married Berta Hoerner. In 1949 the Haders won the Caldecott Medal for their book, The Big Snow. Other titles include: Big City, Friendly Phoebe, Little Antelope; An Indian for a Day, Lost in the Zoo, Midget and Bridget, Wish on the Moon. JBA-1, JBA-2

HAGER, Alice Rogers 1894-
Born in Peoria, Illinois, she has lived in Colorado, Arizona, and California. She has been president of the Woman's National Press Club, and Information Officer in the Foreign Service at the American Embassy in Brussels. As a war correspondent in World War II, she received a War Department Citation. As a reporter, she has flown many miles, and this experience provided her with the incentive to write about aviation. Her book, Canvas Castle, was the winner of the Julia Ellsworth Ford foundation award for children's literature. She also wrote Washington, City of Destiny. CA-5/6

HAHN, Emily 1905-
Reporter and author, born in St. Louis, Missouri. She graduated from the University of Wisconsin with a degree in Mining Engineering, and continued her studies at Columbia University and at Oxford. She has traveled extensively, and has lived in China, India, the Belgian Congo, and North Africa. She married Professor Charles R. Boxer and has lived in England. Juvenile book titles include: First Book of India, Francie, Francie Again, June Finds A Way (a Junior Literary Guild selection), Leonardo da Vinci, Mary, Queen of Scots. CA-3

HALL, Elvajean
Author and librarian, a native of Illinois. She received her B. A. degree from Oberlin College, and attended Columbia University and the University of

Wisconsin Library School. Miss Hall has been a librarian in Illinois, Wisconsin and Michigan, and was a librarian at Stephens College. She has been co-ordinator of library services of the public schools of Newton, Massachusetts. She has traveled extensively, visiting England fourteen times. Included in her titles for young people are: Land and People of Argentina, The Land and People of Norway.

HALL, Esther Greenacre
Author and journalist. Born on a Colorado cattle ranch, she used this setting for her book, Back to Buckeye. She attended Stanford University, and this experience enabled her to write College on Horseback. She spent a summer in a Kentucky settlement school. Mrs. Hall has collected many antiques, and Woods End Farm, her home in Armonk, New York, has been the setting for them. Helping to establish the public library at Armonk was her proudest achievement. She has written Mario and the Chuna; a Boy and a Bird of the Argentine for boys and girls.

HALSMAN, Philippe
Author and photographer. He has created more Life magazine covers than any other photographer. Plays and books were written while he was living in Europe. In 1949 his first book was published in America. It was called The Frenchman. In order to tell stories to his two daughters, he invented the character of "Piccoli." Piccoli's adventures were not only entertaining but instructive. Encouraged by friends, he assembled the stories into a book entitled Piccoli, a Fairy Tale for all children to enjoy.

HANDFORTH, Thomas Schofield 1897-1948
Born in Tacoma, Washington, he studied art in New York and Paris. He was awarded the Caldecott Medal in 1939 for his book, Mei Li, which was created when Mr. Handforth lived in Peking, China. Before his death in 1948, Mr. Handforth resided in California. His work has been exhibited in many great museums including the Metropolitan Museum of

Art in New York, the Chicago Art Institute, and the Fogg Art Museum in Cambridge, Massachusetts. He wrote and illustrated Mei Li. JBA-2

HARKINS, Philip 1912-
Author, free-lance writer, sports enthusiast. He was born in Boston, Massachusetts. His education has consisted of private and public schools and study abroad at the University of Grenoble in France and the School of Political Science in Paris. He has been very interested in sports, and at one time played semi-professional hockey in Paris. Also, Mr. Harkins has been a news reporter, a free-lance writer for magazines, and a seaman in the Merchant Marine. In 1943 his first book, Coast Guard, Ahoy! was published. Other titles include: Big Silver Bowl, Bomber Pilot, Double Play, Fight Like a Falcon, Knockout, Road Race, Young Skin Diver. MJA

HARNETT, Cynthia
English author-illustrator. As a young girl in Kensington, England, long hours were spent in the company of her brother visiting castles and old churches. When she was only ten years old, she was publishing her own magazine. In 1951 she was awarded the Carnegie Medal for her book, Nicholas and the Wool Pack. Also, she wrote Caxton's Challenge.

HARPER, Wilhelmina
Librarian-author, born in Farmington, Maine. She has held important library posts in New York, California, and France. She was the first county children's librarian to be appointed in California. This position was in the Kern County Free Library at Bakersfield. In addition to serving in libraries, she has been a teacher of children's literature at the San Jose, California, State Teacher's College, Riverside Library School, and at the University of California School of Librarianship. She compiled: Easter Chimes; Stories for Easter and the Spring Season, The Harvest Feast; Stories of Thanksgiving, Yesterday and Today, Merry Christmas to You!

HARRINGTON, Lyn

Librarian-author. She spent her childhood in the Great Lakes region and Sault Ste. Marie, Ontario. She has been a children's librarian in the Soo and in a boys' club in Toronto. As a result of accompanying her husband on his photographic expeditions, she has learned a great deal about the Arctic. She wrote Ootook, Young Eskimo Girl (photographs by Richard Harrington).

HARRIS, Joel Chandler 1848-1908

Born in Georgia, Mr. Harris began working as a typesetter on a newspaper at the age of fifteen. This weekly newspaper was published at a plantation, and it was during this period of his life that he heard the many stories from the Negroes which later became so well-known as his "Uncle Remus" tales. Later, he and his son published the Uncle Remus' Magazine. He wrote: Aaron in the Wildwoods, Told By Uncle Remus; New Stories of the Old Plantation. JBA-1

HARSHAW, Ruth (Hetzel)

She has been educational director for Carson, Pirie, Scott store in Chicago, and started the popular radio book program called "The Hobby Horse Presents." In collaboration with Dilla MacBean who was director of School Libraries in Chicago, she wrote What Book Is That? Fun With Books at Home, at School.

HAVIGHURST, Walter 1901-

Born in Appleton, Wisconsin. He has studied in colleges both in America and England. At one time he traveled around the world in the United States Merchant Marine. He has been a Professor of English at Miami University in Oxford, Ohio. He has written books with his wife, Marion Margaret Boyd, including Climb a Lofty Ladder. Also, he wrote: Buffalo Bill's Great Wild West Show, First Book of Pioneers: Northwest Territory, The First Book of the California Gold Rush, High Prairie, Life in America: the Great Plains. CA-3, MJA

HAWES, Charles Boardman 1889-1923

He grew up in Bangor, Maine, and spent his college days in Bowdoin. He has always been interested in the sea, and decided to live in Gloucester. In the book, A Critical History of Children's Literature, by Cornelia Meigs, Anne Eaton, Elizabeth Nesbitt, and Ruth Hill Viguers has been written: "In describing his strong, well-balanced personality one friend has said, 'He had the wind with him; whenever he came we saw in our imagination the blue ocean as it is on a clear, cool day...He was himself...the stuff that skippers are made of.' " He worked with The Youth's Companion and the Open Road magazines. In 1924 he was awarded posthumously the Newbery Medal for The Dark Frigate. JBA-1

HAWKES, Hester 1900-

Has lived in Cambridge, Massachusetts, and for seven years in the Orient. She wrote one story based on an important news item, the shipment of "Seeds for Democracy" in 1950. The gift of seeds from the Americans to the Filipinos who were desperately in need of a better diet, inspired her to write a story about Luis and the three seeds in Three Seeds. She wrote Ning's Pony.

HAWKINS, Quail

Born in Spokane, Washington. She studied at the University of California. Miss Hawkins has worked in bookshops and publishing houses including the University of California Press in Berkeley. Juvenile titles include: The Aunt-Sitter, Mountain Courage, Who Wants an Apple.

HAWTHORNE, Hildegarde

Grand-daughter of Nathaniel Hawthorne. She has lived in many parts of the world including England and France. At one time her home was on a plantation in Jamaica. Miss Hawthorne has served on the staff of the New York Times and St. Nicholas. Juvenile contributions include: Born to Adventure; the Story of John Charles Fremont, Give Me Liberty,

The Mineature's Secret, Ox-Team Miracle; the Story of Alexander Majors, Phantom King, the Story of Napoleon's Son. JBA-1

HAYCRAFT, Howard 1905-
Born in Madelia, Minnesota. He graduated from the University of Minnesota. He married Molly Costain, the daughter of novelist Thomas Costain. She wrote First Lady of the Theatre: Sarah Siddons. Mr. Haycraft has been president of the H. W. Wilson Company, and was one of the founders of the Mystery Writers of America. He edited: Boys' Book of Great Detective Stories, Boys' Second Book of Great Detective Stories, Junior Book of Authors (with Stanley Jasspon Kunitz).

HAYES, Florence (Sooy) 1895-
She attended Columbia University, and later wrote Hosh-ki the Navajo following an assignment in a juvenile writing class taught by Dr. Mabel Robinson. Mrs. Hayes has been interested in Indians and Eskimos. She has traveled in Alaska, Central America, Mexico, and lived one year in the Southwest. She once said, "Writing for children is richly rewarding." Her titles for young people include: The Boy in the 49th Seat, Burro Tamer, Good Luck Feather, Skid.

HAYWOOD, Carolyn 1898-
Born in Philadelphia, Pennsylvania, she graduated from the Philadelphia Normal School and also attended the Pennsylvania Academy of Fine Arts. In addition to writing books for boys and girls, she has been a portrait painter. Juvenile titles include: Annie Pat and Eddie, "B" Is For Betsy, Back to School With Betsy, Betsy and Billy, Eddie and Gardenia, Here Comes the Bus! JBA-2

HAZLETT, Edward Everett 1892-
Born in Kansas. He graduated from Annapolis. During World War I, he commanded a submarine chaser squadron in the Adriatic. He has had an illustrious career in the submarine service, and has

taught at Annapolis. His articles have appeared in the Encyclopaedia Britannica and the Naval Institute Proceedings. He wrote for young people "He's Jake!" The Story of a Submarine Dog.

HEINLEIN, Robert Anson 1907-
Science fiction writer for young people. He was born in Butler, Missouri, and graduated from the United States Naval Academy at Annapolis. During World War II, he served in the Navy and met his wife, former WAVE lieutenant Virginia Gerstenfeld. They have lived in Colorado. Juvenile titles include: Between Planets, Citizen of the Galaxy, The Rolling Stones, The Star Beast, Starship Troopers, Tunnel in the Sky. CA-2, MJA.

HENDERSON, Le Grand 1901-
Author-artist. His pseudonym is Le Grand. He was born in Torrington, Connecticut, and studied painting at Yale. He once cruised in a schooner near the coast of Maine, and served as a combination sea-cook and deck hand. This undoubtedly provided research and flavor for his rollicking book, Cap'n Dow and the Hole in the Doughnut. Other juvenile titles include: Augustus and the Desert, Augustus and the River, Augustus Flies, Augustus Hits the Road, Cats for Kansas, How Baseball Began in Brooklyn. CA-5/6, JBA-2.

HEIDERSTADT, Dorothy 1907-
Librarian, author. In the 1890's her great-grandmother was an Indian Agent in Oklahoma. She has been a member of the Oklahoma Historical Society, and has visited many Indian schools. An outstanding occasion was a visit made to Bacone (Indian) College where she heard the Indian choir sing and use sign language for the 23rd Psalm. She has been Director of Children's Work at the Public Library of Bethlehem, Pennsylvania, and has been on the staff of the Public Library of Kansas City, Missouri. Juvenile titles include: Frontier Leaders and Pioneers, Ten Torchbearers. CA-4

HENRY, Marguerite (Breithaupt) 1902-
Grew up in Milwaukee, Wisconsin, and graduated from Milwaukee State Teachers College. After her marriage to Sidney Crocker Henry, she contributed articles to magazines. They have lived near Wayne, Illinois. Her book *Justin Morgan Had a Horse* was given the Junior Scholastic Gold Seal Award and the Award of the Friends of Literature. In 1949 she won the Newbery Medal for her book *King of the Wind.* Juvenile contributions include: *All About Horses,* *Always Reddy,* *Australia in Story and Pictures,* *Benjamin West and His Cat Grimalkin,* *Black Gold,* *Born to Trot.* JBA-2

HEUMAN, William
Born in Brooklyn, New York. His first sale to the publishing world was a juvenile story which brought him $3.50. Since that time, Mr. Heuman has contributed articles to *Collier's,* the *Post,* and *Sports Illustrated.* He has been very interested in sports, and also, has collected antique weapons and guns. His juvenile titles include: *Famous American Athletes,* *Rookie Backstop.*

HEYLIGER, William 1884-
Born in Hoboken, New Jersey. He began his career as a newspaperman on the *Hudson Observer* He worked on newspapers for twenty years, and then devoted full time to his writing. He has written many books for young people on sports and careers. They include: *Gasoline Jockey,* *Son of the Apple Valley,* *SOS Radio Patrol,* *Top Lineman,* *You're On the Air.* JBA-1, JBA-2.

HICKOK, Lorena A.
Born in East Troy, Wisconsin. She attended the University of Minnesota. Later she was on the staff of the *Minneapolis Tribune.* She wrote about political events for the Associated Press, and this led to her friendship with the late President Roosevelt and his wife. She has lived in Hyde Park, New York, near the home of the Roosevelts. She has enjoyed gardening, dogs, history, and the

Dodgers. Her books for young people include: The Road to the White House; F.D.R.: the Pre-Presidential Years, Story of Helen Keller.

HICKS, Clifford B. 1920-
He has been Associate Editor of Popular Mechanics magazine. In this capacity Mr. Hicks has been responsible for a great deal of the atomic energy and missile information which was published in the magazine. He wrote First Boy On the Moon; a Junior Science Fiction Novel as an answer to his own two boys' questions. CA-5/6.

HIGHTOWER, Florence Cole 1916-
Born in Boston, Massachusetts. She graduated from Vassar College. Her husband, James Robert Hightower, was a member of the Far Eastern Language Faculty at Harvard University. At one time, the Hightowers lived in Peking, North China. Her books for young people include: Ghost of Follonsbee's Folly, Mrs. Wappinger's Secret. CA-4

HILL, Lorna
English author. She has lived in Northumberland, the background of many of her books. Also, she has used the Sadler's Wells Ballet School as a setting for several stories. Her books for young people include: The Little Dancer, Veronica at Sadler's Wells.

HILLCOURT, William 1900-
Interested in Scouting and nature study. He earned his M.S. degree in pharmacy. Mr. Hillcourt was only nine years old when his first article on nature was published. He has studied the flora and fauna of both America and Europe. He has served as National Director of Scoutcraft, Assistant Editor of Boy's Life magazine, and has written several Scout manuals. He wrote Field Book of Nature Activities for boys and girls.

HINKINS, Virginia
Farmer-author. She graduated from the School of

Horticulture for Women in Ambler, Pennsylvania. She has managed the Spengler Hall Farm in Strasburg, Virginia, and has been interested in horses and riding. She married Dr. John F. Cadden and has lived in Front Royal, Virginia. She wrote Gently Now.

HINKLE, Thomas Clark 1876-1949
He grew up in Kansas, and remembered the day when he saw the famous horse, "Comanche," at Fort Riley as one of the most exciting experiences of his boyhood. This horse was the only living reminder of Custer's Last Stand at Little Big Horn. Later, he became Dr. Hinkle, physician and ordained Congregational minister. Juvenile titles include: Dapple Gray, Tan, A Wild Dog, Vic, A Dog of the Prairies, Wolf, A Range Dog.

HIPPEL, Ursula von
She was born in Germany. Later, she came to America and graduated from the School of the Museum of Fine Arts in Boston where she was an honor student in sculpture. At one time, Miss von Hippel was a kindergarten teacher. Also, she has worked in puppetry in Boston, Massachusetts. She wrote: Craziest Hallowe'en, The Story of the Snails Who Traded Houses (After a Story by Gertrud von Hippel).

HIRSHBERG, Albert 1909-
Born in Boston, Massachusetts, and attended Boston University. He worked on the Boston Post as a sports writer, and traveled with the Boston Red Sox. Later, he devoted his full time to free-lance writing. He has contributed articles to the Saturday Evening Post, Look, Sport, Reader's Digest, and Sports Illustrated. Mr. Hirshberg has been a member of the Baseball Writers Association of America, the Authors Guild, and the Society of Magazine Writers. He wrote: Basketball's Greatest Stars, The Man Who Fought Back: Red Schoendienst. CA-4

HOBART, Lois

Native of Minneapolis. She graduated from the University of Minnesota. She has been on the staff of Coronet, Esquire, and Glamour magazines. In writing Laurie, Physical Therapist, the author visited rehabilitation centers. In an endeavor to give young readers a true picture of physical therapy as a profession, she had the help of the National Foundation for Infantile Paralysis and the American Physical Therapy Association. Also, she wrote Katie and Her Camera, A Palette for Ingrid. CA-5/6

HODGES, Carl G.

Native of Quincy, Illinois, he has been quite interested in the history of the Civil War, and was instrumental in starting the Springfield (Illinois) Civil War Round Table. Mr. Hodges has been Illinois state director of departmental reports, and regional vice-president of the Mystery Writers of America. He wrote: Baxie Randall and the Blue Raiders, Benjie Ream, Dobie Sturgis and the Dog Soldiers.

HODGES, C. Walter 1909-

Illustrator-author, born in Beckenham, Kent. He studied at Dulwich College, London, and Goldsmith's College School of Art. He has been a designer of scenery for the theatre, worked in advertising, and created the mural (90 feet long) for the Museum of the Chartered Insurance Institute of London. He has lived in Spain, France, and has visited in America. He wrote and illustrated Sky High; the Story of a House That Flew.

HOEHLING, Mary (Duprey) 1914-

Born in Worcester, Massachusetts. After her marriage, she and her husband lived for six months in Europe. Mrs. Hoehling has written scripts for the Puppet Theater at the Stamford Museum in Connecticut, has been a reporter, and written articles on travel. She once said, "As far back as I can remember I had a little notebook in which I wrote stories, real or imagined." She wrote Girl Soldier and Spy; Sarah Emma Edmundson.

HOFF, Sydney 1912-
Author-artist, born in New York City. He attended the National Academy of Design. He has contributed cartoons regularly to the New Yorker where he had sold his first cartoon at the age of eighteen. Also, Esquire and the Saturday Evening Post have published his cartoons. Several collections of his cartoons have been published. Juvenile contributions include: Albert the Albatross, Chester, Danny and the Dinosaur, Grizzwald, Julius, Little Chief, Ogluk, the Eskimo, Oliver, Sammy the Seal, Where's Prancer.
CA-5/6

HOFFMANN, Peggy 1910-
Born in Delaware, Ohio, she studied at Miami University at Oxford, Ohio, and did graduate work at the Chicago Theological Seminary of the University of Chicago. After her marriage to Arnold E. Hoffmann, State Supervisor of Music in the public schools of North Carolina, Mrs. Hoffmann's attention turned to homemaking. After sewing with her daughter, she incorporated her experiences into the book Sew Easy. She has also written Miss B's First Cookbook; 20 Family-Sized Recipes for the Youngest Cook. CA-5/6

HOFSINDE, Robert
Author-illustrator. Born in Denmark, he studied at the Royal Art Academy of Copenhagen. After arriving in America, he did trapping in the forests of Minnesota. When he saved the life of a Chippewa Indian boy, Mr. Hofsinde was made a blood brother of the tribe, and given the name of Gray-Wolf. This episode stimulated a deep interest in Indian culture. Assisted by his wife, Mr. Hofsinde has been a teacher of Indian lore in camps, clubs, and training courses. They have interpreted Indian songs and dances and have made several television appearances. Several magazines and newspapers have published his articles. He has written and illustrated: Indian Beadwork, Indian Games and Crafts, Indian Sign Language.

HOGAN, Inez 1895-
She was born in Washington, D. C., and attended Wilson Teachers College, and studied art at the Corcoran Art School, the National Art School, the Berkshire Summer School of Art, the Cape Cod School of Art, and in Paris. She has been a first grade teacher, and an art supervisor. Juvenile titles include: A Bear Is a Bear, Dinosaur Twins, Eager Beaver, Fraidy Cat, Giraffe Twins, Littlest Satellite, Nicodemus and His Little Sister, We Are a Family. CA-4, MJA

HOGNER, Dorothy (Childs) Nils 1893-
Husband-wife team. Both were born in the East (he was born in Whitinsville, Massachusetts), and they have continued to live in New York and Connecticut. Mrs. Hogner has been a teacher. She has loved horses since she was a little girl and lived on a farm in Connecticut. Nils Hogner attended the Royal Academy of Arts (Stockholm, Sweden), the Rhodes Academy (Copenhagen, Denmark), the Boston School of Painting, and the School of the Museum of Fine Arts (Boston). The Hogners have collected a great deal of information for their books on their farm in Litchfield, Connecticut. Juvenile books written by Dorothy Hogner include: The Bible Story, Butterflies, The Cat Family, The Horse Family. Nils Hogner has written and illustrated: Dynamite, the Wild Stallion, Farm For Rent (a Junior Literary Guild selection), Molly the Black Mare. JBA-2

HOLDEN, Raymond 1894-
Poet, novelist, biographer. He has lived in New Hampshire but was a native New Yorker. He studied at Princeton University. He served with the Cavalry during World War I. His jobs varied from government work to banking, investment houses to travel agencies and book clubs. He has written novels, mysteries, and two volumes of poems. Mr. Holden has written Famous Scientific Expeditions for young people.

HOLLAND, Marion 1908-
Author, illustrator. Born in Washington, D. C., she graduated from Swarthmore College. She married Thomas W. Holland who was an economist and college professor. Children in Washington, D. C. have become acquainted with Mrs. Holland through her chalk talks at libraries and schools. She has written and illustrated: A Big Ball of String, Billy's Clubhouse, The Secret Horse, Teddy's Camp-Out.

HOLLING, Holling Clancy 1900-
Author-illustrator. Born in Henriette, Michigan. He graduated from the Art Institute of Chicago and studied anthropology while associated with the Field Museum of Natural History in Chicago. He has been in advertising and worked on ore boats on the Great Lakes. Besides illustrating children's books, Mr. Holling has executed the drawings and construction of restaurants and a dude ranch. Accompanied by his wife, Lucille Webster Holling, he has obtained first-hand information for his books through travel and collection trips; by research in university and museum libraries; and by consultation with scientific friends in the marine and biology fields. He wrote: Book of Cowboys, Minn of the Mississippi, Pagoo, Seabird, Tree in the Trail. JBA-2

HOLT, Stephen
Born in Western Kansas. He has lived in Nebraska and on a ranch in Alberta, Canada. His education included schools in Canada, high school in California, and the University of Southern California. This author's books can be found in libraries under the name of Harlan Thompson. His thorough knowledge of horses helped in his writing career. Juvenile contributions include: Outcast, Stallion of Hawaii, Prairie Colt, Spook, the Mustang, Whistling Stallion.

HONNESS, Elizabeth (Hoffman) 1904-
Daughter of a civil engineer, born in Boonton, New Jersey. The greater part of her childhood was spent around water since her father was an engineer

and had helped in creating New York City's water supply. After graduation from Skidmore College in Saratoga Springs, she wrote advertising copy for publishers. Later, she was the managing editor of The American Girl. After her marriage to J. A. McKaughan, she lived in Pennsylvania where she continued her writing and painting. Some of her books are: Mystery at the Doll Hospital, Mystery in the Square Tower, Mystery of the Auction Trunk, Mystery of the Diamond Necklace, Mystery of the Wooden Indian.

HOUGH, Richard Alexander 1922-
Author, racing journalist, naval historian. Born in Brighton, England, he received his education at Frensham Heights. He has been a sports reporter for a London newspaper. Auto racing has been his main interest, and he has often attended the Grand Prix. During World War II, he was a fighter bomber pilot in the R.A.F. Juvenile titles include: Fast Circuit, Four-Wheel Drift, Great Auto Races, Speed Six. CA-5/6

HUNGERFORD, Edward Buell 1900-
He grew up on the seacoast of New England. He was a naval officer stationed in the Pacific during World War II. He has been an English professor at Northwestern University and has lived in Kenilworth, Illinois. Juvenile titles include: Emergency Run, Escape to Danger, Forge for Heroes.

HUNT, George Pinney 1918-
Born in Philadelphia. He graduated cum laude from Amherst College. During World War II, he served overseas with the famed 1st Division of the United States Marine Corps. He was awarded the Silver Star and the Navy Cross. His book Coral Comes High was based on his own war experiences at Pelilieu. He has been on the staff of Fortune magazine and Co-editor of the Military Affairs Department of Life. He has written Story of the U.S. Marines for juvenile readers.

HUNT, Mabel Leigh 1892-
Librarian and author. Born in Indiana. She spent her early life in Greencastle, a college town, in the environment of books and people who liked books. She has been a librarian in the Indianapolis Public Library. Miss Hunt once said: "Writing for children is a delightful occupation. It is important. There is something very precious about it, almost sacred - this care one expends, this joyous responsibility one feels in creating, between two gay book covers, a complete and imaginary child world for the delight and enchantment of the real child world." Among her titles are: Benjie's Hat, Double Birthday Present, John of Pudding Lane, Little Grey Gown, Lucinda; a Little Girl of 1860 (her first book to be published), Sibby Botherbox, Susan Beware. JBA-2

HUNTINGTON, Harriet E. 1909-
At one time she studied to be a dancer. Accompanied by a photographer, a director, and a sound technician, Harriet Huntington traveled around the world filming native dancing. This film was later made into a travelogue. One of her books, Let's Go Outdoors, was inspired by an assignment which she had been given in a course in Parent Education and Nursery School Procedure. Her assignment was to write down all that a child said or did during a half hour, and her son talked to her about insects. She has lived in Los Angeles, California. Juvenile titles include: Aircraft U.S.A., Let's Go to the Brook, Let's Go to the Desert, Let's Go to the Seashore, Praying Mantis. MJA

HURD, Clement 1908- Edith (Thacher) 1910-
This husband-wife team has collaborated on many books for boys and girls. Edith Hurd studied in Switzerland, attended Radcliffe College and the Bank Street College of Education in New York City. She married illustrator Clement Hurd. He was born in New York City, and attended Yale University. Also, he has studied painting in Paris. Many books have been illustrated by Clement Hurd (including

Gertrude Stein's only children's book, The World Is Round). The Hurds have lived in Mill Valley, California. Books written by the Hurds include: Cat From Telegraph Hill, Johnny Littlejohn, Mr. Charlie, The Fireman's Friend. Books written by Edith Hurd and illustrated by Clement Hurd include: Christmas Eve, It's Snowing, Mary's Scary House, Stop, Stop. MJA

HYLANDER, Clarence John 1897-

Teacher and author, he received his Ph.D. degree from Yale University. Mr. Hylander has been a teacher of botany, general science, and zoology, and at one time, was on the faculty of Colgate University. During World War II, he served as an officer with the U.S. Navy, and wrote manuals for navy pilots. Both adults and children have enjoyed and gained much information from books written by Clarence Hylander. Juvenile titles include: Animals In Fur, Flowers of Field and Forest, Insects On Parade, Sea and Shore, Trees and Trails.

I

IWAMATSU, Jun 1908-

Taro Yashima is his pseudonym. Japanese artist-author. He has lived in Los Angeles, California where he has had his own art school. He created a mural for the Bayshore Library in Long Beach, California. He has been a close friend of Hatoju Muku who has been head of a library in Kagoshima where Mr. Yashima attended high school. Mr. Muku and Mr. Yashima created The Golden Footprints. Juvenile titles include: Crow Boy, Umbrella, Village Tree.

J

JACKSON, Caary Paul 1902-

His pseudonyms are Colin Lochlons and Jack Paulson. He was born in Urbana, Illinois, and graduated from Western Michigan University. He received his master's degree from the University of Michigan. Mr. Jackson has been a teacher, and has been interested in sports. Juvenile contributions include: All-Conference Tackle, Barney of the Babe Ruth League, Bud Baker Racing Swimmer, Bullpen Bargain, Dub Halfback.

JACKSON, Robert B.
Author and photographer. Born in Hartford, Connecticut. He received his education at Williston Academy and Amherst College, and obtained a master's degree in Library Science from Columbia University. He has been Co-ordinator of Readers' Service at the East Orange, New Jersey, Public Library where he has lived. Interest in sports cars led Mr. Jackson to write a book which "he hopes... will correct what he feels is the large amount of misinformation prevalent about sports cars." He has written Sports Cars for young readers.

JAMES, Will 1892-1942
Author, illustrator, born in Montana. Orphaned by the death of his parents, he was adopted by a French Canadian trapper, a friend of his father. Will James used charcoal from a branding fire in order to make his first drawings. An accident in which a horse fell on him caused his retirement from cowpunching. He submitted an article about bucking horses to Scribner's Magazine, and then continued writing until his death in 1942. His book, Smoky, the Cowhorse, won the 1927 Newbery Medal. He has also written: Look-See With Uncle Bill, My First Horse. JBA-1, JBA-2.

JERR, William A.
Born in Massachusetts. He studied botany at Yale. He has worked for the National Audubon Society as a Tour Leader and Warden. Mr. Jerr has been a bird watcher since childhood, and has traveled extensively. While he was serving in the Navy, Mr. Jerr became interested in tropical and sub-tropical wildlife. In his books he has endeavored to create the same interest in nature in his reader. For

juveniles he has written The Adventure Book of Birds.

JOHNSON, Gerald White 1890-

Author and newspaperman, born in Riverton, North Carolina. He received his B.A. degree from Wake Forest College in North Carolina. He has lived in Baltimore, and has been a news commentator and Professor of Journalism at the University of North Carolina. Also, he has been a contributing editor of The New Republic. He decided to use his knowledge of American history and write books about his favorite subject so that his grandson Peter would know that "it is in some ways better and in some ways worse to be an American than to be an Englishman, or a Frenchman, or a man of any other nationality." His titles for young people include: America Grows Up; a History for Peter, America is Born; a History for Peter, The Congress, The Presidency, The Supreme Court.

JOHNSON, Siddie Joe 1905-

Author, teacher, librarian. Born in Dallas, Texas. She attended Texas Christian University, received her degree in Library Science at Louisiana State University. She has been Children's Librarian at the Dallas Public Library where she conducted story hours and a Creative Writing Club for boys and girls. Books of verse and a picture history of Texas have been published by Miss Johnson. Juvenile contributions include: Cat Hotel, Cathy, Debby, A Month of Christmases, New Town in Texas.

JONES, Elizabeth Orton 1910-

Author-illustrator, born in Highland Park, Illinois. She studied art at the University of Chicago, and has studied painting at Fontainebleau and in Paris. Her first children's book, Ragman of Paris, was created from her drawings of the city which she remembered and loved. Elizabeth Orton Jones has illustrated many books for various authors. In 1945 she received the Caldecott Medal for Prayer for a Child, written by Rachel Field. She has had a studio in

Highland Park, Illinois, and has lived in Mason, New Hampshire. She has illustrated some books written by her mother, Jessie Mae (Orton) Jones including: Secrets, This is the Way; Prayers and Precepts From World Religions. JBA-2

JONES, Mary Alice 1898-
Author, teacher, lecturer, born in Dallas, Texas. She attended the University of Texas, and received a master's degree in religious education from Northwestern University, and her Ph.D. from Yale University. Mary Alice Jones has been Director of Children's Work for the International Council of Religious Education, and has taught at Yale, Northwestern University, and at Iliff School of Theology. Juvenile books include: Bible Stories, God Speaks To Me, His Name Was Jesus, Jesus and His Friends, My First Book About Jesus, Tell Me About God, Tell Me About the Bible. MJA

JUDSON, Clara (Ingram) 1879-1960
Born in Logansport, Indiana. After her marriage, she lived in Chicago and Evanston, Illinois where she remained after the death of her husband. She has written fairy tales, social studies, and biographies. Mrs. Judson has been the recipient of numerous awards and honors. Clara Ingram Judson died four weeks before she could receive the Laura Ingalls Wilder Award in 1960 from the Children's Services Division of the American Library Association for "a lasting and substantial contribution to children's books." Juvenile books include: Abraham Lincoln, Andrew Jackson, Frontier Statesman, Benjamin Franklin, Bruce Carries the Flag, Christopher Columbus, Mr. Justice Holmes. JBA-2

JULIAN, Nancy R.
Author and teacher. A native of Tennessee, she was educated in San Diego, California. She has visited many European countries, and was a teacher with the Army of Occupation in Frankfurt, Germany. Also, Miss Julian has worked in advertising. She wrote Peculiar Miss Pickett for young readers.

JUSTUS, May 1898-
She was born in Tennessee, and grew up in the Smoky Mountain region. She has taught school, and later, taught handicapped children in her home. In her books she has endeavored to preserve as a permanent record a great deal of the folklore and ballads of the mountain people. She has lived in Summerfield, on the Cumberland Plateau. She wrote: Barney, Bring Your Banjo, Big Log Mountain, Children of the Great Smoky Mountains, Lucky Penny. JBA-2

K

KAHL, Virginia 1919-
Born in Milwaukee, Wisconsin. She graduated from Milwaukee-Downer College. She has been a librarian in Milwaukee, Berlin, and Salzburg, Austria. She began to write and illustrate children's books while living in Austria which she called a "fairy-tale country." Her books for boys and girls include: Away Went Wolfgang! The Baron's Booty, Droopsi, Duchess Bakes a Cake, Habits of Rabbits, Maxie. MJA

KÄSTNER, Erich 1899-
Born in Dresden of Saxony, Germany. He has lived in Munich, and has written books for both children and adults. In 1960 he was awarded the Hans Christian Andersen Prize for his book When I Was a Boy. In presenting the award, Mrs. Jella Lepman, Director of the International Youth Library, said, "...let us hope that this book, as well as his entire work, will gladden the children of the world and further the idea of international understanding through children's literature." Also, he wrote Emil and the Detectives, a Story for Children (translated by May Massee).

KAY, Helen 1912-
Helen Kay is a pseudonym. She has done research work for Time and Fortune magazines, edited trade papers, and has written many books for boys and

girls. Helen Kay has lived in Thornwood, New York. Juvenile titles include: City Springtime, A Duck for Keeps, The House of Many Colors, How Smart Are Animals? CA-2

KEATING, Lawrence Alfred 1903-
He attended Marquette University in Milwaukee, Wisconsin where he studied journalism. During World War II, he served as Assistant Director of Public Information, Midwestern Area, in the American Red Cross. He has traveled extensively and has lived for a year in South America. Mr. Keating has lectured on writing at both Marquette and Northwestern Universities. Juvenile titles include: Freshman Backstop, Junior Miler, Runner-Up, Wrong-Way Neelen.

KEATS, Ezra Jack 1916-
Illustrator-author, born in Brooklyn, New York. During World War II, he was a camouflage expert in the United States Air Corps. He has illustrated many books for children, but The Snowy Day was the first book which Mr. Keats both wrote and illustrated without a collaborator. It was this book which won the Caldecott Medal in 1963. My Dog Is Lost! was written by Ezra Jack Keats and Pat Cherr. MJA

KEELER, Katherine (Southwick) 1887-
She was born in Maine and grew up in Wisconsin. She graduated from Central State Teachers College, Stevens Point, Wisconsin. She continued her studies at the Academy of Fine Arts and the Art Institute in Chicago. Also, she attended the Pennsylvania Academy of Fine Arts in Philadelphia, and was awarded two European scholarships while she was a student there. She married Burton Keeler. Juvenile titles include: Apple Rush, Dog Days, In the Country, Party for Hoppy.

KEITH, Harold 1903-
Native Oklahoman. He studied at Northwestern State Teachers College at Alva, Oklahoma, and at

the University of Oklahoma. He once won the Missouri Valley conference indoor mile and two-mile championships. He has been sports publicity director at the University of Oklahoma, and has written sports stories for The American Boy. In 1958 he was awarded the Newbery Medal for his book, Rifles for Watie. Also, he wrote: Boys' Life of Will Rogers, Sports and Games. MJA

KELLY, Eric Philbrook 1884-
As a boy he lived in New England and Denver, and as a young man he studied at Dartmouth College. He became a newspaperman and has been on the staffs of the Boston Herald and the Boston Transcript. Shortly after World War I, he did relief work in Poland and grew to know and love the Polish people. He has taught at the University of Krakow in Poland. In 1929 his book, The Trumpeter of Krakow, was awarded the Newbery Medal. Juvenile titles include: The Christmas Nightingale, Three Christmas Stories From Poland, In Clean Hay, Land of the Polish People. JBA-1, JBA-2

KELSEY, Alice (Geer) 1896-
Born in Danvers, Massachusetts. She graduated from Mount Holyoke College. After her marriage to Lincoln David Kelsey, they served as relief workers in the Near East. During World War II, Mrs. Kelsey and her husband once again did relief work. After living in Puerto Rico, Mrs. Kelsey wrote Ricardo's White Horse. CA-5/6, MJA.

KENDALL, Carol 1917-
Born in Bucyrus, Ohio. She graduated from Ohio University in Athens, Ohio. She married Paul Murray Kendall who has been a professor of English at Ohio University. Mrs. Kendall once said, "I can't remember a time that I wasn't interested in writing, and I did all the usual things such as columns and feature articles in school newspapers and magazines." She wrote Gammage Cup. CA-5/6

KENYON, Raymond G. 1922-
Teacher-author, born in Gloversville, New York. He received his B.Ed. degree from the State University of New York in Oswego and his M.A. degree from New York University in New York City. He has been a teacher, elementary school principal, and professor of education at the State University of New York at New Paltz. He was with the Combat Engineers in the Third Army during World War II. Mr. Kenyon wrote I Can Learn About Calculators and Computers for young people.

KERR, Laura (Nowak) 1904-
Born in Chicago, Illinois. She began to enjoy writing while she was a student in grade school. She attended the University of Chicago, and married William Kerr in their senior year. She wrote Scarf Dance.

KINERT, Reed
Author-illustrator. He came from Richmond, Virginia where he was manager of the local airport. He has been a weather observer and advertising man for the airways, and has created drawings on aviation. He has been a flight instructor and has participated in numerous air races. Mr. Reed has combined knowledge with experience to create his book American Racing Planes and Historic Air Races.

KING, Martha Bennett
Author, lecturer, teacher. She has taught children's literature at the University of Chicago and was a children's book editor for a newspaper. Children's theaters have produced several of her plays. Interested in children's literature and American folklore, Martha King has written delightful stories for young people. She wrote: The Key to Chicago, Papa Pompino.

KIPLING, Rudyard 1865-1936
Born in Bombay, he spent the greater part of his life in India. He attended school (the United Service College at Westward Ho, Devonshire) in England.

He was on the staff of the Lahore Civil and Military Gazette and was assistant editor of the Pioneer. He was awarded both the Nobel Prize for Literature and the Gold Medal Award of the Royal Society of Literature. Books for young people include: All the Mowgli Stories, "Captains Courageous," The Jungle Book, Just So Stories, Kim. JBA-1

KJELGAARD, James Arthur 1910-
Of Danish descent, he was born in New York City, and has lived in Pennsylvania. He started working as soon as he finished high school. Jim Kjelgaard began writing at the age of ten. Magazines published occasional articles written by him. He has worked in a factory and has been enrolled in college extension courses. Upon receiving five hundred dollars for a story which he had written, he decided to make writing his career. He has lived in Milwaukee. Books include: Big Red, Double Challenge, Fawn in the Forest, Fire-Hunter, Hidden Trail, Irish Red, Son of Big Red, Lion Hound, Outlaw Red. JBA-2

KNIGHT, Clayton 1891-
Author-artist. Born in Rochester, New York. His main interest has always been aviation. He served as a pilot in the famed Lafayette Esquadrille in World War I, and has been a special correspondent with the Associated Press during World War II. He wrote Big Book of Real Helicopters.

KNIGHT, Eric Mowbray 1897-1943
Born in Yorkshire, in northern England. He came to America when he was a boy and received most of his education here. He had wanted to be an artist, but he discovered that he was color-blind. In the World War, he served in the Canadian Army. After his return, Eric Knight pursued his writing career. American and British anthologies have included his short stories. His book The Flying Yorkshireman was a selection of the Book of the Month Club. He also wrote Lassie-Come-Home.

KOCH, Dorothy (Clarke) 1924-
Author and teacher. Born in Ahoskie, North Carolina. She received a B.A. degree at Meredith College and did graduate work at the University of North Carolina. Chapel Hill has been her home before and after her marriage. Experiences as a teacher led Mrs. Koch into writing. Juvenile titles include: I Play At the Beach, Monkeys Are Funny That Way, Gone Is My Goose, Let It Rain, When the Cows Got Out.

KOFFLER, Camilla ?-1955
Ylla is her pseudonym. Born in Austria, she has become very well-known for her photographs of animals. She always felt that the reason behind the popularity of her photographs was that she thought that every animal had a personality of its own. Her work has been classified as: indoor cat and dog photographs and outdoor farm and zoo photographs. As she was photographing a race in India, she fell from a jeep and died on March 30, 1955. Her books include: Animal Babies (story by Arthur Gregor), Polar Bear Brothers (story by Crosby Newell).

KOMROFF, Manuel 1890-
Author, editor, lecturer. Born in New York City. He studied at Yale University and has lectured on the technique of the novel at Columbia University. He has been the author of short stories, biographies, and adult fiction. Also, he has been editor of the Modern Library and the Black and Gold Library. For young people he has written: Mozart, Thomas Jefferson, True Adventures of Spies. CA-4

KRASILOVSKY, Phyllis 1926-
Born in Brooklyn, New York, attended Brooklyn College and Cornell University. She has been a page girl in the New York Stock Exchange and has worked on New Yorker Magazine. She has contributed verses and articles to newspapers and magazines. Her books include: Benny's Flag, The Cow Who Fell in the Canal, Scaredy Cat, Susan Sometimes, The Very

Little Girl. MJA

KRISTOFFERSEN, Eva 1901-
Born of Danish stock she has lived in Germany, Switzerland, Holland, Italy, and Denmark. She attended Junior College, the International Peoples College of Elsinore, Denmark. After arriving in America, she entered the field of library work, and had her start at Princeton University Library. She received the American Library Association scholarship in 1925 and obtained a degree in library science at Drexel Institute. Her husband, Magnus Kristoffersen, also, was a librarian. Juvenile contributions include: Bee in Her Bonnet, Merry Matchmakers; a Story of Sweden.

KRUM, Charlotte 1886-
Born in Bloomington, Illinois, she lived a greater part of her life in Chicago. Miss Krum taught kindergarten and was librarian at the Avery Coonley School. She has written plays and stories for children. Included in her titles are: Four Riders, Read With Me.

KRUMGOLD, Joseph 1908-
Film writer, producer, author, born in Jersey City. He attended New York University. After graduation, his career in films began with Metro-Goldwyn-Mayer studios in Hollywood. He has been both a writer and a producer of documentary films. In New Mexico he produced a picture about "Miguel Chavez." This film resulted in the author writing ...And Now Miguel, the 1954 Newbery Medal winner. The Krumgolds have lived in Hope, New Jersey which was the setting for his book Onion John (which won the Newbery Medal in 1960). MJA

KRUSCH, Werner E.
He grew up in Germany, lived in France, and later, came to Canada. He has lived in Vancouver, British Columbia. Mr. Krusch has said that his hobbies have been photography and travel. With Raymond A. Wohlrabe, he wrote: The Key to Vienna, Land and

People of Austria, The Land and People of Denmark.

KUSAN, Ivan 1933-
Born in Sarajevo, Yugoslavia. During World War II, his family lived in Zagreb where he attended secondary school and graduated from the Academy of Fine Arts. Ivan Kusan began his writing and painting career at an early age. Painting became his hobby and writing his career. Mr. Kusan has had numerous translations published of American, English, French, and Russian authors. The Mystery of Green Hill; translated from the Yugoslavian by Michael B. Petrovich, was his first contribution to the juvenile field.

KUSKIN, Karla Seidman 1932-
A native of New York, she lived in Greenwich Village until her marriage in 1955. She was educated at the Ethical Culture School, The Little Red School House, Elisabeth Irwin High School, Antioch College, and received her B. F. A. from the Yale School of Design. Her first book, Roar and More, was used as part of her thesis on children's books at Yale. Included in her juvenile titles are: ABCDEFGHIJKLMNOPQRSTUVWXYZ, Alexander Soames: His Poems, All Sizes of Noises, The Bear Who Saw Spring, The Dog That Lost His Family, Square As a House. CA-3

L

LAMB, Harold 1892-
Born in New Jersey. He attended Columbia University. He has been interested in the history of the Cossacks for many years. While traveling through Cossack country, he has studied manuscripts of native Ukrainian historians. He wrote Chief of the Cossacks, Genghis Khan and the Mongol Horde. JBA-2

LAMBERT, Janet
Born in Crawfordsville, Indiana. When she was a young girl, she used to visit in the home of General

Lew Wallace, the author of Ben Hur, and Crawfordsville's leading citizen. Before her marriage, she studied for the theatre, and appeared on Broadway opposite Walter Whiteside. After her marriage to Colonel (then a Captain) Lambert, she lived at various army posts. She has written many books for young people including: Boy Wanted, Candy Kane, Dreams of Glory, Extra Special, Five's a Crowd.

LAMPMAN, Evelyn (Sibley) 1907-
Lynn Bronson is her pseudonym. Born in Dallas, Oregon. She received her B. S. degree from Oregon State College. She has been Educational Director for the Portland NBC station. In 1948 Crazy Creek, her first book for young people, was published. Also, she wrote: The Bounces of Cynthiann', The City Under the Back Steps, Coyote Kid, Darcy's Harvest, Elder Brother, Popular Girl, Shy Stegosaurus of Cricket Creek. MJA

LANDECK, Beatrice
Author, music educator. She taught music at the Little Red School House in New York City and in the Mills College of Education. Miss Landeck is a true "music pioneer." Years ago she introduced American folk songs in school rooms. Recognizing the appeal which jazz held for young people, she compiled a selection of songs which contained the origins of jazz. Her juvenile titles include: Children and Music; an Informal Guide for Parents and Teachers, Echoes of Africa in Folk Songs of the Americas.

LANE, Carl Daniel 1899-
Born in New York City. He has lived in Maine. Describing his working environment, he once said, "...I work in a tiny room without ventilation and jammed with ship models, yacht plans and ship chandlery..." He has been interested in boats, and has owned many of them including some which were self-designed. This interest coupled with his concern in Scouting led to the choice of this author to

prepare the second edition of the Sea Scout Manual. Also, he wrote: The Fire Raft, River Dragon.

LANE, Neola Tracy
Originally from Colorado, she has traveled extensively throughout America with her husband who was a Captain in the Air Force. She has been enrolled in extension courses at both Colorado University and Denver University. This author who was born on St. Patrick's Day has enjoyed many hobbies including color photography, painting, and playing the organ. She wrote Get Along, Mules.

LANG, Andrew 1844-1912, ed.
He has been called "editor-in-chief to the British nation." Born in Selkirk, Scotland, he received his education at Oxford. He has achieved fame through his translations and editing of foreign folk and fairy tales. Andrew Lang once said: "Some are born soldiers from the cradle, some merchants, some orators; nothing but a love of books was given me by the fairies." He collected and edited: The Blue Fairy Book, Crimson Fairy Book, Olive Fairy Book, Rose Fairy Book. JBA-1

LANGTON, Jane Gillson 1922-
Her book The Majesty of Grace began as an assignment at the Boston Museum School. This assignment consisted of printing, illustrating, and binding an edition of twenty copies. She married a physicist, and has lived in Lincoln, Massachusetts. Boys and girls who make scrapbooks would enjoy knowing that Mrs. Langton once said: "I, too (as a child) had a royal-family scrapbook and used to dream of the glory of it all." Her titles include: The Diamond In the Window, The Majesty of Grace. CA-4

LANSING, Elisabeth Carleton (Hubbard) 1911-
Born in Connecticut, she attended boarding and preparatory schools. She studied library science at Simmons College, but never worked in a library; however, she kept close to books by working in the book department of a store, a publishing house,

writing for Cue, and reading for movies. Seeing New York was her first book for boys and girls. Mrs. Lansing often wrote under the name of Martha Johnson. Juvenile titles include: Lulu Herself, Ann Bartlett at Bataan; the Adventures of a Navy Nurse, Cathy Carlisle.

LARRICK, Nancy 1910-
Author, teacher, editor, born in Virginia. She has been president of the International Reading Association and was an editor of the Reading Teacher. Dr. Larrick has been the recipient of many awards including the Edison Foundation Award and the Cary-Thomas Award. She married Alexander L. Crosby, and they collaborated on Rockets Into Space. She wrote: Junior Science Book of Rain, Hail, Sleet & Snow, Parents' Guide to Children's Reading, A Teacher's Guide to Children's Books. CA-1

LATHAM, Jean Lee 1902-
Born in West Virginia. She has earned many degrees: B.A. from West Virginia Wesleyan College, B.O.E. from Ithaca Conservatory, M.A. from Cornell University, and a Doctor of Letters from West Virginia Wesleyan. Jean Lee Latham began writing at an early age. In 1956 she was awarded the Newbery Medal for her book, Carry On, Mr. Bowditch. She has lived in Miami, Florida. Juvenile titles include: Drake: the Man They Called a Pirate, Man of the Monitor; the Story of John Ericsson, On Stage, Mr. Jefferson! MJA

LATHROP, Dorothy Pulis 1891-
Illustrator, author, teacher, born in Albany, New York. She attended Teachers College, Columbia University, Pennsylvania Academy of Fine Arts, and the Art Students League. Mrs. Lathrop has illustrated many books by different authors and in 1938 she received the first Caldecott Medal for the illustrations in Animals of the Bible. She has lived in Albany, New York. Other titles include: Angel in the Woods, Follow the Brook, Let Them Live, Littlest Mouse, Presents for Lupe, Puppies for

Keeps, Who Goes There? JBA-1, JBA-2

LATTIMORE, Eleanor Frances 1904-
Born in China, and at the age of sixteen, she moved to the United States. Her first book was published in 1931. She once said: "I only write about, or draw, the things I have actually seen or experienced." Her books about Chinese children have been very popular, and the book, Bayou Boy was written after the author lived for six months on the Bayou Terre Aux Boeufs in St. Bernard Parish, Louisiana. She married Robert Armstrong Andrews, and lived on Edisto Island, South Carolina. Her juvenile titles include: The Bittern's Nest, The Chinese Daughter, Cousin Melinda, First Grade. JBA-1, JBA-2

LATTIN, Harriet (Pratt) 1898-
Native of Corning, New York, historian, and author. She graduated from Smith College, and has her Ph.D. from Ohio State University. She has written the English translation of Gerbert's Letters and Papal Privileges. She married Norman D. Lattin who has been a professor of law at Western Reserve University. Mrs. Lattin has held membership in many historical societies. Her books for young people include: The Peasant Boy Who Became Pope; Story of Gerbert.

LAUBER, Patricia
She graduated from Wellesley College. Writer of fiction and non-fiction, Patricia Lauber has been an editor of a science magazine for young people. She has lived in New York City, and has written these books for young people: Adventure at Black Rock Cave, All About the Ice Age, All About the Planets, Clarence, the TV Dog, Famous Mysteries of the Sea, The Friendly Dolphins.

LAUGHLIN, Ruth
She graduated from Colorado College, and has studied in Rome and Paris. Also, she has traveled in Mexico, Cuba, and Puerto Rico. As a member of

the staff of the School of American Research, at one time she went to Guatemala on an archaeological survey. Also, she has held office in the Archaeological Society of New Mexico, and written articles for the New York Times and the Christian Science Monitor. She wrote Caballeros.

LAVINE, Sigmund A. 1908-
His parents were members of John Craig's stock company, and he was both actor and stage manager as an undergraduate in college. Also, he wrote about Boston University's sports activities for two wire services. After receiving his M.A. degree, he taught at Belcourt, North Dakota, in a United States Government Indian School where he learned to speak the Cree and Sioux languages. Mr. Lavine has been both a teacher and assistant principal in the Boston school system. His titles for young people include: Famous Industrialists, Kettering: Master Inventor, Strange Travelers, Wonders of the Beetle World. CA-3

LAWSON, Don 1917-
Editor and author who grew up in the Chicago area. He attended Cornell College, Iowa, and did graduate work at the University of Iowa Writer's Workshop. During World War II, he served with the Air Force Counterintelligence in Europe. Following this, he collected books, including rare editions, on World Wars I and II. Mr. Lawson has been Managing Editor of Compton's Pictured Encyclopedia. His titles include: The United States in World War I; the Story of General John J. Pershing and the American Expeditionary Forces, Young People in the White House. CA-1

LAWSON, Marie (Abrams)
Born in Georgia. Her grandfather had been an officer in the Confederate Navy, and he used to sing old sailor songs to her. Mrs. Lawson once said: "...I saw Jamestown when it was merely a remote little island, not a national shrine. From the first it held a singular fascination for me. It seems al-

most uncanny that so many years afterward I should be given the privilege of writing of that first colony." She married illustrator Robert Lawson. She wrote: Pocahontas and Captain John Smith; the Story of the Virginia Colony, Sea is Blue. JBA-2

LAWSON, Robert 1892-1957
Native New Yorker. He attended school in Montclair, New Jersey and received training in art at the New York School of Fine and Applied Art. During World War I, he served in the Camouflage Section of the United States Army in France. He has lived near Westport, Connecticut in a house called "Rabbit Hill" (on a hill and frequented by rabbits). It is fitting as he was awarded the Newbery Medal in 1945 for his book, Rabbit Hill. Juvenile contributions include: Ben and Me, Fabulous Flight, Great Wheel, I Discover Columbus, Mr. Revere and I. In 1941 he was awarded the Caldecott Medal for They Were Strong and Good. JBA-2

LEAF, Munro 1905-
Born in Maryland, graduated from the University of Maryland, and received his M. A. degree from Harvard. He has been a teacher and a director in a publishing company. It was in 1934 that his first children's book, Grammar Can Be Fun, was written. Since that time, he has written many books for boys and girls including everybody's favorite, The Story of Ferdinand. His books include: Arithmetic Can Be Fun, Let's Do Better, Robert Francis Weatherbee, Wee Gillis. JBA-2

LEAR, Edward 1812-1888
He was a painter, but he became well-known for his nonsense verse. He painted birds, was a landscape artist, and taught drawing (Queen Victoria was one of his students). His first book of nonsense appeared in 1846. Included among the nonsense titles: The Jumblies, and Other Nonsense Verses, Edward Lear's A Nonsense Alphabet, Edward Lear's Nonsense Book, Nonsense Omnibus. JBA-1

LEAVITT, Jerome Edward 1916-
He graduated from New Jersey State Teachers College, and received his doctorate from Northwestern University. He has taught at Northwestern and has been Assistant Professor of Education, Oregon State System of Higher Education. He was sent on a special mission to Cyprus by the United States Government in 1961. His books for young people include: America and Its Indians, True Book of Tools for Building. CA-4

LEEMING, Joseph 1897-
Born in Brooklyn, New York. He attended Williams College. Mr. Leeming has been interested in the sea. He has served in the navy, and as a seaman on cargo vessels, has traveled to Brazil, Argentina, British, Dutch, and French Guiana, Cuba, and Jamaica. He has written easier how-to-do-it books than those which he read as a boy ("everything was too large or difficult or expensive"). His many titles include: The Costume Book, First Book of Chess, Fun With Artificial Flowers, Fun With Wire, Fun With Wood, Holiday Craft and Fun. JBA-2

Le GALLIENNE, Eva 1899-
Distinguished actress who was born in London. In an introduction to her edition of Andersen's fairy tales, she wrote that her Danish mother had sat on Hans Christian Andersen's lap when he told stories to her class in school. Her father was an author. She received her education in Paris. She founded the Civic Repertory Theatre in New York City in 1926. In the winter of 1964 she toured with the National Repertory Theatre. She has lived in Westport, Connecticut. Her collection from Andersen was called Seven Tales; translated from the Danish by Eva Le Gallienne.

LEMMON, Robert Stell 1885-
Naturalist, author. He was quite young when he began to be interested in birds, insects, fish and wildflowers. As a result of this interest, he has traveled throughout North America and into the tropical

regions south of the equator. He has lived in Connecticut. His titles include: All About Monkeys, All About Strange Beasts of the Present, All About Moths and Butterflies.

L'ENGLE, Madeleine 1918-
Actress, author. During World War I, her father had been a foreign correspondent for Collier's. She graduated from Smith College, and worked in the theater. "I was more interested in writing than in anything else in the world, so I managed to get jobs in the theater, as I thought it an excellent school for writers." She married Hugh Franklin. It was in 1963 that she was awarded the Newbery Medal for her book, A Wrinkle in Time. Also, she wrote: Meet the Austins, The Moon by Night. CA-3, MJA

LENS, Sidney 1912-
Mr. Lens has been a union official for many years, and during the 1930's he was a union organizer. As a result of his deep interest in the labor movement, he has lectured and written many articles for magazines on this subject. His wife has been a teacher; and they have lived in Chicago, Illinois. He wrote Working Men: the Story of Labor. CA-4

LENSKI, Lois 1893-
Born in Springfield, Ohio. She graduated from Ohio State University, and studied at the Art Students League in New York and at the Westminster School of Art in London. In 1946 she was awarded the Newbery Medal for her book, Strawberry Girl. In June 1962 the Woman's College of the University of North Carolina conferred on Lois Lenski (Mrs. Arthur Covey) the Honorary Degree of Doctor of Humane Letters. In an "appreciation booklet" issued by the college, she wrote: "A book should illumine the whole adventure of living." Her books include: Bayou Suzette, Blueberry Corners, Cowboy Small. JBA-1, JBA-2

LENT, Henry Bolles 1901-
Born in New Bedford, Massachusetts. He attended Yale and Hamilton College. He has been a copy supervisor in a large advertising agency. In order to bring authenticity to his books, he took flying lessons and wrote Eight Hours to Solo. He traveled to Quebec and made a study of pulpwood, then wrote From Trees to Paper. He has lived in Woodstock, Vermont. His titles include: The Bus Driver, Clear Track Ahead, Diggers and Builders, Flight Overseas. JBA-1, JBA-2

LESSER, Milton 1928-
Born in New York, he graduated from the College of William and Mary in Virginia. He has been a writer for television, and a consultant on science fiction articles; also, he has written stories for magazines. He wrote Stadium Beyond the Stars.

LESSIN, Andrew
Born in Brooklyn, New York. He graduated from Long Island University, and did graduate work in Secondary Art Education at New York University School of Education. He has been art director of Boys' Life magazine. He wrote Here Is Your Hobby: Art.

LEVINE, Israel E. 1923-
Native New Yorker, he attended City College of New York, and eventually became Director of Public Relations there. During World War II, he was a navigator on a B-24 Liberator and completed thirty-two bombing missions. He has written many biographies for young people, and had this to say about it: "Since we expect young people to meet the challenge of tomorrow, I think it is important for them to have a sense of the drama of history, as reflected in the lives of the important figures who helped mold the past." His titles include: Champion of World Peace: Dag Hammarskjold, Inventive Wizard: George Westinghouse. CA-3

LEVINGER, Elma (Ehrlich) 1887-
Born in Chicago, Illinois. She attended the University of Chicago, and studied drama with George P. Baker at Radcliffe. She has written plays, short stories, and textbooks. Mrs. Levinger's son was a physicist, and has taught in the Physics Department of Cornell University. He provided her with a great deal of assistance when she was writing her book Albert Einstein.

LEWELLEN, John Bryan 1910-1956
He lived in Chicago, Illinois. Mr. Lewellen was a man of varied interests and accomplishments. He had been a farmer, reporter, and a photographer for Life magazine. Also, he had been producer and writer of various radio and television programs including "Quiz Kids" and "Down You Go." He flew a plane, and taught his son to fly when he was only eight years old. Juvenile titles include: Atomic Submarine, Earth Satellite; Man's First True Space Adventure, Tee Vee Humphrey, Tommy Learns to Fly, True Book of Farm Animals. MJA

LEWIS, Alice Hudson
She and her husband were missionaries in China for eighteen years. She has worked in the Youth and Publications Departments of the Board of Foreign Missions, Presbyterian, in the United States. Also, she has been managing editor of The YWCA Magazine. She wrote Day After Tomorrow.

LEWIS, Clive Staples 1898-1963
Born in Belfast, Ireland. He was Fellow and Tutor of Magdalen College, Oxford, England. Many people in America admired his novel, The Screwtape Letters. Boys and girls who prefer magic and fantasy have enjoyed reading Mr. Lewis' books about the land of Narnia. They include: Last Battle, The Lion, the Witch and the Wardrobe; a Story for Children, Magician's Nephew, Prince Caspian. MJA

LEWIS, Elizabeth (Foreman) 1892-
Born in Baltimore, Maryland. She studied art at Maryland Institute, Baltimore, and received training in religious education in New York. The Methodist Women's Board later sent her to China in order to work with the missions there. In Nanking she taught at the Huei Wen School for Girls and at the Boys' Academy. Also, it was in that city that she married John Abraham Lewis whose father had been Methodist Bishop of China. In 1933 her book, Young Fu of the Upper Yangtze, was awarded the Newbery Medal. Also, she wrote: China Quest, To Beat a Tiger, One Needs a Brother's Help.
JBA-1, JBA-2

LEWIS, Mildred and Milton
Husband and wife team, both are native New Yorkers. Before their marriage, Mrs. Lewis did public relations work, and Mr. Lewis was a reporter for the New York Herald Tribune. Each was on an assignment when they met. Mr. Lewis became top general assignment reporter for the New York Herald Tribune. His specialty has been crime stories. They wrote Famous Modern Newspaper Writers.

Le WITT, Jan 1907-
European painter and graphic artist. He has lived in London, and his works have been shown on the Continent and in the United States. He has designed tapestries for Tabard at Aubusson, glass sculptures in Italy, and sets and costumes for London's Sadler's Wells Ballet. In 1954 he was awarded a Gold Medal for book illustrations at the Milan Triennale. He wrote and illustrated The Vegetabull.

LEY, Willy 1906-
Born in Berlin, Germany. He studied at the Universities of Berlin and Konigsberg. In 1927 he was one of the founders of the German Rocket Society. When Hitler came into power in Germany, Mr. Ley left his country, and became an American

citizen. He has been a member of the American Rocket Society, American Association for the Advancement of Science, and the Institute of the Aeronautical Sciences. His books on rockets and space include: Conquest of Space, Space Travel.

LEYSON, Burr Watkins 1898-
Pilot, author, born in Medical Lake, Washington. He graduated from many military schools including: School of Military Aeronautics, U. S. Army; the Royal School of Military Aeronautics, R. A. F.; the Royal School of Aerial Gunnery, R. A. F.; the Royal School of Air Fighting, R. A. F.; the Royal Air Force Gosport Instructor's Course. During World War I, he was a fighter pilot. Juvenile titles include: It Works Like This, Modern Wonders and How They Work, The Warplane and How It Works.

L'HOMMEDIEU, Dorothy (Keasbey) 1885-
She has enjoyed living in the country where she has raised a variety of livestock. She has been fond of animals since she was a little girl. She started the Sand Spring Kennel of Cocker Spaniels in New Jersey near Morristown in 1920. Her popular books on dogs include: Leo, the Little St. Bernard, Nipper, the Little Bull Pup, Pompon, Spot, the Dalmatian Pup.

LICHELLO, Robert 1926-
He was born in Parkersburg, West Virginia, and attended West Virginia University where he majored in creative writing. He has been a disc jockey, news announcer, and reporter. At one time, he was on the staff of the National Enquirer, and an editor of different men's magazines. He wrote Ju-Jitsu Self Defense for Teen-Agers.

LIEB, Frederick George 1888-
Born in Philadelphia, Pennsylvania. He has watched many World Series baseball games including several occasions when he was chief scorer (at three series) and alternate at another. Mr. Lieb has been a columnist, baseball writer, and newspaper editor.

He has frequently contributed articles to The Sporting News. He wrote Story of the World Series; An Informal History.

LILLIE, Amy Morris
Born in Elizabeth, New Jersey. She attended the Philadelphia Musical Academy and Teacher's College, Columbia University. She has been a teacher in a girls' school in Philadelphia. Miss Lillie has contributed stories to Child Life and Story Parade. Her interests have included: writing, music, religious activities, and working with children. Her books for young people include: Book of Three Festivals; Stories for Christmas, Easter and Thanksgiving, I Will Build My Church, Judith, Daughter of Jericho.

LINDGREN, Astrid (Ericsson) 1907-
Swedish author, born in Vimmerby. She was the first person to be awarded the Nils Holgersson Plaque which is the "finest mark of distinction in Sweden for any writer of books for children and young people." Also, she received the Hans Christian Andersen Medal in 1958. Her titles include: Bill Bergson, Master Detective (translated by Herbert Antoine), Christmas in the Stable, Pippi Longstocking (translated by Florence Lamborn). MJA

LINDMAN, Maj Jan
Swedish author. She grew up in Örebro, Sweden, and studied at the Royal Academy of Arts. In 1922 she created her first book about the three brothers named Snipp, Snapp, Snurr. She has lived in Djursholm, Sweden. American children have enjoyed reading such books as: Dear Little Deer, Flicka, Ricka, Dicka and the Big Red Hen, Flicka, Ricka, Dicka and the Three Kittens, Snipp, Snapp, Snurr and the Big Farm, Snipp, Snapp, Snurr and the Buttered Bread. JBA-2

LINDQUIST, Jennie Dorothea 1899-
Librarian and author, born in Manchester, New Hampshire. She has been Children's Librarian in

Manchester, Consultant in Work with Children and Young People at the University of New Hampshire Library, and Head of the Children's Department of the Albany Public Library. Also, Miss Lindquist has been Editor of The Horn Book magazine. Her book, The Golden Name Day, contains many incidents drawn from her own childhood memories. "She remembers adults who made a spring birch gathering as lovely an experience as it was for Nancy." She wrote The Little Silver House. MJA

LIONNI, Leo
Art director, author. Mr. Lionni has been art director of Fortune magazine, and the recipient of many awards including the Gold Medal for Architecture. He has been interested in painting, graphic arts, and travel, especially Italy where he designed his own house which overlooks the Gulf of Genoa. Several of his books have been included in the fifty best books named by The American Institute of Graphic Arts. He created: Inch by Inch, Little Blue and Little Yellow; a Story for Pippo and Ann and Other Children, Swimmy.

LIPKIND, William 1904-
Born in New York, and graduated from the College of the City of New York. During World War II, he served with the Office of War Information in England. Following the war, he made a study of Bavarian society for the American Military Government and lived in Germany. Also, he has studied jungle tribes in Brazil, and the Winnebago language of the Indians in Nebraska. Juvenile titles include: Boy of the Islands, Boy With a Harpoon. Also, with the illustrator, Nicolas Mordvinoff, he has produced many outstanding picture books. This team, called Will and Nicolas, created Finders Keepers, Caldecott Medal winner in 1952. MJA

LIPPINCOTT, Joseph Wharton 1887-
Born in Philadelphia, Pennsylvania. He graduated from Wharton School of the University of Pennsylvania. Young people who have preferred to read

about animals and the outdoors have enjoyed Mr. Lippincott's books. He has been chairman of the board of the publishing house, J. B. Lippincott Company. After hunting and fishing for many years in the Florida wilds, he used this background and knowledge in order to write the book, The Wahoo Bobcat. Also, he wrote: Gray Squirrel, Long Horn, Leader of the Deer, The Phantom Deer, The Red Roan Pony. MJA

LOBEL, Arnold 1933-
Born in Los Angeles, California. He graduated from Pratt Institute in Brooklyn, New York. He began his career as an illustrator in the field of children's books, but in 1961 he wrote and illustrated A Zoo for Mister Muster. He illustrated Greg's Microscope, by Millicent E. Selsam, and Little Runner of the Longhouse by Betty Baker. CA-4

LOBSENZ, Amelia Freitag
"Ham" radio operator, author, born in Greensboro, North Carolina. She received her "ham" radio license in 1941 after passing the FCC test. During World War II, she did public relations work for an electronics firm, and taught Morse code to civil defense organizations. Her husband has been managing editor of Quick magazine. Mrs. Lobsenz wrote Kay Everett Calls CQ.

LOCKWOOD, Myna
Born in Rome, Iowa, and studied at the Chicago Art Institute and in France and Italy. She has been a portrait painter, and has lived in Kew Gardens, Long Island, New York. Her books for young people include: Free River; a Story of Old New Orleans, Indian Chief; the Story of Keokuk, Macaroni, an American Tune.

LOFTING, Hugh 1886-1947
Born in Maidenhead, England. He received his education from the Jesuits in England and later attended the Massachusetts Institute of Technology in Ameri-

ca. During World War I, he eased the tension of war by writing illustrated letters to his children. A civil engineer became a favorite author for boys and girls. His letters became The Story of Doctor Dolittle which was published in 1920. The Newbery Medal was awarded to him in 1923 for his book, The Voyages of Doctor Dolittle. Some of the titles in this popular series: Doctor Dolittle and the Green Canary, Doctor Dolittle In the Moon. JBA-1, JBA-2

LOISY, Jeanne 1913-
French author, born in a little village near Lyons. In addition to writing books, she has been both teacher and lecturer. In 1956 she won the Prix Jeunesse for the original French edition of Don Tiburcio's Secret; it was translated by James Kirkup.

LONERGAN, Joy 1909-
Born in Toronto, Canada, the daughter of a minister. She attended Denison and Syracuse Universities. She has been a teacher and has worked in a bookstore. She married artist John Lonergan. Her juvenile titles include: When My Father Was a Little Boy, When My Mother Was a Little Girl. CA-3

LONGSTRETH, Joseph 1920-
Author, actor, critic, composer. He was born in Indiana. He received his M.A. degree from Princeton University and studied at the Royal Academy of Dramatic Art in London and at the Conservatory of St. Cecilia in Rome. Mr. Longstreth has been a pilot in the Army Air Force. His books for young people include: Little Big-Feather, Penguins Are Penguins.

LONGSTRETH, Thomas Morris 1886-
Perhaps, the boys who attended the school in Westtown, Pennsylvania, have contributed authenticity and realism to this author's books. He lived near their school for many years. After traveling throughout Canada, and studying the Canadian

Mounted Police, he wrote The Scarlet Force. Boys (girls, too) have enjoyed this author's books which include: Bull Session, The Calgary Challengers, Camping Like Crazy, Doorway in the Dark, Elephant Toast. MJA

LOOMIS, J. Paul

Born in Juneau, Alaska. He attended Kansas State College. Mr. Loomis has said that he was born "under the sign of the Itching Foot." He has lived in Canada, California, Alaska, and Siberia (with the Canadian Expeditionary Force). He has been a rancher, contractor, carpenter, and boatbuilder. His interests have been horses and canoes. He wrote Salto, a Horse of the Canadian Mounties.

LOOMIS, Robert D.

Born in Ohio, and graduated from Duke University in North Carolina. He has always been interested in planes. During World War II, he was a cadet in the Air Force. Later, he enjoyed flying a Piper Tri-Pacer in and out of Teterboro Airport in New Jersey. He has lived in Greenwich Village. He wrote Story of the U.S. Air Force.

LOVELACE, Delos Wheeler 1894-

He was born in Minnesota, and attended the University of Minnesota and Cambridge University, England. He has been a newspaperman, and worked on the Fargo Courier-News, the Minneapolis Tribune, and the New York Daily News. Also, he has been assistant city editor of the New York Sun, and a staff writer on the New York World-Telegram and Sun. He married author Maud Hart Lovelace. He wrote "Ike" Eisenhower; Statesman and Soldier of Peace, That Dodger Horse.

LOVELACE, Maud (Hart) 1892-

She was born in Mankato, Minnesota, and attended the University of Minnesota. She married newspaperman and author Delos Lovelace. When she was in high school in Mankato, she kept a diary (in fact, four diaries, one for each year). In later years, these diaries were read and enjoyed by Mr. and Mrs. Lovelace and their daugher Merian. After writing about the childhood of Betsy, Tacy, and Tib, the diaries gave her ideas for this threesome's adventures in high school. Titles in the popular series include: Betsy and Joe; a Betsy-Tacy High School Story, Betsy-Tacy, Betsy, Tacy and Tib, Betsy's Wedding. JBA-2

LOW, Joseph 1911-
He attended the University of Illinois and the Art Students League in New York. Mr. Low has operated the Eden Hill Press in Newtown, Connecticut. This has been a private press for the publication of prints and books, many of which have been purchased by colleges and special libraries. Also, they have been shown in The American Institute of Graphic Arts' traveling exhibit. His books for young people include: Adam's Book of Odd Creatures, Mother Goose Riddle Rhymes, with help from Ruth Low.

LOWREY, Janette (Sebring) 1892-
Born in Orange, Texas, the daughter of the Superintendent of Schools. She graduated from the University of Texas, and taught school. Also, she has been associated with the advertising business. She married an attorney, and they have lived in San Antonio, Texas. She wrote: Annunciata and the Shepherds, Lavender Cat, Margaret, Tap-a-Tan!

LUBELL, Cecil Winifred (Milius)
He married illustrator Winifred Milius. Cecil Lubell has been associated with the publicity department of the Institute for Motivational Research. Also, he has contributed many articles to magazines. With his wife Winifred, he wrote: Rosalie; the Bird Market Turtle, Tall Grass Zoo, Up a Tree. She has illustrated many children's books, and has taught art to children. She illustrated Millicent E. Selsam's Birth of an Island.

LUMM, Peter
Author and friend of Faith Grigsby Norris, Peter Lumm was enthusiastic and excited when invited to write a children's book with her. He has been a teacher at Oregon State College. The Lumms have lived in Greenwich Village, New York City, but they have preferred the type of living offered in the state of Oregon as compared to life in a big city. Kim of Korea was the result of his collaboration with Faith Norris.

M

MacAGY, Douglas
He attended the University of Toronto, and continued his studies in art in London, Philadelphia, and Cleveland. During World War II, he was Chief of the Japan Section of the Propaganda Analysis Division of the Far East Bureau of the OWI. He has held many important posts in the art world including: Curator of the San Francisco Museum of Art, Director of the California School of Fine Arts in San Francisco, Consultant to the Director of the Museum of Modern Art, and Director of Research for the Wildenstein Galleries. He wrote Going For a Walk With a Line; a Step in the World of Modern Art, by Douglas and Elizabeth MacAgy.

McCAHILL, William P.
He studied at Marquette University in the College of Journalism, and has been associated with the Milwaukee Associated Press Bureau. During World War II, he was a junior public relations officer in the Marine Corps in Washington, D. C. Later, he was assigned to the Marine Base at San Diego, California. He wrote First to Fight.

McCLINTOCK, Marshall 1906-
Editor and author. One of the notable achievements of his career as an editor was the publication of the first two Dr. Seuss books, And to Think That I Saw It On Mulberry Street and 500 Hats of Bartholomew Cubbins. Mike McClintock has written many

books on subjects as varied as science and adventure. He wrote: A Fly Went By, Here Is a Book, Leaf, Fruit and Flower; a Nature Primer, Millions of Books; the Story of Your Library, Stop That Ball!

McCLOSKEY, Robert 1914-
Born in Hamilton, Ohio, he studied at the National Academy of Design in New York. During World War II, he was in the Army where he drew training pictures. He has been the recipient of several awards including the Prix de Rome in 1939, and the Caldecott Medal in 1942 and again in 1958. The award in 1942 was given to him for his book, Make Way for Ducklings, and in 1958, for his book, Time of Wonder. The McCloskey family has lived on an island off the coast of Maine. His titles include: Blueberries for Sal, Centerburg Tales, Homer Price, Lentil, One Morning in Maine. JBA-2

McCLUNG, Robert M. 1916-
He majored in biology at Princeton University, and received his M.S. degree in science education from Cornell University. During World War II, he served as a landing-signal officer on aircraft carriers. He has been Curator of Mammals and Birds at the Bronx Zoo. Mr. McClung has written and illustrated many books about animals all of which were based upon years of observation and study. His titles include: Bufo; the Story of a Toad, Little Burma, Mammals and How They Live, Possum. MJA

McCORMICK, Alma Heflin
Born in Winona, Missouri. She graduated from Eastern Washington College of Education in Cheney, and attended the School of Aviation in Dallas, Texas. After receiving her commercial pilot's license, she flew throughout the United States, and to Alaska, Mexico, and Canada. She wrote Merry Makes a Choice.

McCORMICK, Wilfred 1903-

Born in Newland, Indiana, he attended the University of Illinois. During World War II, he served in the army. He has been a lecturer, professional baseball player, state president of the Crippled Children's Society, and Finance Chairman for the Boy Scouts of America. He has lived in Albuquerque, New Mexico, with his wife and two children. He wrote: The Automatic Strike, a Rocky McCune Baseball Story, Bases Loaded, a Bronc Burnett Story, First and Ten; a Dyke Redman Story. CA-2

McCRACKEN, Harold 1894-

Although he was born in Colorado Springs, he spent his boyhood in Idaho and Iowa. When he was twenty-two years old, he made a trip of exploration to British Columbia. He has collected many specimens for natural history museums. It was the Stoll-McCracken Siberian Arctic Expedition of the American Museum of Natural History which he wrote about in his book, Toughy; Bulldog in the Arctic. Also, he wrote: Alaska Bear Trails, Biggest Bear on Earth, Caribou Traveler, Flaming Bear. JBA-2

MacDONALD, Betty (Bard) 1908-

Born in Boulder, Colorado, the daughter of a mining engineer. She studied art at the University of Washington. After her marriage, she lived on a chicken ranch on the Olympic Peninsula in Washington, and from these experiences came her best-selling book, The Egg and I. It was published in the fall of 1945. Her titles for young people include: Hello, Mrs. Piggle-Wiggle, Mrs. Piggle-Wiggle, Nancy and Plum.

MacDONALD, George 1824-1905

He was a friend of Lewis Carroll. Mr. Carroll used to tell stories to the MacDonald children, and Mr. MacDonald advocated the publication of Alice in Wonderland. George MacDonald's youngest daughter became Lady Winifred Troup who lived in Kensington. In the book, A Critical History of Children's Literature, by Cornelia Meigs, Anne Eaton, Elizabeth Nesbitt, and Ruth Hill Viguers has been written: "Macdonald was a visionary, and his children's stories, while not allegories, were filled with spiritual meaning." He wrote: At the Back of the North Wind, The Light Princess, The Princess and Curdie. JBA-1

McDONALD, Lucile (Saunders) 1898-
Born in Portland, Oregon, and attended the University of Oregon. Also, she has taken courses in writing from Columbia, and the University of Washington. She has been on the staff of the New York World, The Oregonian, and the Seattle Times. It was on an assignment in Oregon that she first met her husband, H. D. McDonald. She has written many books for young people with Zola Helen Ross including: Friday's Child, Pigtail Pioneer, Wing Harbor. CA-3

MacDONALD, Zillah Katherine
Born in Halifax, Nova Scotia. She received her education at Dalhousie University. She has been a teacher in the School of Business at Columbia University. Her father worked for the Government in Nova Scotia and Cape Breton, and they often took trips together throughout this part of the country. These experiences plus research provided her with the information to write Flower of the Fortress. Also, she wrote Nurse Todd's Strange Summer, Rosemary Wins Her Cap.

MACFARLAN, Allan A.
Born in Canada. He has been a camp director, international camp commissioner, and director of recreation. He has introduced many Indian programs for the Campfire and Council Ring of the Boy Scouts of America. He has been a Fellow of the Royal Geographical Society, and has taken many camping trips with American and Canadian Indians. He wrote Book of American Indian Games, Indian Adventure Trails; Tales of Trails and Tipis, Ponies, and Paddles, Warpaths and Warriors.

McGAVRAN, Grace Winifred
Born in India, daughter of missionaries. She graduated from Butler University and received her M.A. degree from Boston University. Miss McGavran once said that her "greatest joys were children and the great outdoors." Her books include: All Through the Year; a Devotional Reader for Boys and Girls, Ricardo's Search, Stories of the Book of Books, They Live in Bible Lands.

McGEE, Dorothy Horton
Born at West Point, New York. Her father taught law at the United States Military Academy. She attended the Green Vale School, Glen Head, the Brearley School in New York City, and the Fermata School in Aiken, South Carolina. She has been very interested in sailing, and has sailed on many types of boats from dinghies to cup-defenders. She wrote Herbert Hoover, Engineer, Humanitarian, Statesman.

McGINLEY, Phyllis Louise 1905-
Born in Ontario, Oregon. She attended the University of Utah. At one time she taught school in New Rochelle, and has worked in an advertising agency. She married Charles Hayden. Phyllis McGinley has been a recipient of the Pulitzer Prize. Her books for young people include: All Around the Town, Blunderbus, Horse Who Had His Picture in the Paper, Plain Princess. JBA-2

McGOVERN, Ann
She has been a production assistant and editor in a publishing company. Also, she has been Assistant Editor of the Arrow Book Club for children, sponsored by Scholastic Magazines. She wrote Why It's a Holiday.

McGRAW, Eloise Jarvis 1915-
Born in Texas, she graduated from Principia College, Elsah, Illinois. Later, she studied art at Oklahoma and Colorado Universities. She has been a teacher of portrait painting at Oklahoma City University, and has had articles published in Parents'

Magazine and Jack and Jill. Her titles for young people include: Crown Fire, Moccasin Trail, Sawdust in His Shoes. MJA

MacGREGOR, Ellen 1906-1954
Librarian and author. She graduated from the University of Washington at Seattle. She continued her library education in the Graduate School at the University of California at Berkeley. She has supervised the work of elementary school libraries in Hawaii, and has worked in Special Libraries. She has lived in Chicago, Illinois, and has belonged to the Illinois Women's Press Association and the Chicago Children's Reading Round Table. Her books include: Miss Pickerell Goes to the Arctic, Mr. Ferguson of the Fire Department, Theodore Turtle. MJA

McGUIRE, Frances
Born in Crawfordsville, Indiana. She attended Ferry Hall at Lake Forrest, Illinois, and received her Ph.B. at the University of Chicago. She has been closely associated with both radio and television. She has been director of Women's Activities for a radio station in Philadelphia, Pennsylvania, and was one of the first women commentators in television. Later, she had her own television program, "Meet Frances McGuire," on WFIL-TV. She wrote Arizona Hide-Out, The Case of the Smuggled Ruby.

McILVAINE, Jane (Stevenson) 1919-
She was born in Pittsburgh, Pennsylvania, and graduated from Miss Porter's School in Farmington, Connecticut. She married Robinson T. McIlvaine. She has been a writer for the Washington Times-Herald, and a member of the staff of Fortune magazine. Mrs. McIlvaine and her husband have been editors of the Archive of Downingtown, Pennsylvania. She was the recipient of the 1949 Pennsylvania Women's Press Association Award. She wrote Copper's Chance, Stardust for Jennifer. CA-2

MacKELLAR, William
He was born in Glasgow, Scotland. At the age of eleven, he came to America and later, became an American citizen. He has written many articles for teen-age magazines. Juvenile titles include: Ghost in the Castle, Two for the Fair, Wee Joseph, The Team That Wouldn't Quit.

McKELVEY, Gertrude Della
Her husband has been the pastor of the Lansdowne Methodist Church. Mrs. McKelvey has taught Christian Education, and has traveled extensively in Palestine and Jerusalem. She wrote Gertrude D. McKelvey's Stories to Grow On; Five Everyday Parables for Boys and Girls, Stories to Live By.

McKENNY, Margaret
She was born in Olympia, Washington. She has been interested in botany since she was in high school. Although she has written many science books, the first book which she planned was one about trees. She has photographed and studied trees throughout the United States. She wrote: Book of Wayside Fruits, by Margaret McKenny and E. F. Johnston, Trees of the Countryside.

McKINNEY, Roland Joseph 1898-
Born at Niagara Falls, New York. He attended Niagara University and the Art School of the Art Institute of Chicago. Also, he has studied abroad. Mr. McKinney has been director of the Baltimore Museum of Art, the Los Angeles County Museum, and has been Consultant to the Department of American Art, the Metropolitan Museum of Art. He has enjoyed collecting prints, paintings, and drawings which relate to Niagara's past. He wrote: Famous French Painters, Famous Old Masters of Painting.

McKOWN, Robin
She was born in Denver, Colorado. Mrs. McKown graduated from the University of Colorado, attended Northwestern's School of Drama, and the University of Illinois (where she studied short story writing).

She has lived in France and has traveled in South America. Robin McKown has done sales promotion work and has written radio scripts plus a column for newspapers. Her novel, Janine, was recipient of the 1961 Child Study Association Award, and a Junior Literary Guild Selection. She once said: "In the course of my travels I've seen other beautiful mountains, but nothing else has ever quite replaced for me the excitement of my own Colorado mountains." She wrote The Fabulous Isotopes, Marie Curie, Roosevelt's America. CA-3

MacLEOD, Beatrice (Beach)
Native New Englander, she graduated from Swarthmore College and Yale Drama School. She has been a theater director and secretary of an educational trust. Her husband has been Professor of Psychology at Cornell University. She wrote On Small Wings.

McMEEKIN, Isabel (McLennan) 1895-
She was born in Louisville, Kentucky, and attended the University of Chicago. She has written many books for children on her own, and she has written some in collaboration with Dorothy Park Clark. Their books may be found under the pseudonym of Clark McMeekin. Her book, Journey Cake, won the $2000.00 award in 1942 of the Julia Ellsworth Ford Foundation for Children's Literature Contest. Mrs. McMeekin once said: "History can only be visualized by arbitrarily picking one small group of people and seeing their particular time and corner of the world through their own eyes..." She wrote: Kentucky Derby Winner, Robert E. Lee, Knight of the South. CA-5/6, MJA

McMILLEN, Wheeler
Farmer, editor, author. Mr. McMillen was born on a farm in Ohio, and attended Ohio Northern University. He has been executive director of President Eisenhower's Commission on Increased Industrial Use of Agricultural Products, and vice-president of the National Council of the Boy Scouts of America. He

has been editor of Country Home and the Farm Journal. He wrote Land of Plenty; The American Farm Story.

McNEER, May Yonge 1902-
Born in Tampa, Florida. She studied at Columbia University where she met Lynd Ward whom she married. After their marriage, they lived in Europe. When they returned to America, May McNeer (Mrs. Ward) began to write books for children. Her titles (illustrated by her husband) include: The Alaska Gold Rush, America's Abraham Lincoln, America's Mark Twain. They both wrote many books including: Armed With Courage, John Wesley, Martin Luther. JBA-2

McPHEDRAN, Marie (Green) 1904-
Born in Canada, she attended the University of Toronto. She married Dr. Harris McPhedran who has been a Professor of Medicine at the University of Toronto. She has taken several freighter trips on the Great Lakes which has furnished her with invaluable information for her book, Cargoes On the Great Lakes. Other titles include: David and the White Cat, Golden North.

MACPHERSON, Margaret L.
Born in Scotland. At one time she was the only woman editor of a newspaper in New Zealand. After a conversation with Bernard Shaw, she traveled to Antipodes to study the social conditions, people, and places of interest. She has lectured, broadcast, and written about Australia. She wrote Australia Calling.

McSWIGAN, Marie 1907-
Born in Pittsburgh, Pennsylvania. She graduated from the University of Pittsburgh, and did graduate work at Columbia University. An extensive traveler, she was in Spain when the revolution took place in 1931. She has been a reporter for the Pittsburgh Press and the Pittsburgh Sun-Telegraph. Also, she did newspaper publicity work during the summer for

Kennwood Park, a Pittsburgh amusement park. It was through this work that she became acquainted with the Carl Wallenda high wire troupe, the Great Peters, and many others. Her books for young people include: All Aboard for Freedom!, Five On a Merry-Go-Round, Small Miracle at Lourdes, Snow Treasure. MJA

MACE, Katherine (Keeler) 1921-
She was born in New York City, and graduated from Swarthmore College. Her mother was author, Katherine Keeler. She married a cartoonist, Harry Mace, who illustrated her books, Chief Dooley's Busy Day and Mr. Wiggington Joins the Circus. Also, she wrote: A Tail is a Tail, Let's Dance a Story.

MACE, Wynn
He graduated from Princeton University. He has won the Southern California Tennis Championship, and the Intercollegiate Doubles Championship with George Meyers Church. He has been a tennis instructor at the Annandale Golf Club in Pasadena where many of his students later became well-known tennis stars. He wrote Tennis Techniques Illustrated.

MALKUS, Alida Sims 1895-
She was born in New York state, but grew up in Michigan. She has traveled in Mexico and South America studying Mayan ruins and visiting museums. Mrs. Malkus has been interested in archaeology since the time when she was sixteen and visited the southwest. Juvenile contributions include: Along the Inca Highway, Constancia Lona, The Sea and Its Rivers, Sidi, Boy of the Desert, Young Inca Prince. JBA-1, JBA-2

MALONE, Mary
Born in Lambertville, New Jersey. She attended Trenton State Teachers College, Rutgers, and Columbia University. She has been both a public and a school librarian. Also, she has been a children's

book reviewer for Library Journal. Her book, This Was Bridget, was a winner in the Dodd, Mead Librarian Prize Competition. Also, she wrote: Deenie's Coat, Here's Howie, Three Wishes for Sarah. CA-1

MALOT, Hector Henri 1830-1907
Born in France in the province of Normandy. Although he studied law, he left it in order to pursue a literary career. He was a news correspondent in London, and a literary critic for L'Opinion Nationale. His autobiography, Roman de mes Romans, was published before he died at Vincennes, France, in 1907. He wrote: Nobody's Boy (translated by Florence Crew Jones), Nobody's Girl (translated by Florence Crew Jones).

MALVERN, Gladys
She has been an actress, advertising manager of a large store, and a radio script writer. She has enjoyed writing for young adults whom she has considered "the most discerning and critical audience." Her book, Valiant Minstrel: The Story of Harry Lauder, won the Julia Ellsworth Ford Foundation Award in 1943. Her sister, Corinne Malvern, has illustrated many of her books. Her books for young people include: Behold Your Queen!, Eric's Girls, The Foreigner; The Story of a Girl Named Ruth, Meg's Fortune, So Great a Love. JBA-2

MAMMEN, Edward William 1907-
Born in Brooklyn, New York, and received his Ph.D. degree from Columbia University. He has taught speech at Columbia, and has been Assistant Professor of Public Speaking at the City College of New York (C.C.N.Y.). In his book, Turnipseed Jones, he based part of the character of Mrs. Turnipseed on a lady who was able, at ninety-five, to mow the lawn. He wrote: Turnipseed Jones.

MANTON, Jo 1919-
She has been editor and producer for the British Broadcasting Company's School Broadcasting Depart-

ment. During World War II, she served in the Women's Auxiliary Territorial Service of England. She married poet Robert Gittings. Her book, The Story of Albert Schweitzer, was awarded one of the five medals given each year by Boys' Clubs of America. She wrote Portrait of Bach. CA-5/6

MARAIS, Josef 1905-
He was born in South Africa. Since the time when he was a small boy, he has been interested in the folk songs of Africa. At the age of nineteen, he possessed a large collection of native Africaans folk songs. He has presented them on programs of both the British Broadcasting Company and the National Broadcasting Company. He wrote Koos, the Hottentot; Tales of the Veld.

MARCUS, Rebecca B. 1907-
Native New Yorker who graduated from Hunter College and attended Teacher's College, Columbia University. She was a science teacher in the New York City junior high schools for many years. With her husband, Abraham Marcus, she wrote Power Unlimited! Also, she wrote The First Book of Glaciers. CA-5/6

MARINO, Dorothy (Bronson) 1912-
She was born in Oregon and graduated from the University of Kansas. When she was five years old, her family moved to Missouri where they lived on a farm prior to locating in a small town. This experience of living on a farm made a lasting impression on Dorothy Marino. She has enjoyed writing stories about farms for boys and girls. Juvenile titles include: Buzzy Bear and the Rainbow, Buzzy Bear Goes South, Good Night Georgie. She illustrated Miss Hattie and the Monkey by Helen D. Olds.

MAROKVIA, Mireille
French author. She studied at the Sorbonne. When she came to America, she attended Columbia University. She has been a teacher, translator, and writer. Jannot was her first book for boys and girls

(also, her first publication in English). She wrote: Belle Arabelle by Mireille Marokvia and Artur Marokvia, Jannot; a French Rabbit.

MARKS, Mickey Klar
Sand sculptress, author, born in Brooklyn, New York. Her sand sculptures have been sold at America House in New York City. Also, she has been interested in ballet, painting, and the theater. At one time, she was a member of a repertory company. She wrote: Fine Eggs and Fancy Chickens, Sand Sculpturing, Slate Sculpturing; Sculptures by Frank Eliscu.

MARKUN, Patricia (Maloney)
Born in Minnesota, and graduated from the School of Journalism at the University of Minnesota. When she was twelve years old, she won first prize in a children's short story contest conducted by a Duluth newspaper. After her marriage to a lawyer, she lived in the Panama Canal Zone. Her husband has been Assistant General Counsel for the Panama Canal Company. She wrote: The First Book of Central America and Panama, First Book of the Panama Canal.

MARRAN, Ray J.
He was born in New York City. When he was a small boy, his family moved to a suburb near Kansas City. Later, he became a cub reporter on the Kansas City Star. Also, he has worked in railroad freight offices, in advertising, and in the display advertising department of newspapers. Juvenile titles include: Games Outdoors, Making Models of Famous Ships, Playthings for Indoor and Outdoor Fun.

MARRIOT, Alice Lee 1910-
Ethnologist-author. She has spent a great portion of her life in the study of the American Indian. She graduated from Oklahoma City University and the University of Oklahoma. She has been a specialist in the Indian Arts and Crafts Board of the Department of the Interior. Miss Marriott has made a

study of the Northwest tribes as a field research fellow of the Laboratory of Anthropology of Santa Fe, and has been associated with the Rockefeller and Guggenheim Foundations in ethnological study of the Southwest. Juvenile titles include: Black Stone Knife, The First Comers; Indians of America's Dawn, Indians of the Four Corners, Sequoyah: Leader of the Cherokees.

MARSHALL, Catherine
She was born in Yonkers, and graduated from Mt. Holyoke. She has been secretary in a welfare organization, and has done promotion work for textbooks. Also, she has worked in the Children's Room of the Yonkers Public Library. Teen-age readers have enjoyed her book, Julie's Heritage.

MARTIN, Charles Morris 1891-
"Chuck" Martin left his home in Ohio at the age of seventeen, and went to work on a 250,000-acre cattle ranch in California. Later, he owned his own ranch, the "Boot Hill," in Oceanside, California. He has written columns for newspapers, Western stories, and has done publicity work for rodeos. He once said: "Kids all up and down the valley want my opinion on their calves, steers and horses. You can't love those kids like I do, and stay long away from them. 'Here comes the old cowboy!' they shout. They all want to know when 'their book' is coming out." Juvenile titles include: Cowboy Charley, 4-H Champ, Orphans of the Range.

MARTIN, George
Born in New York City, he graduated from Harvard College and the University of Virginia Law School. Also, he has studied at Trinity College, Cambridge, England. In order to write his book, The Opera Companion, he resigned his position in a New York law firm. Mr. Martin has been a Director of the Metropolitan Opera Guild. He wrote The Battle of the Frogs and the Mice; an Homeric Fable.

MARTIN, Patricia Miles
As a child, she lived on a farm near Coffeyville, Kansas, and later, made her home in Denver. At one time, she was a country school teacher in eastern Colorado. She has felt that most children pass through a phase of "wondering why they have to learn." So she wrote not only to entertain, but "to show that there is power in the written word." She has lived in San Mateo, California. She wrote Pointed Brush.

MARTINI, Teri 1930-
Her mother operated a book shop in Teaneck, New Jersey, so this author has grown up in an atmosphere of books. After attending college, she has devoted her time both to teaching and writing for children. Juvenile titles include: True Book of Cowboys, True Book of Indians, What a Frog Can Do. CA-5/6

MASANI, Shakuntala
She received her M.A. degree from Lucknow University, and studied art at the Lucknow Art School. Mrs. Masani has been on the staff of a Bombay newspaper, and has been the head of the children's book section in a publishing house in India. She married M.R. Masani who has been Ambassor of India in Brazil, and who was the author of Our India. She wrote Nehru's Story.

MASON, Frank W. 1901-
Military man, author, born in New England. As a young boy, he lived in many capitals of Europe with his grandfather who was consul in Paris and Berlin. When he was a young man, he transferred from the French Army to the A.E.F., and achieved the distinction of being the sixth generation of his family to serve in the U.S. armed forces. He graduated from Harvard, and became an importer. He wrote Pilots, Man Your Planes! CA-5/6

MASON, George Frederick 1904-
He grew up on a farm near Worcester, Massachu-

setts. He graduated from art school, and later, joined the staff of the American Museum of Natural History. He has been very interested in Alaska, and has been on several expeditions there studying its animals for the Museum. Mr. Mason has been Assistant Curator of the Department of Education in the Museum. Juvenile titles include: Animal Clothing, Animal Habits, Animal Sounds, Animal Tails, The Deer Family.

MASON, Miriam Evangeline 1900-
She was born in Goshen, Indiana, and grew up on a farm in southern Indiana. She decided that she would be a writer when she was eight years old. Her first poem was published when she was in the fourth grade, and her first story about cats was published a little later in a farm magazine. There has hardly ever been a nine or ten year old little girl who has not thoroughly enjoyed Miriam Mason's books. Juvenile titles include: Caroline and Her Kettle Named Maud, Freddy, Herman the Brave Pig, Katie Kittenheart. CA-2, MJA

MASSIE, Diane Redfield
She was born in Los Angeles, California, and studied art at Los Angeles City College. Mrs. Massie has been first oboist with the Pasadena Symphony, and with the Honolulu Symphony. Her husband has been an instructor in mathematics at New York University. She wrote The Baby Beebee Bird.

MAULE, Hamilton 1915-
He is known to young readers as Tex Maule. He graduated from the University of Texas. Mr. Maule has been publicity director for the professional football club, the Los Angeles Rams, and an associate editor of Sports Illustrated in charge of pro football. His titles for young people include: The Rookie, The Shortstop. CA-1

MAXWELL, Gavin 1914-
He received his education at Stowe and Hertford College, Oxford. During World War II, he served in

the Scots Guards and in Special Forces. When the war was over, he bought the Island of Soay in the Hebrides. His first book, Harpoon Venture, was the result of his experiments with commercial shark-fishing. He has been a member of the Royal Geographic Society and the American Geographic Society. He wrote The Otters' Tale for boys and girls. This was a retelling and shortening of the author's Ring of Bright Water.

MAXWELL, William 1908-
He was born in Lincoln, Illinois. One summer when he was sixteen, he worked on a farm in Wisconsin. This experience later provided him with the inspiration to write Heavenly Tenants. He has taught freshman composition at the University of Illinois, and has been an associate editor of The New Yorker magazine. He has contributed short stories to Harper's Bazaar, The New Yorker, and The Atlantic Monthly magazines. He wrote Heavenly Tenants.

MAY, Charles Paul 1920-
He has his B.A. degree from Drake University, and his M.A. from Oklahoma Agricultural and Mechanical College. He has traveled throughout the United States, Canada, Europe, Asia, and Africa. Mr. May has been on the editorial staff of the Grolier Society, and has lived in New York City. Juvenile titles include: Box Turtle Lives in Armor, Women in Aeronautics. CA-1

MAY, Julian 1931-
Author of science books. He has written thousands of encyclopedia articles in the fields of science, technology, and natural history. His books have been the result of careful and thorough research. He has lived with his wife and three children in Chicago, Illinois. His books include: There's Adventure in Atomic Energy, There's Adventure in Chemistry, There's Adventure in Jet Aircraft, There's Adventure in Marine Science. CA-2

MAYER, Jane (Rothschild) 1903-
She has lived in the Chicago suburb of Glencoe, Illinois, where she has been a member of the Board of Education. As a mother of three, she has been very interested in teachers, schools, and the many aspects of education. She was assigned by Encyclopedia Britannica, Jr. to write a booklet called Getting Along in the Family. Later, this was published by Teachers College, Columbia University. She wrote Betsy Ross and the Flag, Dolly Madison.

MAYNE, William 1928-
English author. He has lived in Leyburn, a village in Yorkshire. He has called himself a "Yorkshireman first, an Englishman second." One of his books, The Blue Boat, which has been published in the United States was selected by the American Library Association as one of the 1960 notable books for young people. He wrote A Grass Rope, Over the Horizon; or, Around the World in Fifteen Stories, by William Mayne [and others].

MEAD, Margaret 1901-
Born in Philadelphia, Pennsylvania, she graduated from Barnard College, and received her M.A. degree from Columbia University. She has been assistant curator and associate curator of ethnology at the American Museum of Natural History, and the recipient of many awards including the Viking Medal in anthropology in 1958. She wrote for young people People and Places. CA-3

MEADER, Stephen Warren 1892-
He was born in Rhode Island, attended high school in New Hampshire, and graduated from Haverford College near Philadelphia. After graduation, he became an investigator for the Society for the Prevention of Cruelty to Children in Newark, New Jersey. Also, he has been associated with the advertising agency of N.W. Ayer & Son in Philadelphia. Juvenile titles include: Buffalo and Beaver, Bulldozer, The Commodore's Cup, Everglades Adventure, Phantom of the Blockade. CA-5/6, JBA-1, JBA-2

MEADOWCROFT, Enid (La Monte) 1898-
Teacher, author, born in New York City. She taught her first class of boys and girls in Harrington Park, New Jersey. Since that time, she has worked with children at the Browning School for Boys in New York and at the Bergen School for Girls in New Jersey. Also, she has acted as supervising editor of all of the Signature Books. Close association with young people has paid rich dividends for this author as her books have been loved and understood by many young readers. They include: By Secret Railway, Story of Andrew Jackson, The Story of Crazy Horse, Texas Star. JBA-2

MEANS, Florence (Crannell) 1891-
She was born in Baldwinsville, New York, the daughter of a minister. She has lived in Denver, and has visited Hopi and Navajo Indians in the Southwest. She was given the Hopi name, Tawahonsi. She married a lawyer, Carleton Bell Means, and they had a daughter named Eleanor. It is particularly appropriate at this time for young people to be able to read books written by an author who believed in the equality of races. Juvenile titles include: Alicia, Moved Outers, Reach For a Star, Tolliver. CA-4, JBA-1, JBA-2

MEEKS, Esther K. 1909-
She has lived in Chicago, Illinois. In addition to writing many books for boys and girls, Mrs. Meeks has been Children's Book Editor for Wilcox & Follett Company. As her books testify, this author has been very fond of animals: "We like cats, but we don't happen to have any right now. Our English Springer Spaniel, Duke, is the family pet, and he is very impartial--and lavish--with his affection." Her titles include: Bow Wow! Said the Kittens, The Curious Cow, Friendly Farm Animals.

MEIGS, Cornelia Lynde 1884-
Born in Illinois, but has lived in Iowa and New England. Storytelling has played an important part in her life. Her father and grandfather used to enjoy

telling stories about America's past, and the children enjoyed hearing them. When she was an instructor in a boarding school, Cornelia Meigs made up short stories to tell to the younger children, and from these came her first book, The Kingdom of the Winding Road. Juvenile titles include: The Covered Bridge, Critical History of Children's Literature by Cornelia Meigs [and others], Dutch Colt, Invincible Louisa (winner of the 1934 Newbery Medal), Wind in the Chimney. JBA-1, JBA-2

MEIGS, Elizabeth Bleecker 1923-
She studied at a convent in France, and later, attended Cornell University where she took veterinary medicine and animal husbandry. When she wrote The Silver Quest, she said that it was based on real people who lived about thirty miles south of the Rio Grande on the Laredo Trail. She continued: "This is the most beautiful country I have ever seen, the land of my heart's choosing." Juvenile titles include: Candle in the Sky, Crusade and the Cup, Scarlet Hill, Sunflight, White Winter; a Story of Scarlet Hill.

MELLIN, Jeanne
She was born in Stamford, Connecticut, and received a B.A. of Fine Arts in painting from the Rhode Island School of Design. She once said: "Horses have always influenced my drawing and painting. I have specialized in them since I first began to draw, always trying to get the true character and action of the animal." She married an artist, and has lived in New Canaan, Connecticut. She wrote and illustrated Horses Across America.

MEMLING, Carl 1918-
Born in New York City, and studied at Brooklyn College. During World War II, he was with infantry communications. Mr. Memling has been an editor and writer on the staff of the Bank Street College of Education. He married a school psychologist, and the Memlings have lived in East Meadow, New York. He wrote Seals for Sale. CA-4

MEREDITH, Nicolete
She has been interested in all facets of welfare work and has been on the Governor's Board in Iowa, "helping to implement several phases of the welfare law." She has contributed articles to many magazines including the Reader's Digest and Humpty Dumpty. She wrote the Story of the Philippines which was the recipient of the annual award from the Missouri Writer's Guild. She has been a member of the Missouri's Writer's Guild and the Gallery of Living Catholic Authors. Also, she wrote Welcome Love.

MERRILL, Jean Fairbanks 1923-
She came from Rochester, New York, and has lived in New York City. Miss Merrill has been a magazine writer and editor. She has traveled extensively in Europe and the Far East. Her books for young people include: Emily Emerson's Moon, by Jean Merrill and Ronni Solbert, The Superlative Horse.
CA-1

METCALFE, June M.
She was born in Saskatchewan, Canada, and later, became a United States citizen. She has been a member of the Society of Woman Geographers and an associate member of the American Institute of Mining and Metallurgical Engineers. Mrs. Metcalfe has served with Teachers College, Columbia University, as a specialist on simplified writing. Also, she has taken part in the Writer's Conference at Columbia. She wrote Mining Round the World; Stories of Mines, Minerals and Men.

MEYER, Franklyn E. 1932-
Born in St. Louis, Missouri, he graduated from the University of Missouri. After graduation from college, Mr. Meyer served as a second lieutenant in the Marine Corps Reserve. He has been a teacher in Sarasota, Florida. He wrote Me and Caleb.
CA-4

MEYER, Gerard Previn
Author, teacher, born in New York. He has written and produced radio and television scripts for

WNYE, the New York City Board of Education Station. Also, he has devoted part of his time to teaching College English. As a result of his radio program "How It Began," he wrote the book Pioneers of the Press; the First Newspapers in America.

MEYER, Jerome Sydney 1895-
Born in New York City, he studied engineering at Columbia University. He served in World War I. Mr. Meyer entered the field of advertising with eventual ownership of his own agency. The first radio quiz program was credited to him. Magazines have published articles written by him, and several of his books have been on the best seller lists. Among his juvenile contributions can be found: Boys' Book of Modern Science [by] S.M. Jennings [pseud], Engines, Fun With Mathematics, Machines, Paper, Picture Book of Electricity, Prisms and Lenses, World Book of Great Inventions. CA-2

MIERS, Earl Schenck 1910-
Born in Brooklyn, New York. He graduated from Rutgers University. American history has always claimed his interest. Mr. Miers collaborated with Paul M. Angle, to edit a one-volume edition of the writings of Abraham Lincoln. Juvenile contributions include: America and Its Presidents, Our Fifty States, Rainbow Book of American History, Storybook of Science. CA-3

MILHOUS, Katherine 1894-
Illustrator, author, native of Philadelphia. She attended the Pennsylvania Museum's School of Industrial Art and the Academy of Fine Arts. She was the recipient of a Cresson traveling scholarship and went abroad. Miss Milhous has served as supervisor on a Federal Art Project. Many of her stories have had a Pennsylvania Dutch background. She received the Caldecott Medal in 1951 for her delightful story, The Egg Tree. Other titles include: Appolonia's Valentine, First Christmas Crib, Herodia, the Lovely Puppet, Patrick and the Golden

Slippers, With Bells On; a Christmas Story. JBA-2

MILLER, Donald G. 1909-
Teacher and author, a graduate of Greenville College, Illinois. He received his M.A. and Ph.D. degrees from New York University. Donald G. Miller has been Walter H. Robertson Professor of New Testament at Union Theological Seminary, Richmond, Virginia. He taught in Pyengyang Foreign School in Korea. He has written Conqueror in Chains, a Story of the Apostle Paul. CA-5/6

MILLER, Helen Louise
Teacher, playwright, author. She has been an English teacher in York, Pennsylvania, and developed the first course of study in English for the York junior high schools. Also, she has contributed to Plays, The Drama Magazine for Young People. Various civic organizations in her community have used her plays, pageants, and dramatic sketches. She married school administrator, Samuel A. Gotwalt. Her books include: Gold Medal Plays for Holidays; Thirty Royalty-Free One-Act Plays for Children, Plays for Living and Learning; Twenty-Five Dramatic Programs for Classroom and Assembly.

MILLER, Helen Markley
Author, teacher, born in Iowa. A graduate of Iowa State Teachers College, she had been a teacher of speech and English before her marriage. After the death of her newspaper-editor husband, Mrs. Miller returned to the teaching profession. Upon the publication of her first book, Helen Miller traveled by trailer to view some of the Idaho ghost towns. This trip provided the background for her book, Promenade All. Also, she has written: Dust in the Gold Sack, The Long Valley, The Lucky Laceys, Miss Gail (A Junior Literary Guild selection), Westering Women.

MILLER, Helen (Topping) 1884-
"To me the unchanging loveliness of the holy days is proof of the unchanging love of God," was part

of a Christmas message presented by Helen Topping Miller. Her series of books about Christmas in the lives of great Americans have made her a popular author. Included in these are: Christmas at Monticello, With Thomas Jefferson, Christmas at Mount Vernon, With George and Martha Washington, Christmas With Robert E. Lee.

MILLER, Mark
Mr. Miller's stories of action have been contributed to the author's experience of working in newspaper city rooms. He has been a cub reporter, editor, publisher, and has worked on such newspapers as: The Duluth (Minn.) News Tribune, St. Paul Dispatch, Minneapolis Journal, Milwaukee Sentinel, and Brownsville, (Texas) Herald. He has been interested in stamp collecting, Indian lore and legends. His juvenile titles include: The Singing Wire, a Story of the Telegraph, White Captive of the Sioux.

MILLER, Mary Britton 1883-
Author and poet. This author sometimes writes under the name of Isabel Bolton. Give a Guess and All Aboard, two books of her poems, were well-received by the critics. "Distinguished for the simplicity that comes with the passion for perfection," was the comment written in the New York Times. Juvenile books include: Jungle Journey, Listen - the Birds; Poems. CA-2

MILNE, Alan Alexander 1882-1956
Born in London, studied at Cambridge, and became editor of its undergraduate paper, the Granta. He has been assistant editor of Punch during which period of his life he married Dorothy de Sélincourt. The Milnes had a son named Christopher Robin (often called "Billy Moon") who inspired his father to create verses for boys and girls. After the publication of Winnie-the-Pooh and The House at Pooh Corner, everyone felt that the boy in these stories, Christopher Robin, was a personal friend. Juvenile contributions include: House at Pooh Corner, Now We Are Six, When We Were Very Young, Winnie-the-Pooh.

JBA-1, JBA-2

MILNE, Lorus Johnson 1910 - Margery Joan (Greene) 1914-

Husband-wife team. Mr. Milne was born in Toronto, Canada, and later, became an American citizen. He attended the University of Toronto, and received his M.A. and Ph.D. degrees at Harvard. New York was Margery Milne's birthplace. She obtained her M.A. at Columbia and a Ph.D. at Radcliffe. Durham, New Hampshire, has been their home. Both have written for literary and nature magazines. Also, Mr. and Mrs. Milne have taught biology and have enjoyed field trips as a hobby. Together, they wrote Famous Naturalists.

MIMS, Sam 1887-

Author, farmer, born in Webster Parish, Louisiana. He studied at Louisiana Polytechnic Institute, Ruston, Louisiana, and the Louisiana State University, Baton Rouge. His writing career began after his return from World War I. The Taming of the Cur, his first story, was purchased by The Youth's Companion. Mr. Mims has been employed by a municipal bond company. Also, he has been a newspaper columnist, and manager of a writers' colony. He married his secretary, Frances Elizabeth Perry. He wrote Chennault of the Flying Tigers.

MINARIK, Else Holmelund

She was born in Denmark. Mrs. Minarik has lived in Chatham, New York. As a former teacher, she said: "I never felt that I had enough books to give my first graders that they could really read by themselves, quietly at home...Therefore, I wrote some." Her "I Can Read" series include: Little Bear's Friend, Little Bear's Visit, No Fighting, No Biting. Also, she wrote The Little Giant Girl and the Elf Boy.

MIRSKY, Reba Paeff 1902-

Author, traveler, lecturer, teacher. She studied music at Radcliffe College and did graduate work at

Harvard. Also, she has studied ancient instruments at the Schola Cantorum in Basle. She married Dr. Alfred Mirsky of the Rockefeller Institute. Mrs. Mirsky has been a teacher of old instruments (the harpsichord, clavichord, and recorder), and has lectured on primitive cultures and music. Authentic facts in her first biography, Beethoven, were acquired by much research and travel to the places where he lived and composed. She also wrote Mozart. CA-2

MITCHELL, Isla
Born in Times Square, New York City, she began her education in a one-room school in Cocoa, Florida, and later attended Oxford University. She lived in London for fifteen years. At one time she planned a six-week holiday in Ireland, but it resulted in her staying there for seven years. Family experiences during her long visit formed the basis for her book, Irish Roundabout.

MOLLOY, Anne Stearns (Baker) 1907-
Author, traveler, she studied at Brimmer School in Boston and at Mt. Holyoke College. At one time she lived in a dormitory at Exeter Academy where her husband taught. She has lived in New Hampshire, and racing homer pigeons has been her hobby. Since she has studied and raised pigeons, this author was well qualified to write The Pigeoneers. Other titles include: ...A Bird in Hand, Celia's Lighthouse, Christmas Rocket, Decky's Secret, Secret of the Old Salem Desk, Shooting Star Farm.

MONTGOMERIE, Norah
Author, illustrator, born in London. She attended art school, and later, married Scottish poet and teacher, William Montgomerie. Together, they edited Scottish Nursery Rhymes, Sandy Candy, and the Scottish folk tales, Well at the World's End. Mrs. Montgomerie collaborated with Kathleen Lines to compile Poems and Pictures which she also illustrated. She has been a designer of textiles. She wrote Twenty-Five Fables; Retold and illustrated by

Norah Montgomerie.

MONTGOMERY, Elizabeth (Rider) 1902-
Teacher and author, daughter of an American missionary. She was born in Huaraz, Peru. She was a student at Western Teachers College and the University of California. She has written textbooks, articles, and plays. Other interests of Mrs. Montgomery have been water-color painting and rug-making. As a first grade teacher, she was dissatisfied with the type of reader which was being used so she decided to "write a better one." The Montgomerys have lived in Seattle, Washington. Her juvenile books include: *Second-Fiddle Sandra,* *Story Behind Great Books,* *Story Behind Modern Books,* *Susan and the Storm,* *Three Miles an Hour.* CA-2

MONTGOMERY, Rutherford George 1896-
He was born in North Dakota. He served in the Air Corps of the U.S. Army during the World War. This experience provided him with a good background in order to write stories of aviation. Also, Rutherford Montgomery has been a teacher and judge. His knowledge of wild horses, coupled with his love for the Western terrain, resulted in his writing *The Capture of the Golden Stallion.* He has enjoyed the outdoor life as a hobby. His many titles include: *Amikuk,* *Beaver Water,* *Golden Stallion and Wolf Dog* (A Junior Literary Guild selection), *Jets Away.* MJA

MOODY, Ralph O. 1898-
Born in New Hampshire, he received his education in Colorado. Later, he resided in San Francisco. When he was a boy in Colorado, Mr. Moody used to hear stories about Geronimo from men who had fought in the war against the Indian. Also, he has made friends with many Indians from the Ute, Navaho, and Apache tribes. He has written: *The Fields of Home,* *Geronimo, Wolf of the Warpath,* *The Home Ranch,* *Kit Carson and the Wild Frontier,* *Wells Fargo.*

MOON, Grace (Purdie) 1883?-1947, Carl-
Husband (illustrator)-wife (author) team. Born in Indianapolis, Indiana, Grace Moon has always displayed a great interest in Indians. Her husband Carl Moon was an "Indian" artist, and the Pueblo Indians were the models for his painting and photography. The Moons have lived with the Indians in New Mexico and Oklahoma for long periods of time. During this time, they accumulated a great deal of information for their books. Mr. and Mrs. Moon wrote One Little Indian. Also, she wrote: Chi-Weé; the Adventures of a Little Indian Girl, Chi-Weé and Loki of the Desert, illustrated by her husband. JBA-1

MOORE, Anne Carroll 1871-1961
Born in Limerick, York County, Maine, the daughter of a lawyer. She attended Limerick Academy, Bradford (Massachusetts) Academy, and later, graduated from the Library School of Pratt Institute. She was Children's Librarian of the Pratt Institute, Free Library (their Children's Room was the "first room of its kind to be included in an architect's plan"), the first Supervisor of Work with Children in the New York Public Library. Anne Carroll Moore has been and will continue to be a leading authority in the field of children's literature. Her death occurred on January 20, 1961, inauguration day of the late President John F. Kennedy. Juvenile contributions include: Cross-Roads to Childhood, My Roads to Childhood, Views and Reviews of Children's Books, The Three Owls; a Book About Children's Books, Their Authors, Artists and Critics. JBA-1, JBA-2

MOORE, David William
Born near Highland, Ohio, he studied at Ohio Wesleyan University, and Columbia University. Although he has been well-known as a short story writer, he has also contributed editorials to magazines. In discussing a school assignment, Mr. Moore and his son decided that it would be interesting to tell what became of Long John Silver. As a result, he wrote The End of Long John Silver. He also has written

The End of Black Dog.

MOORE, Lamont
He studied art at the Newark Museum, Newark, New Jersey. He has been Director of Education at the National Gallery of Art, Washington, D. C., and Director of the Art Gallery of Yale University. As an officer in the Monuments and Fine Arts Section of Military Government during World War II, Mr. Moore assisted in the preservation of European architecture and works of art. He was awarded membership in the Legion of Honor in recognition of his services by the French government. For young readers he wrote The First Book of Architecture.

MOORE, Lillian
Mrs. Moore has devoted much of her time to the improvement of children's reading. She has been a teacher and reading specialist with the Board of Education of New York City. Also, Mrs. Moore has been editor of the Arrow Book. Club. Humpty Dumpty Magazine for Little Children has published articles written by her. Juvenile titles include: Bear Trouble, A Child's First Picture Dictionary, My First Counting Book, A Pickle for a Nickel, Snake That Went to School. She collaborated with Leone Adelson to write Old Rosie; the Horse Nobody Understood.

MOORE, Nancy
Actress, author, monologist, lecturer. Miss Moore was a professional actress before the start of a writing career. In addition to writing plays for adults and children, she has written for radio and television. An enthusiastic traveler she has said, "I write to travel, and I travel to write." She has enjoyed ballet and collecting antique paper weights. Juvenile books include: Ermintrude, Miss Harriet Hippopotamus and the Most Wonderful, by Nancy Moore and Edward Leight, Unhappy Hippopotamus.

MOORE, Patrick Alfred
Astronomer and author. He was a member of the British Astronomical Association at the age of elev-

en. Mr. Moore has lectured in Russia about the moon and has appeared on BBC television. Also, he has conducted children's programs. He has been Secretary of the Lunar Section in the British Astronomical Association and has belonged to British and foreign astronomical societies. He wrote: The Boy's Book of Space, Isaac Newton, The Picture History of Astronomy.

MOORE, Vardine
Author and teacher. She has been a kindergarten teacher in Evansville, Indiana, and has written and conducted a children's story hour on radio. Also, she has operated a nursery school. Mrs. Moore's stories have been published in American Childhood, Child Life, Jr., Jack and Jill, and others. She has collaborated with Fleur Conkling to write Billy Between.

MORAN, Eugene Francis 1872-
The son of the founder of the Moran Towing and Transportation Company, he became company president, and later, Chairman of the Board. Mr. Moran has been Chairman of the Rivers, Harbors and Piers Committee of the Maritime Association of the Port of New York and has been one of the Commissioners of the Port of New York Authority. He wrote Famous Harbors of the World for boys and girls.

MORDVINOFF, Nicolas 1911-
Author, artist, born in Petrograd, now known as Leningrad. His pseudonym is Nicolas. He graduated from the University of Paris. Nicolas began drawing at an early age and continued to do so when he lived in the South Pacific. In Tahiti, writer William Stone asked him to illustrate a book which later influenced Nicolas in coming to America. Bear's Land was the first book written by the author. He has combined his talent with that of William Lipkind, and together they have created distinguished books for children. In 1952, this team, known as Will and Nicolas, won the Caldecott Medal for Finders Keepers (illustrations by Mr. Mordvinoff). MJA

MORENUS, Richard 1897-

Author and lecturer. Authentic knowledge of the frozen Northland was obtained by the author's lonely existence for several years in northern Ontario. Also, his experiences with fur-trapping, Indians, and trading posts, have given his books a certain spirit of adventure. Also, he has worked in the advertising field. Mr. Morenus and his wife have lived in Fennville, Michigan. His books include: Dew Line; Distant Early Warning: The Miracle of America's First Line of Defense, Hudson's Bay Company.

MORGAN, Alfred Powell 1889-

Author, illustrator, electrical engineer. Born in Brooklyn, New York, and attended the Massachusetts Institute of Technology. He has written and illustrated numerous books, and magazines have published his articles. His background and experience as an electrical engineer enabled him to write authentic books of science. Mr. Morgan has designed and made equipment for the United States Army and Navy. He has written and illustrated: Aquarium Book for Boys and Girls, Boys' Book of Engines, Motors and Turbines, Boys' Book of Science and Construction, A First Electrical Book for Boys. MJA

MORISON, Samuel Eliot 1887-

Author, teacher, born in Boston. He graduated from Harvard University where he obtained his B.A. and Litt.D. degrees. A well-known historian, he has taught American Colonial History at Harvard. Also, he has taught at the University of California, and has held the chair of American History at Oxford. Mr. Morison was the authorized Naval Historian for World War II. During the war, he received seven battle stars and the Legion of Merit with Combat Clasp. For children he has written Story of the "Old Colony" of New Plymouth (1620-1692). CA-2

MORRIS, Richard Brandon 1904-
An eminent authority on the American Revolution, he has been a Professor of History at the Columbia University Graduate School. Also, he has taught history at City College, New York and Princeton University Graduate School where he belonged to the Institute for Advanced Study. Mr. Morris has been editor of the Encyclopedia of American History. For young people he has written: The First Book of the American Revolution, First Book of Indian Wars.

MOSCOW, Alvin 1925-
Traveler and author, he has lived in Stamford, Coneticut, with his family. He attended St. John's University, the City College of New York, and obtained his Bachelor's degree in journalism from the University of Missouri. Mr. Moscow served as a U.S. Navy radioman during World War II. In obtaining research for his book, Collision Course, he interviewed the officers and crew of many luxury liners. Also, he was present at the Andrea Doria - Stockholm hearings as a reporter for the Associated Press. He has written City at Sea for children. CA-2

MOWAT, Farley 1921-
After a trip with an uncle into the far north, this author caught "virus arcticus" which he explained as a disease that makes its victims leave a warm home in order to live in the cold arctic. During World War II, he served in the Canadian army. After the war, Mr. Mowat and a young native traveled over 1200 miles of the Barrenlands. After his marriage, his wife was the first white woman to view the central Barrens. He wrote: Lost in the Barrens, Owls in the Family. CA-3

MUKERJI, Dhan Gopal 1890-1936
Born near Calcutta, India, he attended the universities of Calcutta and Tokyo, and Stanford University in California. His memories of religious tales and fables about India told to him by his mother, and his own experiences provided the background and in-

spiration for his books. In 1928 his book Gay Neck; the Story of a Pigeon, was the winner of the Newbery Medal. Other titles include: Fierce-Face; the Story of a Tiger, Hari the Jungle Lad, Kari the Elephant. JBA-1

MULCAHY, Lucille
Born in Albuquerque, New Mexico. She attended the New Mexico State College. Magazines have published her short stories for children. Mrs. Mulcahy's interests in Indian pottery and ceramics helped her to write Magic Fingers. CA-5/6

MUNARI, Bruno
A native of Milan, he has been an artist, sculptor, photographer, and designer. His slides and drawings have been shown in the Museum of Modern Art in New York City. He has written ABC and Bruno Munari's Zoo.

MUNRO, Eleanor C. 1928-
Author and editor, she was born in Brooklyn, New York. She attended the Hathaway-Brown School in Cleveland, Ohio, and received her B.A. degree at Smith College. Also, she studied at the University of Paris on a Fulbright grant. Miss Munro has been Associate Editor of Art News Annual. Horizon and Perspectives USA magazines have published her articles. She married Dr. Alfred Frankfurter, a distinguished art critic and editor. She wrote The Golden Encyclopedia of Art...With A Glossary of Artists and Art Terms. CA-4

MUNSON, Gorham
Writer, editor, and teacher, a graduate of Wesleyan University. As a teacher, he was well-known for his course in professional writing at the New School for Social Research. Writer's Conferences also benefited by his teaching. Mr. Munson has been a free-lance writer and has had his articles published in many magazines. He has been managing editor of magazines and has worked in publishing firms. Gorham Munson was chosen by the late Robert Frost to

write a critical biography about the poet, namely, Robert Frost: A Study in Sensibility and Good Sense. As a teacher and author, Mr. Munson has discredited the old saying: "Those who can, write; those who can't, teach." For children he wrote Making Poems for America: Robert Frost.

MURPHY, Mabel (Ansley) 1870-
She graduated from State Teachers' College, Indiana, Pennsylvania, and also, attended Knox College, Galesburg, Illinois, and Columbia University. Not only did she write for children, but she has written articles about travel and religious education. Her literary page in Holland's Magazine, Dallas, Texas, appeared under her pen name, Anne S. Lee. In 1920, her first book, Great Hearted Women, was published. Mrs. Murphy wrote They Were Little Once for children.

MUSCIANO, Walter A.
Born in New York City, he was a student at Haaren Aviation High School and attended the Brooklyn Polytechnic Institute. A builder of scale model airplanes, he has become well-known in the field of model construction. He has designed and constructed model airplanes, boats, and cars, and has won many prizes for his models. Also, the author's articles about model construction have been published in Mechanix Illustrated, Young Men, Model Airplane News, and others. He has written for young people: Building and Operating Model Cars, Model Plane Manual, which he also illustrated.

MUSGRAVE, Florence
Teacher, author, daughter of a Methodist clergyman. The state of West Virginia was her childhood home. She graduated from Fairmont State Teachers College, Fairmont, West Virginia, and obtained a Master's degree from New York University. Her teaching career was concluded when Florence Musgrave decided to write full-time. The author combined experiences from her own life with fiction to write Oh Sarah. Also, she wrote: A Boy for You, A Horse

for Me, Catherine's Bells, Like a Red, Red Rose, Robert E, Sarah Hastings, Trailer Tribe.

MYERS, Madeleine Neuberger 1896-
Author and teacher, she grew up in New York City. Mrs. Myers has taught occupational therapy and has done a great deal of work with underprivileged children. After her family was grown, Madeleine Myers returned to writing. For children she wrote Pocketful of Feathers and The Courting-Lamp Mystery.

MYLLER, Rolf
Architect and author. He has designed furniture and planned university campuses. He received a ten thousand dollar award as one of the finalists in the Franklin Delano Roosevelt Memorial Competition. Mr. Myller has had his own architectural practice and has been an Assistant Professor of Architecture at Pratt Institute. He wrote How Big is a Foot? for children.

N

NASH, Ogden 1902-
Poet and author, born in Rye, New York. He studied at St. George's School and Harvard. Wall Street claimed a brief period of his life before he entered the literary field. He collaborated with S. J. Perleman and the late Kurt Weill to write the musical comedy, One Touch of Venus. Mr. Nash has been a member of the National Institute of Arts and Letters. He learned from his two daughters (also, successful authors) what young readers enjoy. His books include: The Adventures of Isabel, Custard the Dragon, Custard the Dragon and the Wicked Knight, Girls Are Silly, The New Nutcracker Suite, and Other Innocent Verses.

NEAL, Harry Edward 1906-
Born in Pittsfield, Massachusetts. He retired in 1957 as Assistant Chief of the United States Secret Service, Treasury Department, in order to devote his time to writing. He received the Exceptional

Civilian Service Award, the highest civilian award that is given by an Executive Department. Mr. Neal did a great deal of research on telescopes and has produced a simple and understandable book, The Telescope, for young people. Stories written by him have appeared in the Saturday Evening Post, Cosmopolitan, Esquire, Family Circle, and other magazines. His books include: Disease Detectives; Your Career in Medical Research, Engineers Unlimited; Your Career in Engineering, ...Nature's Guardians, Story of the Kite. CA-5/6

NEILSON, Frances Fullerton (Jones) 1910-
Born in Philadelphia. She spent her summers at Dorking, England, the setting for her first book. She married Winthrop Neilson, also an author, who wrote Story of Theodore Roosevelt. The Neilsons have lived on Long Island, and their interests have included deep-sea fishing and sailing. Their two sons once said, "There's always a book growing on the typewriter." She wrote Look to the New Moon for children.

NELSON, Cholmondeley M. 1903-
Born in London, he received his education at the Royal Naval Colleges. Before the war, he was Assistant Head of the Story Department at MGM. He returned to England and served in the British Army as a private. He was raised to the rank of colonel, and during the Normandy Invasion he was Assistant Adjutant General to Field Marshall Montgomery. Mr. Nelson returned to the United States at the end of the war and became a citizen. He has been U.N. Representative for the Motion Picture Industry, past President of the American Association for the United Nations, and Director of the Los Angeles World Affairs Council. He wrote With Nelson at Trafalgar. CA-5/6

NEVILLE, Emily
She was born in Manchester, Connecticut, and graduated from Bryn Mawr College where she majored in economics. She married newspaperman Glenn Neville

and has lived in Gramercy Park in New York. Mrs. Neville had chosen research as her career, but became a copy-girl on the New York News and following this, on the New York Mirror. It's Like This, Cat, was the recipient of the 1964 Newbery Medal. The author said, "I wrote it because I have to write, and after about twenty years of experimenting I found that I have to write about a place I know very well." She wrote It's Like This, Cat.

NEVINS, Albert J. 1915-
Author, lecturer, priest, born in Yonkers, New York. He attended Cathedral and Venard colleges, and the Maryknoll Seminary. Father Nevins did editorial work before and after his ordination. He has lectured and contributed articles to secular and religious publications. Also, he has written and produced films, including The Miracle of Blue Cloud Country, The Kid Down the Block, and Little Lady Unwanted. Father Nevins has worked with the Catholic Press Association of the United States and the Catholic Institute of the Press. He wrote: Adventures of Men of Maryknoll, Adventures of Wu Han of Korea, Away to East Africa. CA-5/6

NEWBERRY, Clare (Turlay) 1903-
Author, illustrator. Born in Enterprise, Oregon. She attended the University of Oregon, the art school of the Portland Art Museum, and the San Francisco School of Fine Arts. At an early age she began to draw. Her love of cats made them her favorite subjects to sketch. Most of her illustrations were done from life or life studies. Mrs. Newberry has written and illustrated: Frosty, Herbert the Lion, Ice Cream for Two, Lambert's Bargain, Marshmallow, Mittens, Pandora, Widget. JBA-2

NEWCOMB, Covelle 1908-
Born in San Antonio, Texas. She attended Incarnate Word College in San Antonio, Washington University in St. Louis, Hunter College, New York University, and Columbia. She was awarded an honorary degree of Doctor of Letters from Incarnate Word College.

She married artist-author Addison Burbank who has illustrated many of her books. She has belonged to the American Writers' Association, the New York Pen and Brush Club, the Gallery of Living Catholic Authors, and the Authors' Leagues of America. Juvenile contributions include: Cortez, the Conqueror, Red Hat; a Story of John Henry Cardinal Newman, Secret Door; the Story of Kate Greenaway, Silver Saddles. JBA-2

NEWELL, Homer Edward 1915-
He has written books for children and adults. Dr. Newell and his family have lived in Kensington, Maryland. Space and rockets have claimed much of his time. He has been Assistant Director in charge of Space Science of the National Aeronautics and Space Administration, Head of the Rocket Sonde Branch, Vice Chairman of the Technical Panel on Rocketry of the United States National Committee for the International Geophysical Year, and has served with the U. S. N. C. 's Technical Panel on the Earth Satellite Program. For young people he has written: Express to the Stars; Rockets in Action, Guide to Rockets, Missiles and Satellites.

NEWELL, Hope (Hockenberry) 1896-
Nurse and author, born in Bradford, Pennsylvania. She served in the Army Nurse Corps during World War I and later, did public health nursing. Prior to the war, she studied nursing in Cincinnati. Also, she has attended Columbia University. Mrs. Newell has worked with the National Nursing Council for War Service. She wrote: The Little Old Woman Carries On, Mary Ellis, Student Nurse, Story of Christina. MJA

NICKERSON, Jan
She was an actress in summer stock and has written articles, books, and poems. Miss Nickerson graduated from Radcliffe. She married Arthur S. Hall and has lived in Quincy, Massachusetts. She has written: Answer for April, Circle of Love, When the Heart is Ready. CA-4

NICOLAY, Helen 1866-
Author and painter. Born in Paris, the daughter of John G. Nicolay, the American Consul General. Later, he served as President Lincoln's private secretary, and with John Hay wrote a ten-volume life of Abraham Lincoln. In addition to writing, she has enjoyed painting. Miss Nicolay has lived in Washington, D.C. Juvenile books include: Born to Command; the Story of General Eisenhower, The Boys' Life of Abraham Lincoln, Boys' Life of Washington, The Bridge of Water, the Story of Panama and the Canal, China's First Lady. JBA-1, JBA-2

NIEHUIS, Charles C.
Born in Buck Grove, Iowa. Sports Afield published his first outdoor story. Also, stories of his own hunting and fishing experiences have appeared in Sports Illustrated, Outdoor Life, Field and Stream, and other magazines. Mr. Niehuis has edited the Arizona Wildlife-Sportsman magazine. He has been interested in the conservation of natural resources. For young readers he wrote Trapping the Silver Beaver.

NIXON, Kathleen Irene (Blundell)
Illustrator, author. Her pseudonym is K. Nixon. Born in London, she has lived in India. Also, she has visited the United States, Canada, Australia, China, and Japan. As a "natural" animal artist, she has had her work exhibited in London, India, Melbourne, Singapore, and Paris. She has written and illustrated: Poo and Pushti, Pushti.

NOBLE, Iris 1922-
She grew up in Canada. At the age of eleven her family moved to Oregon. She graduated from the University of Oregon and found her first job as a secretary in Los Angeles. She has been a publicity director, and after her marriage, she did free-lance writing. She has a long list of books to her credit, including: Clarence Darrow, Defense Attorney, The Courage of Dr. Lister, Great Lady of the Theater: Sarah Bernhardt, One Golden Summer,

Stranger No More (A Junior Literary Guild selection), The Tender Promise. CA-3

NOLAN, Jeannette (Covert) 1896-
Author and reporter, born in Evansville, Indiana. She has been a reporter on the staff of the Courier. After the death of her husband, she began to write a great deal not only as therapy but in order to provide an education for her children. Mrs. Nolan has conducted classes in Creative Writing in the extension department of the University of Indiana. Her books include: Abraham Lincoln, Dolley Madison, Florence Nightingale, John Brown, Patriot In the Saddle, The Story of Joan of Arc. JBA-2

NORLING, Ernest Ralph 1892- and Josephine (Stearns) 1895-
Husband-wife team. Ernest Norling studied at the Chicago Art Institute and the Chicago Academy of Fine Arts. He has been a free-lance artist and has worked for the art department of the Seattle Times. Also, he has been Art Director of the Preliminary Design Unit of the Boeing Aircraft Company. Mr. Norling was the illustrator, and his wife was the writer of their stories. Josephine (Jo) Norling graduated from State Teachers College, Ellensburg, Washington and studied psychology at the University of Washington. She has been a teacher and has served with the American Red Cross Military Welfare Service. The Norlings books include: First Book of Water, Pogo's Farm Adventure, a Story of Soil, Pogo's Lamb, a Story of Wool, Willie Skis. CA-2

NORMAN, Charles 1904-
Author, teacher. He grew up in New York City and was a student (and later, a teacher) at New York University. Mr. Norman has lived in Europe. He has been a staff writer for the Associated Press, Time magazine, and the Columbia Broadcasting System. He served in the Army during World War II. He wrote: The Flight and Adventures of Charles II, Orimha of the Mohawks; the Story of Pierre Esprit

Radisson Among the Indians.

NORRIS, Faith Grigsby
Author, teacher, the Orient was her home until she was sixteen. She has been a teacher at Oregon State College. Correspondence with Korean missionary friends and students convinced Mrs. Norris to collaborate with Peter Lumm to write Kim of Korea. The purpose of the book was to help American children understand the country of Korea and its people.

NORTH, Sterling 1906-
He spent his boyhood fishing, swimming, canoeing, camping, and reading Mark Twain's books. He has been General Editor of North Star Books and literary editor of the New York World Telegram and Sun. St. Nicholas magazine published his first poem when he was eight years old. His novel, So Dear to My Heart, has been read in twenty-six countries, and was made into a film by Walt Disney. Other titles include: Abe Lincoln; Log Cabin to White House, Birthday of Little Jesus, The First Steamboat on the Mississippi, Mark Twain and the River, Young Thomas Edison. CA-5/6

NOURSE, Alan Edward 1928-
Doctor and author, he has lived in North Bend, Washington. He took a leave of absence from medicine in order to write full-time. Magazines have published his short stories and novels. He has concentrated on science fiction. He has written: The Counterfeit Man; More Science Fiction Stories, Raiders From the Rings, Rocket to Limbo, Scavengers in Space, Star Surgeon. CA-1

NUGENT, Frances Roberts 1904-
Artist and author, born in New York. With scholarships received from the Student Art League, she attended children's classes at the Brooklyn Museum and Pratt Institute. Miss Nugent wanted to be a "master painter," but abided by her father's wishes and became an art teacher. She has taught in the Art Department of UCLA, in the Santa Monica schools, and

in the Division of Education at the Los Angeles County Art Museum. She has written: Jan Van Eyck: Master Painter. CA-5/6

O

OAKES, Virginia Armstrong
Traveler, correspondent, teacher, author. Her pseudonym is Vanya Oakes. Born in Nutley, New Jersey, she attended the Boston schools and graduated from the University of California at Berkeley. She has traveled extensively as a correspondent for the United Press and the Christian Science Monitor. At Los Angeles City College she has conducted classes in World Affairs, Journalism, and Children's Literature. She has lectured on the Orient and has written for several periodicals. Her books for children include: By Sun and Star, Footprints of the Dragon; a Story of the Chinese and the Pacific Railways, Hawaiian Treasure, Willy Wong American.

O'BRIEN, John Sherman 1898-1938
Born in Duluth, Minnesota, he attended the University of Minnesota and Fordham University. He has been known as Jack O'Brien to young people. He was a chief surveyor with the Byrd Antarctic Expedition, and was in charge of huskies on prospecting trips into Northern Canada. Jack O'Brien acquired a great love for dogs, and it was only natural that he should write about them. He belonged to the Adventurers' Club, and the National Geographic Society made him an honorary member. Juvenile contributions include: Return of Silver Chief, Rip Darcy, Adventurer, Royal Red (published after his death), Silver Chief, Dog of the North, Silver Chief's Revenge, Valiant, Dog of the Timberline. MJA

O'CLERY, Helen
Author, nurse, born in Donegal, Ireland. She attended schools in Ireland and France. She served as a nurse in Dublin, and at twenty-one, she traveled around the world. She married a civil engineer

and lived near Dublin with her family. Her children's book Mystery of Black Sod Paint was a Junior Literary Guild selection.

O'DELL, Scott 1903-
Born in Los Angeles, California. He attended Occidental College, the University of Wisconsin, and Stanford University. Sir Walter Scott was his great-grandfather's cousin. He has been a newspaperman, and has studied the history of California. In 1961 he was awarded the Newbery Medal for his book Island of the Blue Dolphins. MJA

ODENWALD, Robert P. 1899-
Author, psychiatrist. He has practiced psychiatry in Washington, D. C. Dr. Odenwald has done extensive study in the United States and abroad. Medical, scientific, and Catholic publications have published his articles. In 1952 he was awarded the Family Catholic Action Award by the National Catholic Welfare Conference. He wrote How You Were Born for children. CA-2

OFFORD, Lenore (Glen) 1905-
Born in Spokane, Washington, and has resided in Berkeley, California. She graduated from Mills College and attended the University of California. She has written adult mysteries and has been associated with the Mystery Writers of America, Inc., and the San Francisco Chronicle. Mrs. Offord attributed her interests in young people's stories to her daughter and her friends, and accepted their "technical advice" when she was writing a book. She wrote Enchanted August.

OLDEN, Sam
Author, teacher, born near Yazoo City, Mississippi. He graduated from the University of Mississippi, and was a teacher of history there. He has lived in Nigeria where he represented the Mobil International Oil Company. Also, Mr. Olden has been in foreign service in South America, served with the Navy during the war, and was with the U. S. Occupation

Forces in Austria. His books for young people include: Getting to Know Africa's French Community, Getting to Know Argentina, Getting to Know Nigeria.

OLDRIN, John 1901-
Author, banker, real-estate broker. He was born in Connecticut where he spent most of his life. During World War II, he served as a major in the Air Transport Command. He has been quite interested in old automobiles. John Oldrin wrote Eight Rings on His Tail; a Round Meadow Story, which has delighted young readers.

OLDS, Elizabeth 1897-
Author, illustrator. Her interest in oil led her to do research on the subject at the Baton Rouge refineries in Louisiana. As a result, she wrote Deep Treasure; a Story of Oil, a Junior Literary Guild selection. The author's illustrations have appeared in Fortune Magazine, and she has held one-man shows in New York City. Other titles include: Big Fire, Feather Mountain (runner up for the Caldecott Medal). CA-5/6

OLDS, Helen (Diehl) 1895-
Author and teacher, she grew up in Ohio and has lived on Long Island and in New York City. She attended the University of Texas and obtained her B.A. degree from Wittenberg College at Springfield, Ohio. Mrs. Olds' articles have appeared in many magazines. Also, she has taught Juvenile Writing at Queens College and at Huckleberry Workshop in North Carolina. She has written: Christmas-Tree Sam, Detour for Meg, Don and the Book Bus, Fisherman Jody, Silver Buttons, What Will I Wear? CA-4

OLSON, Gene 1922-
Author, newspaperman, teacher. Born in Montevideo, Minnesota, he attended the University of Oregon and received his master's degree in Journalism and Education from Pacific University. He has worked on a farm, served in the Army, and has

been a teacher, novelist, and television writer. His books include: The Ballhawks, The Red, Red Roadster, The Tall One; a Basketball Story, The Tin Goose (a Junior Literary Guild selection).

O'MALLEY, Patricia
Author and aviation enthusiast. She has been associated with the Civil Aeronautics Administration, and has been an instructor of flying. Miss O'Malley has been Manager of the Public Information Department for Transcontinental and Western Air, Inc., in Washington, D.C. Also, she has been a member of a Presidential Commission, called the "Finletter Board." This Commission compiled the report, "Survival in the Air Age." She has written: Faraway Fields, the Career of an Airline Publicity Girl, Happy Landings for Ann, Wider Wings.

O'NEILL, Hester 1908-
Author, traveler. As a result of her extensive travels, Miss O'Neill has been able to create color and atmosphere in her books. During the war, she worked with the government information services. Her books for children include: Picture Story of Denmark, Picture Story of Norway, Picture Story of the Philippines, Picture Story of Sweden.

O'NEILL, Mary 1908-
Author, career woman, homemaker. She grew up in Berea, Ohio. At an early age, she began to write and direct plays for her brothers and sisters. Mary O'Neill has been a copywriter for a department store and has contributed stories to magazines. When she became a partner in an advertising agency, she moved to New York City. She has written: Hailstones and Halibut Bones; Adventures in Color. CA-5/6

O'REILLY, John 1906-
Author, newspaperman. He attended Columbia University. Mr. O'Reilly served as a war correspondent during World War II. He has been head of the Paris Bureau of the New York Herald Tribune. He

wrote The Glob after telling the story of evolution to his daughters.

ORTON, Helen (Fuller) 1872-
Author, teacher, born in New York. Her early education consisted of a little red schoolhouse, a village school, and a high school in Lockport, New York. After her marriage to Jesse F. Orton, she lived in Ann Arbor, Michigan. Mr. Orton was a teacher of economics and a student of law at the University of Michigan. Mrs. Orton studied economics, history, and psychology. After telling stories to her children, Mrs. Orton began to write them. Her first book was published in 1921. Juvenile titles include: The Gold-Laced Coat; a Story of Old Niagara, Hoof-Beats of Freedom, Mystery at the Little Red Schoolhouse, Mystery in the Apple Orchard, Mystery in the Old Cave, Mystery in the Pirate Oak. JBA-1, JBA-2

OSMOND, Edward 1900-
Author, illustrator. Born at Oxford, England, the son of a clergyman. He studied in London at the Regent St. School of Art, and with the scholarships, he completed seven years of full time study. Mr. Osmond was the recipient of the National Diploma in Painting and Illustration, and a University Extension Diploma in Art History with Honors. He married a sculptress who also was an author. He has been interested in animals, and he wrote Animals of the World... for children.

OTTO, Margaret (Glover) 1909-
Mrs. Otto and her husband lived in Westport, Connecticut. She has worked in a bookstore in Philadelphia, and in a children's book department of a publishing house in New York City. After helping many authors and artists, she opened her own literary agency. Later, she began to write books for boys and girls. Her titles include: Little Brown Horse, The Little Old Train, The Man in the Moon, Mr. Kipling's Elephant, Mr. Magic, Syrup.

OWEN, Russell 1889-1952

Author and reporter. As a staff member of the New York Times, Mr. Owen accompanied Admiral Byrd on his first Antarctic Expedition. He received the Pulitzer Prize for his 1929-30 articles reported about the expedition. Along with twelve other Times reporters he wrote a part of the book, We Saw It Happen. He wrote Conquest of the North and South Poles; Adventures of the Peary and Byrd Expeditions, which was published after his death.

OWEN, Ruth (Bryan) 1885-

Author and traveler, daughter of William Jennings Bryan. Born in Jacksonville, Illinois, she studied at Monticello Seminary, and the University of Nebraska. She was awarded honorary degrees of Doctor of Laws and Doctor of Humane Letters. Ruth Owen has been engaged in various phases of politics. She has represented Florida in Congress and has been our country's Minister to Denmark. She married Captain Børge Rohde, and they lived in New York City and West Virginia. Her interests have included music and world travel. She wrote: Denmark Caravan, Picture Tales from Scandinavia; Selected and Retold by Ruth Bryan Owen.

P

PALAZZO, Tony 1905-

Author, illustrator, art director. He was born in Manhattan and attended New York City schools and colleges. He has been director of art for Esquire, Coronet, Collier's, and Look magazines. Exhibitions of his works have been held in the Chicago Art Institute, the San Diego Museum, the Pennsylvania Academy of Fine Arts, Buffalo's Albright Gallery, and the Museum of Modern Art in New York City. Writing children's books began as a hobby but developed into a full-time career. His titles include: An Elephant Alphabet, Federico, the Flying Squirrel, Mister Whistle's Secret, A Monkey Alphabet.

PALMER, Helen Marion
Author and teacher, graduate of Wellesley College and Oxford University. Writing children's books started after her teaching career. She has edited juvenile manuscripts and has contributed many of her own to the field. She married another author of children's books, Theodor Seuss Geisel, better known as Dr. Seuss. They have lived in California. She wrote: A Fish Out of Water, I Was Kissed By a Seal at the Zoo, two of her Beginner Books.

PALMER, Robin 1911-
Born in New York, she received her education at Vassar. She married Dr. Douglas S. Riggs, who was a professor at Harvard Medical School. Robin Palmer has contributed stories to magazines, including Jack and Jill, Child Life, and Story Parade. For children she wrote Wise House.

PARADIS, Adrian Alexis 1912-
Born in Brooklyn, New York. He received a B.A. degree from Dartmouth and a B.S. degree in Library Science from Columbia University. He has lived in Westport, Connecticut, where he was Assistant Secretary in charge of corporate work at American Airlines, Inc. As a businessman, Mr. Paradis has considered writing his hobby. Young people who have been interested in careers have provided the inspiration for many of his books. Juvenile contributions include: Business in Action, ...Dollars for You; 150 Ways for Boys to Earn Money, Librarians Wanted; Careers in Library Service, ...The New Book in Banking. CA-4, MJA

PARADIS, Marjorie Bartholomew
Author and teacher. Born in Montclair, New Jersey. A graduate of Erasmus Hall, she has attended Columbia University. She married Adrian F. Paradis. She was a teacher of juvenile fiction at Chautauqua Writers Workshop and conducted a short story class at the YWCA. Mrs. Paradis has written children's books, plays, and adult fiction. One novel was made into a movie. Her interests have included civic af-

fairs, hooking rugs, portrait painting, and travel. Some of her titles are: Maid of Honor, Mr. De Luca's Horse, Timmy and the Tiger.

PARISH, Peggy
Author and teacher. Manning, South Carolina was her birthplace. She has been a teacher in the Panhandle area, in coal-mining districts, and in a private school in Manhattan. Also, Miss Parish has worked in an advertising agency. She wrote Let's Be Indians for children.

PARKE, Margaret Bittner
Author and Teacher. Born in Mauch Chunk, Pennsylvania (now known as Jim Thorpe, Pennsylvania). She has been a Professor of Education at Brooklyn College; also, she was a Fulbright lecturer associated with the University of Sydney. She belonged to the Women's Press Club and the Women's National Book Association. She wrote Getting to Know Australia.

PARKER, Alfred Eustace
He lived in Berkeley, California. He has been associated with the schools, and was counselor at Burbank Junior High School. A close friendship with Los Angeles police chief, August Vollmer, resulted in his writing Crime Fighter: August Vollmer. These two men, also, were co-authors of two adult books concerning crime and the police.

PARKER, Bertha Morris 1890-
Author and teacher. Born in Rochester, Illinois. She attended Oberlin College and graduated from the University of Chicago. Miss Parker has been a teacher of science in Springfield, Illinois, and in the Laboratory Schools of the University of Chicago. She has been president of the National Council on Elementary Science and Chairman of the Elementary Science Section of the Central Association of Science and Mathematics Teachers. Her articles have appeared in magazines, and she has written numerous science books. Book titles include: Fire, Fishes,

Golden Book of Science, The Golden Treasury of Natural History, ... Living Things. MJA

PARKER, Fania M. Pockrose
Born in Latvia. She received her Ph.D. from Columbia University. Dr. Parker has traveled extensively in Europe and Russia. She has lived in Rockville Center, New York, with her husband and two children. She was Associate Professor of Russian at the Brooklyn College, Brooklyn, New York. This, combined with her travels, enabled her to create The Russian Alphabet Book.

PATON, Alan
Author and teacher. Born in Natal, South Africa, he graduated from the University of Natal. He has been a school teacher and a principal of Diepkloop Reformatory, an institution for African delinquent boys. Mr. Paton has written magazine articles concerning the Negro in America. Also, he wrote the famous novel, Cry, the Beloved Country. For young people he wrote The Land and People of South Africa.

PATTERSON, Lillie G.
Author, librarian, teacher. She has been a Specialist in Library Services with the Department of Education in the Baltimore Public Schools. Also, she has been Chairman of the Elementary Book Reviewing Committee. Miss Patterson has especially enjoyed telling stories to young people, and they have enjoyed reading her book, Halloween.

PAULI, Hertha Ernestine 1909-
Born in Vienna, she attended the College and Academy of Arts there. At the age of twelve she began writing, and two of her novels were published in Vienna. American history always interested her, and she wrote books about it. Hertha Pauli arrived in the United States in 1940. She has lived on Long Island. Her book titles include: The First Christmas Tree, The First Easter Rabbit, Lincoln's Little Correspondent, The Most Beautiful House, and Other

Stories. CA-2

PAULL, Grace A. 1898-
Author, illustrator. Born in Cold Brook, New York. She received her education in Utica, Glens Falls, and Montreal, Canada. She studied art at Pratt Institute in Brooklyn, New York. Her interests have included flower gardening, lithography, and water coloring. Museums and galleries have exhibited her works. The Pennell Fund for the Library of Congress purchased one of her lithographs; also, Miss Paull was the recipient of a First Purchase Award at Laguna Beach, California. She has written and illustrated: Come to the Country, Freddy the Curious Cat, Some Day, Squash for the Fair. JBA-2

PEARCE, Ann Philippa
Daughter of a flour-miller, she was born in Cambridgeshire, England. She graduated from Girton College, Cambridge University. She has held various positions, including government service, scriptwriter, and producer. Also, she has worked in the Education Department of the Oxford University Press. For children she wrote: The Minnow Leads to Treasure, Mrs. Cockle's Cat, Tom's Midnight Garden.

PEARE, Catherine Owens 1911-
Author, free-lance writer, teacher. Born in New Jersey, she received her education at State Teachers College in Montclair. She has worked with the National Urban League, the Wall Street House, and has been a teacher. Writing became her full-time job, and in 1962 she received the Sequoyah Children's Book Award for The Helen Keller Story. Other titles include: Albert Einstein; a Biography for Young People, Charles Dickens; His Life, The FDR Story, Jules Verne, His Life, Melor, King Arthur's Page, William Penn; a Biography. CA-5/6, MJA

PEARL, Richard M.
Author, teacher, gemologist. He graduated from the University of Colorado, and later studied at Har-

vard University. He became the second Certified Gemologist in the United States. He has been a Professor of Geology at Colorado College, Colorado Springs. Mr. Pearl was instrumental in starting the Colorado Mineral Society, the American Federation of Mineralogical Societies, and the Rocky Mountain Federation of Mineral Societies. He has written many books and articles, and has received many awards. For young people he wrote Wonders of Gems.

PEASE, Howard 1894-
Author, teacher. Born in Stockton, California, and attended Stanford University. At the age of twelve, his first short story Turn Back, Never, was written as a class assignment. From that particular teacher, he gained an impression that remained with him, "Writing is a craft to be studied and practiced and learned." Also, Mr. Pease has been a teacher. Howard Pease has received awards from the Child Study Association and the Boys' Clubs of America. Book titles include: ...Jungle River, Long Wharf; a Story of Young San Francisco, Mystery on Telegraph Hill, Night Boat, and Other Tod Moran Mysteries, Thunderbolt House. JBA-2

PEASE, Josephine Van Dolzen
Author, teacher. Born in Au Sable, Michigan. She grew up in an atomosphere of lumber and sawmills due to her father's lumber business. She has been a teacher and has done substitute teaching in the Grosse Pointe schools. Miss Pease has written children's stories and poems. She wrote This is Our Land.

PEATTIE, Donald Culross 1898-
Author and editor. He studied the natural sciences at Harvard. In 1935 he was awarded the first Gold Medal of the Limited Editions Club for An Almanac for Moderns. He has been a peripatetic editor of The Reader's Digest, and has lived in Santa Barbara, California when not traveling on an assignment. He wrote: A Child's Story of the World, From the

Earliest Days to Our Own Times, Rainbow Book of Nature.

PEET, Creighton 1899-
Author and reporter. He has lived in New York City, the place of his birth. He graduated from Columbia University, and has studied abroad. His work has appeared in magazines and newspapers. Mr. Peet has been a reporter on the Philadelphia Evening Bulletin. Hard work and curiousity about "what makes the wheels go round," were the necessary ingredients which enabled him to write books for young people. Juvenile titles include: Dude Ranch; the Story of a Modern Cowboy, First Book of Bridges, ... This Is the Way We Build a House.

PEET, William Bartlett 1915-
Author, illustrator. Born in Grandview, Indiana. He studied at the John Herron Art Institute in Indianapolis, and received a special citation as an outstanding student. He has been associated with the greeting card business in Ohio, but later moved to Los Angeles, California. He has written and illustrated Huge Harold, Smokey.

PELS, Gertrude Jaeckel
Author, puppeteer, teacher. She has always enjoyed working with children and has said: "They are grand to get along with - eager, exuberant, imaginative, buoyant, and inquisitive." Mrs. Pels has conducted children's classes in drawing and painting at the Pels School of Art operated by her husband Albert Pels. Also, she has been an instructor of puppetry for adults working in the Bellevue Hospital Speech Therapy Clinic in New York and the Westchester Rheumatic Fever and Polio Wards. She wrote The Care of Water Pets, Easy Puppets; Making and Using Hand Puppets.

PENDER, Lydia 1907-
She was born in England and has lived in Australia. Her poetry has been published in Australian magazines and books. Her daughter who was a teacher

served as her critic. Mrs. Pender has said of her family: "We have always loved the best of children's books, and have read them together." She has written: Barnaby and the Horses, Dan McDougall and the Bulldozer. CA-5/6

PERKINS, R. Marlin 1905-
Born in Missouri and lived in Kansas. He interrupted his studies at the University of Missouri to work at the St. Louis Zoo. His main interests have been the studying and training of animals. Mr. Perkins has been director of the Buffalo Zoo and the Chicago Lincoln Park Zoo. He has received awards and wide acclaim for his television program, "Zooparade." He wrote Marlin Perkins' Zooparade for children.

PERSON, William Thomas 1900-
Author and teacher. Born in Mt. Pleasant, Mississippi. He graduated from Southwestern Presbyterian University. He has contributed numerous stories to periodicals. Mr. Person has been a teacher in Tennessee and Mississippi. Also, he has taught English and Creative Writing at Bay County High School in Panama City, Florida. Juvenile titles include: Bar-Face, Sedge-Hill Setter.

PETERSHAM, Maud (Fuller) 1890- Miska 1889-
Authors and illustrators, this husband and wife team have contributed many books for children. Maud Petersham was born in Kingston, New York, the daughter of a minister. A graduate of Vassar, she did further study at the New York School of Fine and Applied Arts. Born Petrezselyem Mihaly in Hungary, he changed his name to Miska Petersham after his arrival in England. He attended night classes in London in order to study art and later, came to New York where he continued his painting. In 1946 the Petershams received the Caldecott Medal for The Rooster Crows. Also, they wrote: American ABC, Box With Red Wheels, Boy Who Had No Heart, The Christ Child, As Told by Matthew and Luke, Circus Baby, The Story Book of Corn. JBA-1,

JBA-2.

PETERSON, Russell Francis
Author, illustrator. Born in Montclair, New Jersey. He received his education at the Tilton School, Harvard University, and the College of Charleston. In World War II he served with a ski regiment. As a mammalogist, Mr. Peterson traveled to New Guinea, Australia, the South Seas, and the Arctic regions. He belonged to the American Society of Mammalogists, the Australian Mammal Society, and the Explorers Club. Also, he has been associated with the Mammal Department of the American Museum of Natural History. He has written and illustrated The Story of a Natural History Expedition.

PETRY, Ann (Lane) 1911-
Old Saybrook, Connecticut, was her birthplace and has been her home. She graduated from the College of Pharmacy at the University of Connecticut. Ann Petry wrote Harriet Tubman, Conductor on the Underground Railroad, as the result of her personal convictions about slavery.

PHELAN, Josephine
Author and librarian. She has lived in Toronto and has been a librarian there. Miss Phelan has written adult books about her favorite subject, Canadian history. She has been honored with numerous awards, including the Governor-General's Medal in 1952. For young readers she wrote The Bold Heart; the Story of Father Lacombe.

PHILLIPS, Mary (Geisler) 1881-
Author, editor, teacher. A native of Philadelphia, she received a degree in biology from the University of Pennsylvania. She married Everett Franklin Phillips, an authority on bees, which resulted in wide travel that included a three months stay in Russia. Mrs. Phillips has been a high school teacher, script writer for radio, and a professor emeritus of Cornell University. Book titles include: Dragonflies and Damselflies, The Makers of Honey. CA-5/6

PHLEGER, Fred B. 1909-
Author and teacher. Dr. Phleger has believed that teaching should be classified among the two most significant professions, the other in his opinion, scientific research. He has been Professor of Oceanography at the Scripps Institution of Oceanography; also, an observer of the California Gray Whale. His own research and experience has been put to good use in the pages of his Beginner Books, Ann Can Fly and The Whales Go By. He also wrote Red Tag Comes Back. CA-2

PICARD, Barbara Leonie 1917-
Born in England, she has lived in Lewes, Sussex, England. She has been interested in mythology and comparative religion, archaeology, and folk culture. These interests followed by research, have resulted in the publication of her many books. Included in her titles are: French Legends, Tales and Fairy Stories, German Hero-Sagas and Folk-Tales, Retold by Barbara Leonie Picard, The Odyssey of Homer, Retold by Barbara Leonie Picard.

PIERCE, Philip Nason
Lt. Colonel Philip N. Pierce, USMC, has had his books and articles published in magazines in the United States, Canada, England, and Europe. He has been a newspaperman and a Director of Media at Marine Corps Headquarters at Washington, D. C. The author has been a good friend of John Glenn for some time. He wrote John H. Glenn: Astronaut, with Karl Schuon.

PILKINGTON, Roger 1915-
He and his family have enjoyed explorations of several waterways in Europe in his boat, the Commodore. Details of these exciting trips have created delightful reading material. Mr. Pilkington has been a research scientist at Cambridge and has written about science, religion, and travel. He wrote The Eisenbart Mystery. CA-3

PINKERTON, Kathrene Sutherland (Gedney) 1887-
Born in Minnesota, she studied social work at the University of Wisconsin. She resigned her position as Field Secretary for the Wisconsin Anti-Tuberculosis Association after her marriage to Robert Pinkerton. For a time this husband-wife team collaborated and wrote fiction for magazines. Eventually Kathrene Pinkerton devoted her time to books, and her husband devoted his to magazines. Also, she has been associated in business in San Francisco. Her juvenile books include: Farther North, Silver Strain, ...Windigo, Year of Enchantment. Robert Pinkerton wrote First Overland Mail. CA-2

PISTORIUS, Anna
Author-illustrator. The author spent her childhood in the Belmont Yacht Harbor region of Chicago. Canoes and yawls furnished excitement for the Pistorius family when they explored Lake Michigan. She has always been a nature-lover and has spent a great deal of time on collecting trips. Also, Anna Pistorius has become a successful artist. Books which she has written include: What Animal Is It? What Bird Is It? What Butterfly Is It? What Horse Is It?

PIZER, Vernon 1918-
Born in Boston. He lived in New York and attended George Washington University. He served as a Second Lieutenant of Infantry in World War II, and advanced to Lieutenant Colonel. Vernon Pizer's duties with the Army's missile and space programs have involved him in extensive traveling - from New York to Puerto Rico. He has contributed articles to The Saturday Evening Post, Reader's Digest, and Esquire. He has written Rockets, Missiles, and Space for children. CA-4

PLACE, Marian Templeton 1910-
Author, librarian, reporter, free-lance writer. She has resided in Glendive, Montana, and acquired a great knowledge of the state's history. The Montana environment has been used in several of her books. A

graduate of Rollins College in Florida, she obtained a degree in Library Science from the University of Minnesota. Mrs. Place was the recipient of the Spur Award for the best western in children's literature; also, three of her books have been chosen as Junior Literary Guild selections. Juvenile contributions include: The Copper Kings of Montana, Hold Back the Hunter, Young Deputy Smith. CA-1

PLATE, Robert
Born in Brooklyn, New York, he attended Duke University. At the age of twenty he sold his first short story. He has held various jobs including lumberjacking, shipping books, and house painting. Participation in these various jobs formed the basis of valuable training for his eventual position as executive editor of a literary agency. Mr. Plate has always been interested in art and the American Indian. This combination of interests led to his writing Palette and Tomahawk; the Story of George Catlin.

PLISS, Louise
Author, teacher. Born in Gowanda, New York, she graduated from the University of Michigan. She has been head of a book store in Chicago and has taught at the Laboratory School of the University of Chicago. She has contributed That Summer On Catalpa Street to the juvenile field.

POLITI, Leo 1908-
Author-illustrator. Born in Fresno, California. When he was seven, his family moved to Italy. At the age of fifteen, he was awarded a scholarship for the Institute of Monza near Milan. Mr. Politi returned to the United States and has lived in Los Angeles. In 1950 he received the Caldecott Medal for his picture book, Song of the Swallows. Other titles include: Boat for Peppe, The Butterflies Come, Juanita, Little Leo, The Mission Bell, Moy Moy, Saint Francis and the Animals. JBA-2

POLLAND, Madeleine Angela 1918-
Author, librarian. Born in County Galway. Her

holidays as a child were spent in the Irish village of Athenry. During World War II, she served in England with the Radar Division of the W. A. A. F. Mrs. Polland has been a librarian. She has lived in London with her husband and two children. Her titles include: Beorn the Proud, Children of the Red King, Chuiraquimba and the Black Robes. CA-5/6

POOLE, Lynn 1910- and Gray
Husband-wife team. Lynn Poole has been Director of Public Relations at The Johns Hopkins University and producer of their television program, "File Seven." The Pooles have lived in Baltimore, Maryland. His wife Gray Poole has been a free-lance and industrial writer and a magazine journalist. They wrote: Balloons Fly High; 200 Years of Adventure and Science, Danger! Icebergs Ahead! Deep in Caves and Caverns, Volcanoes in Action; Science and Legend. MJA

POPE, Clifford Hillhouse 1899-
Author and herpetologist. Georgia was his birthplace. He has been president of the American Society of Ichthyologists and Herpetologists; also, Curator of the Division of Amphibians and Reptiles at the Chicago Natural History Museum. Mr. Pope has participated in scientific expeditions in China and has been head of others in the United States and Mexico. He and his wife have lived in Winnetka, Illinois, where his writing became a full-time career. For children he wrote Reptiles Round the World; a Simplified Natural History of the Snakes, Lizards, Turtles, and Crocodilians. CA-3

PORTER, Ella Blodwen (Williams)
Author and music teacher. Born on a Iowa farm, she graduated from the Music Department of Coe College, Cedar Rapids, Iowa. She has participated in the musical activities of the 4-H Club. While living in Arizona, Mrs. Porter contributed her talent as a musician to church choirs and choruses. She wrote Sandra Kendall of the 4-H; the Career Story of a Young Home Demonstration Agent.

POSTON, Martha Lee
Author and teacher. Born in Shanghai, China, she was the daughter of a medical missionary. A graduate of the Shanghai-American School, she was a teacher in a Chinese girls' school in Wusih. After her return to America, she graduated from Sweet Briar College in Virginia. She has written Ching-Li and The Girl Without a Country for children.

POTTER, Beatrix 1866-1943
She was the only daughter of an English barrister and spent her childhood in London. She received her education at home. She first wrote The Tale of Peter Rabbit in order to cheer up a friend. Beatrix Potter married lawyer, William Heelis, and they lived at Hill Top Farm at Sawrey. Juvenile contributions include: Appley Dapply's Nursery Rhymes, The Fairy Caravan, Ginger and Pickles, The Roly-Poly Pudding, The Story of a Fierce Bad Rabbit, The Tale of Jemima Puddle-Duck, The Tailor of Gloucester, The Tale of Mr. Jeremy Fisher. JBA-1, JBA-2

POTTER, Miriam (Clark) 1886-
Author-illustrator. She spent her childhood in Minnesota and graduated from the University of Minnesota. At the age of fourteen she sold her first manuscript to Youth's Companion. She has contributed articles to St. Nicholas magazine and others. After her marriage to newspaperman Zenas Potter, she lived in Mexico, India, France, and in Carmel, California where she continued to live after the death of her husband. She has written and illustrated: Goofy Mrs. Goose, Just Mrs. Goose, No, No, Mrs. Goose. CA-5/6

POTTER, Robert Ducharme 1905-
Writer, scientist, teacher. He has taught at Duke and New York Universities. He worked at the Carnegie Institution of Washington in pioneer experiments on atomic fission. The National Association of Science Writers was founded by him, and he has been its President. Recognition for science report-

ing won for him the first George Westinghouse Medal of the American Association for the Advancement of Science. He has been a correspondent at the Bikini A-bomb tests, a Consultant to the U.S. Army Surgeon General, and editor of New York Medicine. He wrote Young People's Book of Atomic Energy.

POUGH, Frederick Harvey 1906-
A native New Yorker. He studied at Harvard and Washington Universities and the University of Heidelberg. Rocks, minerals, and the formation of the earth were his particular interests. He has been on the staff of the American Museum of Natural History. An authority on volcanoes and how they work, Dr. Pough went to Mexico to study a new volcano, Parícutin, which broke out in 1943. This experience provided him with additional material for his book, All About Volcanoes and Earthquakes.

POWER, Effie Louise 1873-
Author, librarian, teacher. Born near Conneautville, Pennsylvania, she obtained her M.A. degree from Allegheny College and studied library science at the Carnegie Library School at Pittsburgh. She has been Supervisor of Work with Children in several libraries, including the St. Louis Public Library. Once she said: "That I was the first children's librarian in the Cleveland Public Library, under William Howard Brett, is my chief claim to distinction." She has been an instructor of library science in several universities. She has written: Work With Children in Public Libraries and collaborated with Florence M. Everson to write Early Days in Ohio.

PRATT, Fletcher 1897-1956
At one time he was a student in Paris. Mr. Pratt has been able to read seven languages. He was one of the originators of the American Interplanetary Society, later to be known as the Rocket Society. He served as a war correspondent with the Navy during World War II. Juvenile contributions include: All About Rockets and Jets, The Civil War, Monitor and the Merrimac.

PRICE, Christine Hilda 1928-
Author-illustrator. Born in London, England, she arrived in the United States at an early age. She received her education at Vassar College, the Art Students League of New York, and the Central School of Arts and Crafts in London. She has lived in Castleton, Vermont. Miss Price has written and illustrated: Made In the Middle Ages, Made In the Renaissance; Arts and Crafts of Exploration. CA-5/6, MJA

PRICE, Olive
Born in Pittsburgh, Pennsylvania. She had a book of plays published when she was only eighteen years old. As a result of this, Miss Price wrote several books of plays, including some that were used by radio and television. Since 1945 her children's books have been published in Denmark, Italy, England, and America. Some have been children's book club selections. Her titles include: The Island of the Silver Spoon, Mystery of the Sunken City, Story of Clara Barton.

PRICE, Willadene (Anton) 1914-
Born in Omaha, Nebraska. After her marriage to an army officer, she lived in various parts of the United States and Europe; later, she located in Boston. Mrs. Price has had articles published and has been the editor of a magazine. She received the Pen Women award for her book Bartholdi and the Statue of Liberty. She has also written Gutzon Borglum: Artist and Patriot. CA-5/6

PRIETO, Mariana (Beeching) 1912-
Author and teacher. Born in Cincinnati, Ohio. She was educated in Cuba and acquired a background which enabled her to speak fluent Spanish. Also, she married Spanish-speaking Martin Prieto. During World War II, she taught Spanish to officers and enlisted men. Also, she has taught evening classes at the University of Miami and at Miami High School. Mrs. Prieto has had numerous articles and stories published in magazines and is the author

of two Spanish textbooks. She wrote El Gallo Sabio. CA-5/6

PROUDFIT, Isabel (Boyd) 1898-
Author and newspaperwoman. Born in Evanston, Illinois, her college days were spent in Boston. She has been a reporter in New York City and London. She has endeavored to maintain authenticity in her writing, and if at all possible, has tried to visit the place about which she has written. Juvenile titles include: James Fenimore Cooper, Noah Webster; Father of the Dictionary, The Treasure Hunter; the Story of Robert Louis Stevenson. MJA

PRUD'HOMMEAUX, Rene
Egypt was his birthplace, and he lived in France before he came to the United States at the age of seven. His education included schools in New York, New Jersey, and Connecticut. He graduated from the University of North Carolina. He has been a sergeant in the Army and spent most of his war duty in Brazil. After his marriage to Patricia Gordon, also a children's author, he lived on Fire Island in New York. The winter freeze of the Great South Bay, created the theme for his book The Sunken Forest. Other titles are: Extra Hand, Hidden Lights, Port of Missing Men.

PURDY, Claire Lee 1906-
Born in Chihuahua, Mexico. She attended the Joanne Ross Seminary in Macon, Georgia, and graduated cum laude with a B.A. degree from the University of Colorado. She has belonged to Phi Beta Kappa, Chi Delta Phi, Delta Zeta, and the American College Quill Club. Her association with marionettes created the desire to write. In collaboration with Benson Wheeler, she wrote My Brother Was Mozart, which won the Julia Ellsworth Ford Foundation award in 1937. She married Rudolf Kohl, who has illustrated some of her music books. Juvenile contributions include: Gilbert and Sullivan; Masters of Mirth and Melody, He Heard America Sing; the Story of Stephen Foster, Song of the North; the Story of Ed-

vard Grieg.

PYNE, Mable (Mandeville) 1903-
Author-illustrator. Almost half a million copies of her books have stayed in print. Two of her books The Little History of the U.S.A. and The Little Geography of the U.S.A., have been very popular in schools and libraries. She has written and illustrated The Hospital and Story of Religion. CA-4

R

RAND, Addison 1896-
Newspaperman, author, born in Eau Claire, Wisconsin. His studies at Eau Claire Teachers College were interrupted by World War I. After the war, Addison Rand continued his education at the University of Wisconsin where he obtained his B.A. degree in journalism. He has worked on newspapers in Buffalo, New York, Miami, Florida, Riverside, California, and other cities. Mr. Rand has been a true fan of baseball both as a player and a spectator. His books include sport stories, westerns, and biographies. He wrote Southpaw Fly Hawk for young readers.

RAND, Paul 1914- Ann -
Husband-wife team. Paul Rand was born in Brooklyn. He has been art director of Esquire and Apparel Arts magazines in New York, a position which he obtained at the age of twenty-three. Also, he has been a free-lance designer, and a teacher at Pratt Institute and at Yale University. Born in Chicago, Ann Rand studied under Mies Van Der Rohe, the noted architect. The Rands designed their home in Weston, Connecticut. The Rands have written: I Know a Lot of Things, Little 1, So Small, Sparkle and Spin, Umbrellas, Hats, and Wheels.

RANDALL, Blossom E.
Composition and journalism were studied at the University of Kansas by this author. The eldest of five children, Blossom Randall acquired a great interest

in people at an early age. Mrs. Randall's "favorite critic" was her lawyer-husband. They have lived in Wichita, Kansas. "Our house is full of stories and will remain so for several years." She wrote Fun for Chris.

RANDALL, Janet 1919-
Born in Lancaster, California, daughter of a newspaper editor. She acquired a great interest in horses and once rode with a drill team. At the University of California in Los Angeles she met her future husband Robert W. Young. He has been a publisher and editor of southern California weekly newspapers while she wrote articles for society columns. After leaving the newspaper field, the Youngs became free-lance writers. She wrote Pony Girl (A Junior Literary Guild selection). CA-5/6

RANDALL, Kenneth Charles
An outdoor man, he has enjoyed hunting and fishing as hobbies. Mr. Randall has been an Associate Professor of English at Michigan State College. Also, he has written for magazines, such as Field and Stream, Sports Afield, Outdoor Life. For children he has written Wild Hunter.

RANDALL, Ruth Painter 1892-
She married James G. Randall, a great Lincoln scholar. In order to write about Mary Todd Lincoln, she has done a great deal of research into the Lincoln papers, the Herndon-Weik papers, and other manuscripts from private collections. "At last, in a book as fascinating as it is scholarly, we have the full truth," was the statement that Allan Nevins made about her adult biography of Mary Lincoln. She has lived in Urbana, Illinois. For children she wrote: I Jessie; a Biography of the Girl Who Married John Charles Fremont, Famous Explorer of the West, I Varina... CA-1

RANSOHOFF, Doris
Author, script-writer, born in Cincinnati, Ohio. Her career as a writer began while she was a student at

Bryn Mawr. She has worked for the New York Herald Tribune and has written feature articles for The Californian. Miss Ransohoff married motion picture director and producer, Leo Seltzer. With her husband she has written scripts of documentary films and television public affairs programs for the United Nations and its agencies, the City of New York, the USO, and the American Cancer Society. Also, she wrote scripts for the United States Information Agency films of Mrs. John F. Kennedy's Pakistan and India trip, and the late President and Mrs. Kennedy's visit to Mexico. She has written Living Architecture: Frank Lloyd Wright, for children.

RANUCCI, Renato 1921-
Comedian, mimic, author, born in Turin, Italy. His pseudonym is Renato Rascel. He has created many radio and television characters, and has directed many musical shows. Also, he wrote "Arrivederci Roma," the hit song which has made him famous. He wrote Piccoletto; the Story of the Little Chimney Sweep.

RAVIELLI, Anthony
Illustrator, author, son of a marine engineer. Anthony Ravielli studied art at Cooper Union and the Art Students League. He began his career as a portrait painter. His illustrations have been seen in magazines and trade publications. His instructional murals and visual training aids were used in the armed forces during World War II. After the war, Mr. Ravielli began a career in medical illustration. Also, he has done etching and wood-engraving. He has written and illustrated: An Adventure in Geometry, The World is Round.

RAYMOND, Margaret Thomsen
Born in Baltimore, Maryland, she graduated from the Friends' Select School in Philadelphia. Her New England ancestors include the Lowells and the "fighting Obrions of Maine." She has been a writer and photographer, and has lived in Chicago, Illinois. She

wrote Linnet on the Threshold.

RECHNITZER, Ferdinand Edsted 1894-
Born in Perth Amboy, New Jersey, the son of a Methodist minister. As an R. A. F. pilot during World War I, and an aviation editor of the New York Telegram, Mr. Rechnitzer possessed the necessary qualifications in order to write books about flying. Also, as a perpetual "dog owner," he decided to write books about dogs. Juvenile contributions include: Bonny's Boy Returns, Captain Jeep, Jinks of Jayson Valley, Midnight Alarm.

RECK, Alma Kehoe 1901-
Librarian, copywriter, author. After reading about Turkey's Candy Festival, she became very interested in foreign festivals, and later, wrote The First Book of Festivals Around the World. She has also written The West From A to Z for children. CA-4

REEDER, Russell Potter 1902-
Born at Fort Leavenworth, Kansas. A West Point graduate, Colonel (Red) Reeder has spent twenty-two years of his life at West Point. He retired in 1945 due to a wound received in action in Normandy. He has held fourteen medals, including a Congressional Life Saving Medal (received at the age of eleven when he saved a friend from drowning), and two French decorations. His books for young people include: The Story of the War of 1812, Clint Lane in Korea, Pointers on Athletics..., The Story of the First World War, West Point First Classman, West Point Story. CA-3

REELY, Mary Katharine 1881-
Teacher, author, born near Spring Green, Wisconsin. She taught and worked in the Unity Settlement House, and succeeded in graduating from the University of Minnesota. Also, she worked "in between times" for the publishing firm, H. W. Wilson Company. Miss Reely has been head of the Book Selection Department of the Wisconsin Library Commission and has conducted a radio program. She has

written: The Blue Mittens, Seatmates.

REESE, John Henry
Born in Sweetwater, Nebraska, he attended Kansas and Nebraska grade schools, and graduated from the Dunbar, Nebraska, High School. Prior to his freelance writing, Mr. Reese had been a Deputy Collector of Internal Revenue, and a newspaperman for the Los Angeles Examiner. While he was ill and confined to bed, the author rewrote the original short story of Big Mutt into a full length book. The Reese family has lived in San Marino, California.

REGLI, Adolph Casper 1896-
He grew up in Eau Claire, Wisconsin, and graduated from the University of Wisconsin. A newspaper career in Wisconsin, Minnesota, Florida, and New York, preceded his career as an author. After the publication of two biographies, Rubber's Goodyear and The Mayos, Pioneers in Medicine, Adolph Regli decided to concentrate on being an author. From his Minneapolis home, he has taken trips West in order to find new material for books. Library and school groups have listened to his book lectures. His book titles include: Fiddling Cowboy, Partners in the Saddle, Real Book About Buffalo Bill.

REILEY, Catherine Conway
Born in Rumson, New Jersey. She received her B.A. degree from Manhattanville College and her M.A. degree from Columbia University. Miss Reiley has been a camp counsellor, volunteer leader, and teacher. She has been associated with the Girl Scouts of the United States of America in several capacities. Also, in 1951, she acted as an Exchange Trainer in Denmark. Miss Reiley's articles have appeared in The Camping Magazine, The American Girl, and the Girl Scout Leader. Other interests have included music and photography. She wrote Group Fun; Games and Activities for Girls - Techniques for Leaders.

REINFELD, Fred 1910-
Champion chess player, author, native New Yorker. Fred Reinfeld began his career in chess at an early age. He has been intercollegiate and New York State champion, and won the Manhattan Club and Marshall Club championship matches. He has written about coin collecting, geology, science, and chess "masters." Included in his many books are: Chess for Young People, Chess Is an Easy Game, Chess: Win in 20 Moves or Less, Coin Collector's Handbook, Creative Chess, Rays, Visible and Invisible, What's New in Science.

RENDINA, Laura (Jones) Cooper 1902-
Traveler and author, born in Northampton, Massachusetts. She attended Smith College. Mrs. Rendina, her artist-husband, and five children have lived on Siesta Key, Sarasota on the Gulf of Mexico. Seventeen and Senior Prom have published her short stories. Included in her books for young people are: Lolly Touchberry, Roommates, Trudi, World of Their Own. MJA

RENICK, Marion (Lewis) 1905-
Born in Springfield, Ohio, she attended Wittenberg College. She has been an editor of My Weekly Reader, a newspaper used in many schools. Also, she has been a teacher of journalism at Ohio State University. Marion Renick has lived in Columbus, Ohio, and has given book broadcasts on the Ohio School of the Air. Juvenile books include: Bats and Gloves of Glory, The Big Basketball Prize, Boy at Bat, Champion Caddy, Heart for Baseball, Nicky's Football Team, Pete's Home Run, Skating Today, Swimming Fever. CA-3, MJA

REY, Margret Elizabeth (Waldstein), Hans Augusto 1898-
Authors, illustrators, husband-wife team. Both were from Hamburg, Germany, and after meeting again years later in Rio de Janeiro they were married. Margret Rey studied art at the Bauhaus in Dessau, the Academy in Duesseldorf, and in Berlin.

H. A. Rey attended Munich and Hamburg universities. He has been a business executive in Brazil and has collected and illustrated Indian folk tales. Many of the Reys' books have been published in other countries. Together they wrote Billy's Picture. Books by H. A. Rey include: Curious George Flies a Kite, Curious George Gets a Medal, Curious George Learns the Alphabet, Find the Constellations. CA-5/6, JBA-2

REYNOLDS, Quentin James 1902-
Sports writer and author, born in Brooklyn, New York. In 1930 he was sent to Berlin on assignment with the International News Service. After he publicized his opinion of the Nazis, he was asked to leave Germany. Later, he worked for Colliers in London. He has always been interested in airplanes and pilots so he decided to write The Wright Brothers, Pioneers of American Aviation. Other books include: Battle of Britain, Custer's Last Stand, The F. B. I., Life of Saint Patrick.

RHOADS, Dorothy
Born in Illinois, she considered this state her home "so far as legal residence is concerned." Her sister's marriage to archaeological director Dr. Sylvanus Morley, provided her with opportunities for frequent visits to the Yucatân. The Carnegie Institution of Washington sponsored Dr. Morley's expeditions and Dorothy Rhoads was present on a number of them. She learned and collected material about the Maya Indians of Yucatân to write her children's book, Corn Grows Ripe.

RICE, Charles D.
Editor, theatrical reporter, and author, born in Cambridge, Massachusetts. He attended Harvard University. Charles D. Rice's specialty has been theatrical reporting; however, he has been on the staff of This Week magazine as a writer and editor. The Rices have lived in Yorktown, New York. In the juvenile field he has written The Little Dog Who Wore Earmuffs.

RICH, Josephine (Bouchard) 1912-

Born in Tamora, Nebraska, she received her education in the Iowa and South Dakota schools. She met and married doctor-radiologist James Sears Rich while enrolled in nurses' training. They have lived in Lexington, Kentucky. She has been very active in civic affairs and was the recipient of the Beta Sigma Phi ("Outstanding Woman of 1958") award. Visits to countries and homes of famous people provided her with material for her books: Jean Henri Dunant: Founder of the International Red Cross, Pioneer Surgeon; Dr. Ephriam McDowell. CA-5/6

RICH, Louise (Dickinson) 1903-

Author and teacher, born in Huntington, Massachusetts. She graduated from Bridgewater State Teachers College, and entered the teaching profession. She has always enjoyed reading and the outdoors. She married Ralph Rich, and has lived in a remote spot (near the Rapid River between two lakes) in Maine. Her children's books include: First Book of New England, The First Book of the Vikings, Mindy, Start of the Trail; the Story of a Young Maine Guide.

RIESENBERG, Felix 1913-

He was the son of the late Captain Felix Riesenberg, noted authority on the sea and writer. He attended Columbia University and has been in the American Merchant Marine. Felix Riesenberg, Jr., has been shipping editor of the San Francisco News and Pacific Coast Correspondent for the Nautical Gazette magazine. He has enjoyed boxing and swimming, and has made models of sailing ships as a hobby. Juvenile books include: Balboa: Swordsman and Conquistador, Crimson Anchor; a Sea Mystery, Phantom Freighter, Story of the Naval Academy, Vanishing Steamer.

RIEU, Emile Victor 1887-

Eminent classicist and author, born in London. He attended St. Paul's School and Balliol College, Oxford. Dr. Rieu has managed the Oxford University

Press in India, has been academic and literary advisor to Methuen and Co., Ltd., and editor of the Penguin Classics. Carpentry, petrology, and mountains have been his interests. He has written The Flattered Flying Fish, and Other Poems for young people. CA-4

RIFKIN, Lillian
Teacher, author, born in Wilkes-Barre, Pennsylvania. She has studied at a teachers training school in Bloomsburg, Pennsylvania, and at Teachers College, New York. During her teaching career, Lillian Rifkin found that there was a need for non-fiction books for young children and wrote Our Planet the Earth, Then and Now. She has traveled extensively and has been interested in drawing and clay modeling. She has also written When I Grow Up, I'll Be a Farmer; ed. by Frederick Grover and Paul Sears.

RINK, Paul 1912-
Scientist, engineer, author, born in San Jose, California. He attended the San Jose State Junior College, University of California, and the Inter-American University in Panama. He has been an engineering watch officer with the merchant marine in the Panama Canal Zone. Also, he served in intelligence for the U.S. Embassy in Panama during World War II. American Heritage, Esquire, and other magazines have published his articles. Also, Paul Rink has written scripts for the motion picture industry and for television. He wrote Ernest Hemingway; Remaking Modern Fiction.

RIPLEY, Elizabeth (Blake) 1906-
Author, compiler, illustrator, born in New Haven, Connecticut. A graduate of Smith College, she also studied in Paris at the Sorbonne. She spent several years in Europe, and later lived in New Hampshire and Connecticut. Children's books of jokes and riddles have been compiled and illustrated by Elizabeth Ripley. She has written many biographies, including: Botticelli, Dürer, Goya, Picasso, Raphael, Rem-

brandt, Titian, Vincent van Gogh. CA-4

RITCHIE, Rita (Krohne) 1930-
Born in Milwaukee, Wisconsin, she graduated from the University of Wisconsin. She has been a library page, copywriter in advertising, camp counsellor, medical bibliographer, and chemical technician. "But writing," she said, "is first, last and forever." Rita Ritchie has traveled in Mexico and Europe. She married free-lance writer Jack Ritchie, and they have lived in Wisconsin on Washington Island. Juvenile books include: Golden Hawks of Genghis Khan, Secret Beyond the Mountains (A Junior Literary Guild Selection). CA-5/6

RIWKIN-BRICK, Anna 1908-
Photographer and author. She was born in Russia but grew up in Sweden where she has lived. Her photographs of children, people, and places have made her well-known everywhere. The Museum of Modern Art has displayed her photo-documentary books in the Family of Man show. Juvenile books include: Dirk Lives in Holland, Elle Kari, Lilibet, Circus Child, Nomads of the North, Sia Lives in Kilimanjaro.

ROBERTSON, Keith 1914-
Born in Dows, Iowa, he obtained his B.S. degree from the U.S. Naval Academy at Annapolis, Maryland. Eleven years of his life were spent in the United States Navy. Keith Robertson has been a electrician, waiter, and salesman. After World War II, he worked for a publishing company, but later resigned to write full-time. Also, Mr. Robertson has written numerous articles and technical booklets and manuals. The Robertsons have lived in Hopewell, New Jersey at "Booknoll Farm." His books include: Crow and the Castle, Henry Reed, Inc., Henry Reed's Journey, The Pinto Deer, Three Stuffed Owls. MJA

ROBINSON, Charles Alexander 1900-
Teacher, lecturer, author, born in Princeton, New Jersey. He has been Professor of Classics at Brown

University. He has lectured at the American Academy in Rome and the American School of Classical Studies in Athens. Also, he has aided in the excavation of ancient Greek cities and has been a member of the Commission for Excavation of the Athenian Agora, and the Committee on the Agora Museum. Professor Robinson has written for boys and girls: The First Book of Ancient Bible Lands, The First Book of Ancient Egypt, First Book of Ancient Rome, The First Book of Ancient Mesopotamia and Persia. CA-1

ROBINSON, Ray
Editor and author, he graduated from Columbia University and returned to study law. Many magazines have published his articles about sports. He has been articles editor of Good Housekeeping, managing editor of Pageant, senior editor of Coronet, and editor of the annual Baseball Stars. Ray Robinson and his family have lived in Manhattan. A former baseball player at Columbia, he has been an enthusiastic San Francisco (formerly New York) Giants fan. He wrote Ted Williams.

ROGERS, Cedric
Of English descent, he was born in Schenectady, New York. He left for England at the age of five to begin his education. He enrolled in prep school and attended Dulwich College and Goldsmith's School of Art. Cedric Rogers was an instructor and test pilot with the R. A. F. during World War II. At the end of the war, he sold his cartoons to Punch. Mr. and Mrs. Rogers and their three children have lived in Bucks County, Pennsylvania. When he was teaching his children the joys of collecting, he wrote Rags, Bottles, and Bones.

ROJANKOVSKY, Feodor 1891-
Illustrator, author, born in Mitava, Russia. He attended the Academy of Art in Moscow. In World War I, he was an officer in the Russian Army. Feodor Rojankovsky has been the art director of the Opera in Pazan, Poland, and an art director in a

Polish publishing house. He came to the United States in 1941. His fame for the illustrations of Daniel Boone and his lithographs for the "Père Castor" books, preceded him to this country. In 1956, he won the Caldecott Medal for Frog Went A-Courtin'. Juvenile books include: Animals in the Zoo, Great Big Wild Animal Book. Numerous authors have used his illustrations in their books. JBA-2

ROLLINS, Charlemae (Hill)
Librarian, author, born in Yazoo City, Mississippi, she studied at Western University, Columbia University, and the Graduate Library School of the University of Chicago. She married Joseph W. Rollins. She has been Children's Librarian in the George C. Hall Branch of the Chicago Public Library, and has lectured on children's literature in many colleges. She compiled the booklet, We Build Together, published by the National Council of Teachers of English. A memorable fall was in 1952 in Springfield, Illinois when Dwight D. Eisenhower campaigned in the public square, and Mrs. Rollins, Chairman of the Children's Section of the Illinois Library Association, introduced Dr. Herbert Zim, luncheon speaker. She compiled Christmas Gif'.

ROOKE, Daphne 1914-
Born in the Transvaal, South Africa. She spent her early years on a cane plantation, and later, visited northern Zululand. Also, she has lived at the foot of Lebombo Mountains, the setting for her book, Twins in South Africa. She wrote another twin book, Twins in Australia.

ROOS, Ann
Born in Brooklyn, New York. She received a Bachelor of Oral English from the School of Speech at Syracuse University. As a staff member of the Girl Scouts, she trained volunteer leaders. This required a great deal of travel in this country and in England. As a member of a Juvenile Writing Class, conducted by Dr. Mabel Robinson at Columbia University, Ann Roos completed her first book, Man of

Molokai; the Life of Father Damien. MJA

ROSENBURG, John M.
Baseball player, coach, sports writer, author. A graduate from Ithaca College School of Physical Education, he has played baseball with amateur and semi-professional teams. Also, he has been a high school basketball, football, and baseball coach. John Rosenburg has been on the staff of the United Press International as a sports writer and general news correspondent. Collier's, Coronet, This Week, and other magazines have published his articles. He has written: Baseball for Boys, The Story of Baseball.

ROSS, Zola Helen (Girdey) 1912-
Born in Dayton, Ohio, and attended MacMurray College for Women. She has been a teacher at the University of Washington. She has written several detective stories and historical novels. She wrote with Lucile McDonald Assignment in Ankara, Friday's Child, Pigtail Pioneer, Wing Harbor.

ROTHERY, Agnes Edwards 1888-
Born in Brookline, Massachusetts, she attended Wellesley College. She married Harry Rogers Pratt, a University of Virginia professor. During the summer, they traveled in South America, Central America, Iceland, and the Scandinavian Peninsula. These trips provided her with a great deal of information for her "Roundabout" books. As a result of a trip to Italy, Agnes Rothery wrote Rome Today. Her interests have included painting, decorating, cooking, gardening, and cats. Juvenile titles include: Central American Roundabout, Iceland Roundabout, Italian Roundabout, Scandinavian Roundabout, Washington Roundabout.

ROUNDS, Glen 1906-
Author, illustrator, he grew up in the Black Hills of South Dakota. He has been a logger, muleskinner, sawmill hand, and cowpuncher. Also, he has worked with a sideshow, studied the trade of a baker, and

has been a sergeant in the Anti-Aircraft. These various occupations served the writer well as his books have been very popular. His books for young people include: Beaver Business..., Hunted Horses, Lone Muskrat, Ol' Paul, the Mighty Logger..., ...Rodeo; Bulls, Broncs & Buckaroos, Stolen Pony, Whitey and the Rustlers. JBA-2

ROWE, Viola Carson
Born in Melrose Park, a suburb of Chicago. She has written a weekly column, "The Feminine Viewpoint," for a suburban weekly, the Maywood Herald. Also, Viola Rowe has written society stories, read proof, and has been an associate editor. She has enjoyed outdoor activities, including ice skating, swimming, and canoeing. After her marriage, she began to write fiction. Her articles and short stories have been published in the United States and Canada, and some of her articles were translated into Portuguese and French. For young people she has written: Free For All, Girl In a Hurry, A Way With Boys. CA-2

RUBICAM, Harry Cogswell, Jr.
Rancher, free-lance writer, reporter, editor, and author, born in Colorado. He has been in charge of the copy department of the advertising agency, Young and Rubicam. Also, Mr. Rubicam has been editor for the Denver Post. After his retirement, the author lived in New York and Vermont, and devoted his time to free-lance writing. He wrote Men at Work in the Great Plains States for children.

RUCHLIS, Hyman 1913-
Teacher, author, a native of New York City. He has been president of the Science Federation and the Physics Club of New York. Also, he has been a mathematics and science teacher in the school system of New York City, and the director of the Educational Materials Department of the Library of Science. Juvenile books include: Clear Thinking, Orbit: a Picture Story of Force and Motion, Story of Mathematics; Geometry for the Young Scientist. CA-4

RUGH, Belle Dorman
Daughter of an American missionary doctor, she spent her childhood north of Palestine in the Lebanon mountains, the setting for her first novel. She received her education at Vassar and Columbia, but returned to the Women's College at Beirut in order to teach English there. She met and married an American teacher in Beirut. After returning to America, they have lived in Newington, Connecticut. She has written Crystal Mountain.

RUKEYSER, Muriel 1913-
Author, artist, born in New York City. She received her education at Vassar and Columbia. Miss Rukeyser has been honored for her writing by achieving a Guggenheim fellowship, a National Academy Grant, and the Harriet Monroe prize. She has been on the Bollingen Award Committee. Also, she had a book included in the Yale Series of Younger Poets. Prior to her books for children, Muriel Rukeyser wrote poetry and biography. For children she has written Come Back Paul.

RUSH, William Marshall 1887-1950
Born in West Virginia, he attended school in Chanute, Kansas. For twenty-two years, he was in the Forest Service of Montana, Wyoming, and Oregon. He has said that the four years assigned to study wild life at Yellowstone Park were his happiest years. His book titles include: Rocky Mountain Ranger, Wheat Rancher, Wild Horses of Rainrock, Yellowstone Scout.

RUSSELL, Solveig Paulson 1904-
Teacher and author, born in Salt Lake City. She has been a teacher in the Oregon rural schools and in a Salem Junior High School. Mrs. Russell has written articles and stories for children's magazines. Book titles include: A is for Apple, and Why; the Story of Our Alphabet, About Fruit, About Nuts, All Kinds of Legs, Navaho Land - Yesterday and Today, Wonderful Stuff; the Story of Clay. CA-3

S

St. JOHN, Philip
Author, sports fan. He has been a free-lance writer. Also, he has done editorial work for Space Science Fiction magazine. For young people he wrote Rocket Jockey.

SAMACHSON, Dorothy and Joseph 1906-
Husband-wife team. A professional pianist, Mrs. Samachson has done a great deal of the research on their books. Also, she has written a book about ballet. Dr. Samachson, who received his Ph.D. degree from Yale University, has been head of a hospital chemical laboratory. He has written scientific articles, a murder mystery, and science fiction. Together, they wrote: Good Digging; the Story of Archaeology, The Fabulous World of Opera (A Junior Literary Guild selection).

SAMUELS, Gertrude
This reporter has covered national and foreign affairs for over twenty years. She has been a staff writer for The New York Times, and has worked on the New York Post, Newsweek, Time, and The Times Magazine. Look and The National Geographic Magazine have published her articles and photographs. The United States Information Service has broadcast her stories to foreign countries. She has been a special observer for UNICEF, and has written about juvenile delinquency and school integration in this country. She has received numerous awards for her work. She wrote B-G: Fighter of Goliaths; the Story of David Ben-Gurion.

SANDERSON, Ivan Terence 1911-
He attended Cambridge University, England. He has written many articles for scientific journals sponsored by the British Museum and the Chicago Museum of Natural History (previously known as the Field Museum). Scientific institutions have sponsored collecting trips to such countries as: Dutch Guiana, Guatemala, Malaya, and Nigeria. Mr.

Sanderson and his wife who has helped in research and writing have lived in New Jersey and New York. He wrote Abominable Snowmen: Legend Come to Life.

SANDOZ, Mari 1907-
Teacher, editor, author. She attended the University of Nebraska, and in 1950 she received an honorary degree of Doctor of Literature from there. Miss Sandoz has been a teacher in rural Nebraska, and has been associate editor of School Executives Magazine, and the Nebraska History Magazine. Also, she was Director of Research at the Nebraska State Historical Society. Mari Sandoz has been head of Advanced Novel Writing at the Writers Institute of the University of Wisconsin, and on the staff of writers' conferences at the Universities of Colorado and Indiana. She wrote: The Horsecatcher, The Story Catcher. CA-2

SANGER, Frances Ella (Fitz)
Born in Summertown, Tennessee, she graduated from State Teachers College in San Diego. Before her marriage, she was a teacher in Chula Vista, California. Later, an extension course at the University of Southern California started her on a writing career. She wrote The Silver Teapot for young people.

SARASY, Phyllis Powell
New York City has been the home of Phyllis Sarasy and her husband. Author and teacher, she has taught in New York City, Connecticut, and Ohio. She has taken part in International Seminars and was instrumental in organizing the first American Seminars between English and Spanish speaking people in South America. For children she wrote Winter-Sleepers.

SARGENT, Shirley 1927-
Shirley Sargent has been a teacher, has operated her own nursery school, and has been a free-lance writer. She has lived in Pasadena, California. She

has written Pat Hawly, Pre-School Teacher. CA-4

SAUNDERS, Blanche

She has been an expert in teaching dog obedience. Blanche Saunders has judged dogs and conducted training clinics throughout the United States, Bermuda, and Canada. At Rockefeller Plaza in New York, she has demonstrated dog obedience during National Dog Week. The author has written several books, produced films, and has written articles for newspapers. In 1946 and 1958, she was chosen "Dog Woman of the Year." She wrote Dog Training for Boys and Girls.

SAVERY, Constance 1897-

Daughter of a vicar, born in the parish of Froxfield, Wiltshire. She grew up both in the country and in an industrial district. She graduated from Somerville College, Oxford. Her career as a teacher ended when she began to help her father with parish activities. American magazines have published many of her short stories. Juvenile titles include: Emeralds for the King, Good Ship Red Lily, Magic in My Shoes, The Reb and the Redcoats. JBA-2

SAVITT, Sam 1917-

Author, illustrator, he studied at Pratt Institute. He served with the U.S. Army Engineers during World War II. Writing about horses has been Mr. Savitt's specialty. Many magazines have published his drawings. He wrote and illustrated Midnight, Champion Bucking Horse. He illustrated Maureen Daly's Patrick Visits the Zoo and Pets at the White House for Carl Carmer. CA-4

SAWYER, Ruth 1880-

Born in Boston, Massachusetts. She attended Columbia University. She was instrumental in developing the storytelling program in the New York Public Library. She has taught school both in South America and Cuba, and has been a reporter for the New York Sun. As a reporter, she traveled in Ireland, Scotland, and Wales. She has collected folklore from many countries including Spain, France, and Mexico. Her book, Roller Skates was awarded the Newbery Medal in 1937. Her juvenile titles include: Journey Cake, Ho! The Least One, Little Red Horse, Picture Tales From Spain. JBA-2

SAXE, John Godfrey 1816-1887
Humorist, poet, lawyer, and lecturer from Vermont. He graduated from Middlebury College, and has been a politician and editor of several newspapers. He was always "well armed with the light artillery of jest and epigram." He wrote The Blind Men and the Elephant.

SAYERS, Charles Marshall 1892-
Born in Kirkcudbright, Scotland, son of a famous cabinetmaker. At the age of seven he began woodcarving, and at fourteen, he was teaching students and creating his own designs. He attended Glasgow Royal Technical College and The School of Art in Glasgow. After his arrival in America, he lived in Carmel, California, and started his own school, The School of Woodcarving. Later, he moved to Walnut Creek, California. He has had exhibitions of his work in many places. For children he wrote The Book of Wood Carving, a Text for Beginners.

SAYERS, Frances (Clarke) 1897-
Born in Kansas, and grew up in Galveston, Texas. She studied at the University of Texas and at the Carnegie Library School in Pittsburgh, Pennsylvania. In addition to being on the staff of the New York Public Library as Superintendent of Work with Children, she has taught in the library school at Berkeley, California, at Pratt Institute, Brooklyn, New York, and at the University of California at Los Angeles. As a leading authority in the field of children's literature, she has been in great demand both as a writer and a speaker, but no one has really heard an "Uncle Remus" tale told unless they have heard it done by Frances Clarke Sayers. She wrote Sally Tait, Tag-Along Tooloo. JBA-2

SCHEALER, John M. 1920-

Born in Boyertown, Pennsylvania, he received his A.B. degree from the University of Pennsylvania. Work in a print shop and an auto body works followed his college years. Also, Mr. Schealer has patented a parlor game and has copyrighted others. He has written for young people: The Sycamore Warrior; a Mystery of Ancient Egypt, This Way to the Stars, Zip-Zip and His Flying Saucer, Zip-Zip Goes to Venus. CA-5/6

SCHEELE, William Earl 1920-

Museum director, author, illustrator, born in Cleveland. He graduated from Western Reserve University. The Cleveland Museum of Natural History's first Bird Art Contest was won by William Scheele, and he was appointed to their staff. After his return from army service, he became one of the youngest museum directors in the country. Mr. Scheele has enjoyed painting natural-history subjects, fossil hunting, and gem cutting. He has lived near Chardon, Ohio. Juvenile books include: Ancient Elephants, Cave Hunters, The Mound Builders, Prehistoric Animals, Prehistoric Man and the Primates.

SCHEIB, Ida

Author-illustrator, born in Brooklyn. She studied at Hunter College, Cooper Union Art School, City College of New York, and the Art Students League. She has made topographic maps for the U.S. Coast and Geodetic Survey. Also, she has written textbooks and science books. Ida Scheib's illustrations for other authors' books involved much research which provided information and ideas for her own books. She wrote and illustrated Elephants in the Garden for children.

SCHERMAN, Katharine 1915-

Writer, editor, author, native New Yorker. She has been associated with the Book-of-the-Month Club, Life, and the Saturday Review. She has been interested in chamber music and mountain climbing. She married Axel Rosin, and they have lived in New

York City. Her travels to other countries formed the basis for her books, Catherine the Great, The Slave Who Freed Haiti; the Story of Toussaint Louverture. CA-5/6

SCHLEIN, Miriam 1926-
Born in Brooklyn, New York, she graduated from Brooklyn College. Previous to writing full-time, Miriam Schlein worked in a publishing house. She married sculptor and illustrator Harvey Weiss, and they have lived in New York City. Her books, Amazing Mr. Pelgrew, Big Cheese, Elephant Herd, and The Pile of Junk have been Junior Literary Guild selections. Other titles include: Bumblebee's Secret, A Bunny, A Bird, A Funny Cat, City Boy, Country Boy, Four Little Foxes, Heavy is a Hippopotamus, The Way Mothers Are. CA-4, MJA

SCHNEIDER, Herman 1905- Nina 1913-
Teachers, authors, husband-wife team. Born in Poland, Herman Schneider has taught at the City College of New York and has been science supervisor of the elementary schools in New York City. Nina Schneider was born in Belgium, and has been a librarian, editor, and teacher. The Schneiders have written teachers' manuals, and articles for American Home, Life, and Parents' Magazine. Also, they have written many books for young people including: Follow the Sunset, How Big is Big? From Stars to Atoms; a Yardstick for the Universe, Let's Look Inside Your House, Plants in the City, Science Fun With Milk Cartons. MJA

SCHOOR, Gene
Sports announcer, coach, author, born in Passaic, New Jersey. He attended the University of Miami. He has been a sports announcer on radio and television. Due to a hand injury, he had to withdraw from the 1936 Olympic trial finals in boxing. He has been a boxing coach at the University of Minnesota and has taught Health Education in New York City. Also, the "Joe DiMaggio Show" on television was originated by Gene Schoor. Books which he

wrote with Henry Gilfond include: Casey Stengel; Baseball's Greatest Manager, The Jack Dempsey Story, The Jim Thorpe Story, America's Greatest Athlete. He wrote: Lew Burdette of the Braves, Mickey Mantle of the Yankees.

SCHULTZ, James Willard 1859-1947
Born in Boonville, New York, he attended Peekskill Military Academy. At the age of eighteen, he traveled to Montana and decided to stay. He married a woman from the Blackfood Indian tribe. James Schultz has endeavored to write books which would be accurate and authentic in their portrayal of the American Indian and his way of life. Juvenile titles include: Gold Dust, The Trail of the Spanish Horse, With the Indians in the Rockies. JBA-1, JBA-2

SCHULZ, Charles Monroe 1922-
Born in Minneapolis, Minnesota, he studied cartooning with Art Instruction, Inc. In 1956 he received the Reuben award for his newspaper comic strip, "Peanuts," given to the Outstanding Cartoonist of the year by the National Cartoonists' Society. During World War II, Charles Schulz was with the 20th Armored Division. After his marriage to Joyce Halvorson, the Schulz family lived north of San Francisco, California in the redwood country. He wrote Happiness Is a Warm Puppy for children (and adults).

SCHUON, Karl
During World War II, Karl Schuon served in the Marine Corps where he was a writer and illustrator for the magazine, Leatherneck. After the war, he was Managing Editor of the magazine. Also, he has written numerous military stories and articles. He collaborated with Philip Nason Pierce to write John H. Glenn: Astronaut.

SCHWALJE, Earl G. 1921- Marjory C.
Authors, teachers, husband-wife team. Both grew up on Long Island, New York, and both received their B. Ed. degrees from State Teachers College in New Paltz, New York. Earl Schwalje served as a

pilot in the U.S. Army Air Force during World War II. At the end of the war, he did graduate work in Educational Administration and received his M.A. degree at Teachers College, Columbia University. Both have been teachers, and have lived in Bedford Village, New York. He and his wife wrote Cezar and the Music-Maker.

SCHWARTZ, Elizabeth Reeder 1912- Charles Walsh 1914-
Biologists, authors, husband-wife team. Elizabeth Schwartz received her A.B. degree from Ohio State University, her A.M. degree from Columbia University, and her Ph.D. from the University of Missouri. Charles Schwartz has been a Ranger-Naturalist in Yosemite National Park, and obtained his A.B. and A.M. degrees from the University of Missouri. Scientific publications have printed many articles on mammals and birds written by Mr. and Mrs. Schwartz. Also, they have won honors for their sound-color motion pictures of wildlife. Their books for children include: Bobwhite From Egg to Chick to Egg, Cottontail Rabbit.

SCHWARTZ, Julius 1907-
Author and teacher, Mr. Schwartz has lived in New York City with his wife and two sons. He has been a science teacher and was an instructor in science education at Bank Street College. Julius Schwartz has been a Consultant in Science both at the Bureau of Curriculum Research, New York City Schools and to the Midwest Program on Airborne Television Instruction. Juvenile books include: The Earth Is Your Spaceship, I Know a Magic House, It's Fun to Know Why; Experiments With Things Around Us.

SCOTT, Robert Lee 1908-
A graduate of West Point, he was born in Macon, Georgia. He has always been interested in guns and big game. Brigadier General Robert Lee Scott's distinguished career in the U.S. Air Force has included commands in Germany and the Flying Tigers in China (during World War II). Also, he has been

Wing Commander of the Jet Fighter School at Williams Air Force Base and was the leader of a Thunderjet Wing over Germany. A training center for jet pilots has been under his command, and he has been Director of Information for the Air Force. He wrote Samburu, the Elephant for young people.

SCRIMSHER, Lila Gravatt
Nebraskan teacher, librarian, author. A graduate from the University of Nebraska, she has been a high school teacher in Lincoln, Nebraska. Later, as a librarian, she saw the need for historical fiction books for children in the upper elementary grades and decided to write. Many magazines have published her articles. She wrote The Pumpkin Flood at Harpers Ferry.

SEAMAN Augusta (Huiell) 1879-1950
Boys and girls have enjoyed mystery stories written by Augusta Seaman for many years. The St. Nicholas published her first mystery story in serial form. Also, her mysteries have appeared in American Girl and Youth's Companion. She married Francis P. Freeman and lived in New Jersey at Seaside Park. Her juvenile books include: Case of the Calico Crab, Crimson Patch, The Half-Penny Adventure, ... The Pine Barrens Mystery, The Vanishing Octant Mystery, When a Cobbler Ruled the King. JBA-1, JBA-2

SEAMAN, David M.
He has been a member of the staff of the Carnegie Museum in Pittsburgh. Also, he has been Associate Curator of Mineralogy at the Harvard Mineralogical Museum, and continued his studies at Harvard University. Also, as a geology and mineralogy specialist, he has been connected with the American Museum of Natural History in New York City. He wrote The Story of Rocks and Minerals, a Guidebook for Young Collectors.

SECHRIST, Elizabeth (Hough) 1903-
Librarian, author. When she was a children's li-

brarian in Bethlehem, Pennsylvania, she became interested in writing. Also, she has been a librarian in Pittsburgh. In addition to her writing, she has lectured on children's books. Mrs. Sechrist has lived in York, Pennsylvania. With Janette Woolsey, she wrote: It's Time for Brotherhood, It's Time for Christmas, It's Time for Easter, It's Time for Thanksgiving. Also, she wrote: Heigh-Ho for Halloween! Red Letter Days; A Book of Holiday Customs.

SEEGER, Ruth Porter (Crawford) 1901-1953
Musician, teacher, author, born in East Liverpool, Ohio, daughter of a Methodist minister. She attended the American Conservatory of Music in Chicago; later, she was a teacher there. She was a recipient of the Guggenheim Fellowship in composition. Many honors have been bestowed upon her, and she has served in many capacities in the world of music. She has lived in Chevy Chase, Maryland. Juvenile books include: American Folk Songs for Children in Home, School, and Nursery School; a Book for Children, Parents, and Teachers, Animal Folk Songs for Children; Traditional American Songs, Let's Build a Railroad.

SELDEN, Samuel 1899-
Director, teacher, author. A graduate of Yale, he did further study in drama at Columbia University. Mr. Selden has held many positions including: Head of the Carolina Playmakers, Chairman of the Department of Dramatic Art at the University of North Carolina, director of outdoor plays, and Chairman of the Department of Theater Arts at the University of California. In 1952, the degree of Doctor of Literature was bestowed upon him at Illinois College. He edited William Shakespeare's, Shakespear: a Player's Handbook of Short Scenes; Selected and arranged by Samuel Selden. CA-1

SELF, Margaret Cabell
Author and riding instructor, born in Cincinnati, Ohio. She received her education at the School of

Fine and Applied Design for Women, and Parsons School of Fine and Applied Arts. Margaret Self started the "New Canaan Mounted Troop, Jr. Cavalry of America." She wrote Ponies on Parade for children.

SELLEW, Catharine F. 1922-
After her graduation from Wheaton College, Catharine Sellew decided to write simplified versions of the myths for boys and girls. Adventures With the Gods was her first children's book. She also wrote Adventures With the Heroes.

SELSAM, Millicent (Ellis) 1912-
Well-known for her books about nature, this author was born in New York City. She received her B.A. degree cum laude from Brooklyn College and her M.A. degree from Columbia University. She has taught biology in the schools of New York City and at Brooklyn College. Among her many juvenile books are: All Kinds of Babies and How They Grow, All About Eggs; and How They Change Into Animals, Birth of an Island, Exploring the Animal Kingdom, Greg's Microscope, How Animals Live Together, Plants That Move, Plenty of Fish, Seeds and More Seeds, Tony's Birds. MJA

SENDAK, Maurice 1928-
Author-illustrator, born in Brooklyn, New York. He attended the Art Students League. During high school he illustrated his first book, Atomics for the Millions, for a teacher. Before writing and illustrating Kenny's Window, his first children's book, Maurice Sendak's illustrations have appeared in other authors' books. Meindert DeJong's, The Wheel on the School, with pictures by Maurice Sendak, won the Newbery Medal in 1955. Other juvenile books include: Nutshell Library, The Sign on Rosie's Door, Very Far Away, Where the Wild Things Are (winner of the 1964 Caldecott Medal). MJA

SENTMAN, George Armor
Editor, free-lance writer, author, native of Mary-

land. He graduated from the University of Missouri. George Sentman has edited several publications, and Today's Woman and Redbook magazines have published his stories. He has traveled throughout Belgium, Germany, and France. He wrote Drummer of Vincennes; a Story of the George Rogers Clark Expedition, for boys and girls.

SEREDY, Kate 1896-
She was born in Budapest, Hungary, where she studied art and nursing (during World War I, she served in front-line hospitals). Later, she came to America and worked as an illustrator. When she decided to write a book about her childhood in Hungary, the result was The Good Master, that perfect example of the type of book which should be written for boys and girls, and one which will be read by many generations. Juvenile titles include: Chestry Oak, Gypsy, Listening, White Stag (winner of the 1938 Newbery Medal). JBA-2

SEVERN, Bill 1914- and Sue 1918-
Husband-wife team. They have lived near Sheffield, Massachusetts. Mr. Severn has been a newspaperman, and his articles and stories have been published in national magazines. Mrs. Severn has been in public relations, a free-lance writer, an editor of a trade magazine, and a reporter for a newspaper. Her hobbies have included the theater and gardening, and his hobbies have been magic and Western Americana. The Severns' books include: How to Earn Money; a Young People's Guide to Spare-Time Income, Let's Give a Show. Bill Severn also wrote Magic and Magicians (a Junior Literary Guild selection). Severn, Bill CA-4; Severn, Sue CA-5/6

SEWELL, Helen Moore 1896-1957
Illustrator, author. She was born at Mare Island Navy Yard, California, and spent part of her childhood on Guam where her father, Commander William E. Sewell, U.S.N., was Governor. She attended Packer Institute, the Art School of Pratt Institute, and Archipenko's Art School in New York. Many of

her illustrations have appeared on the pages of other authors' books. Included among her own books for boys and girls are: Blue Barns, the Story of Two Big Geese and Seven Little Ducks, Three Tall Tales [by] Helen Sewell and Eleska. JBA-2

SEYFERT, Ella Maie
Teacher and author, she was born in Lancaster County, Pennsylvania. After teaching Amish children in the Lancaster schools, she grew to understand and respect the beliefs of the Amish people. She continued her associations with them in Ontario, Canada where her father was an American consul. The history of lace has always fascinated Ella Seyfert, and articles about it have been written by her. She has written Amish Moving Day, Little Amish Schoolhouse for boys and girls.

SHANNON, Monica
Librarian, author, born in Canada, she grew up on a stock farm near the Rocky Mountains, and later, lived in California. She received a degree in library science and has worked in the Los Angeles Public Library. Her book, Dobry, was awarded the Newbery Medal in 1935. Also, she wrote California Fairy Tales. JBA-2

SHANNON, Terry
Feature writer and author, born in Bellingham, Washington. She grew up in the Pacific Northwest and received her education there. She has been a columnist in Hollywood, California. Included in her many children's books are: About Caves, Among the Rocks, Desert Dwellers, A Playmate for Puna, Stones, Bones and Arrowheads, The Wonderland of Plants. CA-2

SHAPIRO, Irwin 1911-
He was born in Pittsburgh, Pennsylvania. He attended Carnegie Tech and the Art Students League in New York. He has been a free-lance writer and on the staff of a magazine. He has become well-known as a writer of American folk-tales. Juvenile

books include: Casey Jones and Locomotive No. 638, Heroes in American Folklore, How Old Stormalong Captured Mocha Dick, Joe Magarac and His U.S.A. Citizen Papers, Steamboat Bill and the Captain's Top Hat, Tall Tales of America, Yankee Thunder; The Legendary Life of Davy Crockett. JBA-2

SHAPIRO, Milton J. 1926-
Born in Brooklyn, New York, he attended the College of the City of New York. During World War II, he served with the Air Force in the Philippines. He has been a copy-boy, sports writer, and movie critic for a New York newspaper. Later, he was editor of GUNsport magazine. He has written for other gun sport enthusiasts, A Beginner's Book of Sporting Guns and Hunting. Also, he wrote: The Dizzy Dean Story, The Gil Hodges Story, Mel Ott Story, Mickey Mantle, Yankee Slugger, Phil Rizzuto Story, Sal Maglie Story, Warren Spahn Story, The Whitey Ford Story.

SHARFMAN, Amalie
Radio announcer and author, born in Baltimore, Maryland. She married a government lawyer and has lived in Washington, D.C. She continued her work in radio, and has produced and moderated two programs on child guidance. During World War II, she was a nursery school teacher, and decided to write books for boys and girls. Mrs. Sharfman's home has been in Worcester, Massachusetts where she has served in the Mental Health Association. She has written A Beagle Named Bertram, Mr. Peabody's Pesky Ducks.

SHARP, Adda Mai (Cummings)
Storyteller and author. Mrs. Sharp has often told stories to her many nieces and nephews and conducted storytelling programs in Denton, Texas. These experiences have provided her with a rich background in order to write books for boys and girls. Her hobbies have included books, games, music, and travel. She learned to love animal and plant life from her

father, a naturalist. Juvenile books include: Daffy, Gee Whillikins, Where Is Cubby Bear?

SHELDON, Walter J.
Native Philadelphian. He has been a short-story writer, novelist, artist, and radio announcer. Also, Mr. Sheldon has been a director-producer in television and a script writer for movies. At one time he was a continuity director for the Far East Network which conducted programs in English for the military forces serving in the Far East. Mr. Sheldon wrote The Key to Tokyo, his first book for boys and girls.

SHERLOCK, Philip Manderson 1902-
He was born in Jamaica, British West Indies, the son of a Methodist minister. He has been headmaster of Wolmer's Boys' School, and has been Secretary of the Institute of Jamaica (a cultural center). The honorary title of Commander of the British Empire was conferred upon Philip Sherlock by Queen Elizabeth II in 1952. Later, he was Vice-Principal and Director of Extra-Mural Studies at the University College of the West Indies. For boys and girls he has written: Anansi, the Spider Man; Jamaican Folk Tales; told by Philip M. Sherlock. CA-5/6

SHIELDS, Karena
Archeologist, author, lecturer, teacher, pilot. She grew up on a rubber plantation on Chiapas, near the Isthmus of Tehuantepec. She attended schools in the United States and studied archeology at the University of Southern California. Mrs. Shields has been an authority on Central American Maya. Also, Karena Shields has been a teacher in naval air navigation and has been a pilot for the Civil Air Patrol. She has lived in Montrose, California. She wrote Three In the Jungle.

SHIELDS, Rita
Teacher and author, born in San Francisco, California. She received her B.A. degree from San

Francisco State College, and has been a teacher. She wrote Cecelia's Locket for young readers.

SHIPPEN, Katherine Binney 1892-
Teacher, lecturer, author, born in Hoboken, New Jersey. She graduated from Bryn Mawr and received her master's degree from Columbia University. She has been a teacher in Orange, New Jersey, and was Curator of the Social Studies Division of the Brooklyn Children's Museum. Her enthusiasm and diligent research in order to write good books for boys and girls have made Katherine Shippen a distinguished and outstanding author of books for young people. Juvenile titles include: Andrew Carnegie and the Age of Steel, Bridle for Pegasus, Bright Design, Great Heritage, Men of Medicine, Moses, New Found World, Portals to the Past; The Story of Archaeology. MJA

SHIRER, William Lawrence 1904-
Author, newspaperman, born in Chicago. After graduating from Coe College in Iowa, William Shirer planned a two-month trip to Europe, but he stayed for twenty years. He has been on radio, and has worked on the Paris editions of the Chicago Tribune and the New York Herald Tribune. Also, he has been a foreign correspondent and has been on the staff of the CBS foreign news in Germany. The Shirer family has lived in New York and Connecticut. Juvenile contributions include: The Rise and Fall of Adolf Hitler, The Sinking of the Bismarck.

SHIRK, Jeannette Campbell 1898-
She was born in Middletown, Pennsylvania, but a great part of her life has been spent around Pittsburgh. She studied illustration and writing at the Carnegie Institute of Technology. Later, she attended library school and received a B. S. in Library Science. Jeannette Shirk has been librarian in the Henry Clay Frick Fine Arts Department of the University of Pittsburgh. Her children's book, The Little Circus, won an Honorable Mention award in the Dodd, Mead Librarian Prize Competition.

SHIRREFFS, Gordon Donald

This author and his family have lived in California in the San Fernando Valley. His hobbies have included archery, rifle and pistol marksmanship, Civil War and Western history. He has written television plays, movies, short stories, and novels. Juvenile titles include: Action Front, The Gray Sea Raiders (a Junior Literary Guild selection), The Rebel Trumpet.

SHORTER, Bani

Mrs. Shorter has spent part of her life in India where she accumulated a great deal of material for her books. She and her husband, a Princeton University professor of economics, have lived near Princeton, New Jersey. Bani Shorter has been a supervisor and a demonstration teacher at the University Elementary School, of the University of California at Los Angeles. Later, Mrs. Shorter again returned to India and Pakistan and wrote India's Children.

SHUTTLESWORTH, Dorothy Edwards 1907-

When she was seventeen years old, she began working in the American Museum of Natural History. Later, as a staff member of the Natural History magazine, she convinced the directors of the Museum to sponsor a similar magazine for children. The Junior Natural History magazine was the result, and she has been its editor and contributing editor. She has lived in East Orange, New Jersey. Included in her book titles for children are: Real Book About Prehistoric Life, Story of Rocks, Story of Spiders. CA-1

SIDJAKOV, Nicolas 1924-

He was born in Riga, Latvia. He attended the École des Beaux Arts in Paris in order to study painting. He has been a free-lance designer and illustrator. He married an American girl in Paris, but they have lived in the United States since 1954. He has maintained a studio in San Francisco. His first illustrations in a children's book appeared in

Laura N. Baker's The Friendly Beasts. Also, he illustrated Ruth Robbins' Christmas story, Baboushka and the Three Kings, winner of the 1961 Caldecott Medal. He has also illustrated The Emperor and Drummer Boy by the same author. MJA

SIEGMEISTER, Elie 1909-
Musician and author. He has been director of the American Ballad Singers and has composed numerous songs. He wrote Doodle Dandy of the U.S.A., a musical show for young people. Also, he has written American folk music and orchestral works. He wrote: Invitation to Music, and edited Work and Sing; a Collection of the Songs That Built America... With Commentary, Annotations and a Critical Bibliography. CA-3

SILLIMAN, Leland 1906-
He was born in New York. Leland Silliman has been a swimming coach, camp director, and an officer with the Navy's physical training and swimming program (during World War II). He received a certificate from the Boys' Clubs of America for his story, The Scrapper. Other titles include: Bucky Forrester, The Daredevil, Golden Cloud, Palomino of Sunset Hill, Purple Tide.

SILVERBERG, Robert
Native New Yorker. He has written many books including the well-known biography of Commander Shepard, First American Into Space. Mr. Silverberg married an electronics engineer, and they have lived in New York City. Juvenile titles include: 15 Battles That Changed the World, Lost Cities and Vanished Civilizations, Lost Race of Mars. CA-3

SILVERMAN, Al
Editor and author, born in Lynn, Massachusetts. A former free-lance writer, Al Silverman has been editor-in-chief of Sport magazine. He has also written for TV Guide, Argosy, Saturday Evening Post, and Saturday Review. Mr. Silverman has written books about sports and baseball players, including

Mickey Mantle: Mister Yankee for boys and girls.

SIMBARI, Nicola 1927-

Painter and author, he has lived in Rome most of his life. At an early age, he was familiar with the art treasures of the Vatican because his father was a builder there. Nicola Simbari attended Rome's Accademia Belle Arti. His work has been shown in Italy, England, and the United States. During a visit to America he decided to write and illustrate his children's book, Gennarino. CA-4

SIMON, Charlie May (Hogue) 1897-

Native of Arkansas. She was the daughter of Wyman Hogue, a teacher and author. She attended the Chicago Art Institute, and also studied in Paris. She married poet John Gould Fletcher, and they have lived in Rowland, Arkansas. Among her children's books are: Bright Morning, Faraway Trail, The Long Hunt, Robin On the Mountain, Roundabout. JBA-2

SIMON, Norma

Author, nursery school teacher and director, Mrs. Simon has lived in Norwalk, Connecticut. As a teacher, she took notes about children's interests, and later used these ideas in writing books for boys and girls. A graduate of Brooklyn College, Norma Simon did graduate work in New York City at the New School and at the Bank Street College of Education. She wrote Daddy Days, Elly the Elephant.

SIMON, Ruth Corabel (Shimer) 1918-

Author and teacher, born in Orosi, California. She attended Visalia Junior College and graduated from San Jose State College. During World War II, Mrs. Simon was with the American Red Cross and served in a hospital at Fort Lewis, Washington. Also, she has been an elementary school teacher. The Simons have lived in Fort Wayne, Indiana. She wrote Mat and Mandy and the Little Old Car for children.

SIMONT, Marc 1915-
Illustrator-author, born in Paris. He attended the Académie Julien, Académie Ranson, the André Lhote School in Paris, and the National Academy of Design in New York. Marc Simont's work has included magazine illustrations, portraits, and visual aids for the Army. Mr. Simont, his wife (Sara Dalton who was a social worker), and son have lived in West Cornwall, Connecticut, and in New York City. In 1957 he received the Caldecott Medal for his illustrations of A Tree is Nice (written by Janice May Udry). Also, he wrote and illustrated Mimi. MJA

SLOBODKIN, Louis 1903-
Sculptor, illustrator, author. He grew up in Albany, New York and studied at the Beaux Arts Institute of Design in New York. He has illustrated children's books for various authors, including James Thurber's Many Moons, the winner of the 1944 Caldecott Medal. Mr. Slobodkin married Florence Gersh. Juvenile contributions include: Adventure of Arab, Amiable Giant, Circus, April 1st., Dinny and Danny, Excuse Me! Certainly! Hustle and Bustle, The King and the Noble Blacksmith, Seaweed Hat, Space Ship Under the Apple Tree, Trick or Treat. JBA-2

SLOBODKINA, Esphyr 1909-
Author-illustrator, born in Cheliabinsk, Russia. She grew up in Siberia and Manchuria. Later, she attended the National Academy of Design in New York. Miss Slobodkina has also been a decorator, painter, designer, and sculptor. Much of her work has been displayed in such museums as The Cocorcan Gallery, the Whitney Museum of American Art, and the Philadelphia Art Museum. She has written and illustrated: The Clock, Jack and Jim, Little Dinghy, The Long Island Ducklings, Pinky and the Petunias. CA-1

SMITH, Agnes
Born in Clarksburg, West Virginia, Agnes Smith decided at the age of sixteen to be a writer. She married newspaper editor Richard Parish, and they have lived on a farm in West Virginia. She has been in-

terested in woodworking, carving, furniture designing, and ceramics (which have been sold in America House in New York). She wrote Edge of the Forest (a Junior Literary Guild selection).

SMITH, Eunice Young 1902-
Author-artist. She attended the Lakeview School of Commercial Art and the Academy of Fine Arts in Chicago. Prior to her career as an author and illustrator, Mrs. Smith designed Christmas cards. She has lived near Mishawaka, Indiana. Juvenile titles include: Denny's Story, Jennifer Dances, The Little Red Drum, Moppet, Sam's Big Worry.

SMITH, Irene 1903-
Librarian, author, born in Kentucky. She grew up in Indianapolis, Indiana, and attended the University of Illinois. She has been Superintendent of Work with Children in the Brooklyn Public Library. Also, she has shared the lectern with Frances Clarke Sayers in teaching a children's literature course at Pratt Institute (1946-47). She married research chemist Louis William Green, and has lived in Dobbs Ferry, New York. She wrote: Down the Road With Johnny, A History of the Newbery and Caldecott Medals, Hubbub in the Hollow, Paris, Santa Claus Book.

SMITH, Moyne Rice
Actress, teacher, author, born in Oskaloosa, Kansas. She graduated from the University of Kansas and Western Reserve University. She has been a high school teacher and has taught college English and dramatics. Many phases of the theater have interested Mrs. Smith, including acting and directing. Also, Childcraft and The Instructor have published her articles on children's theater. She wrote Plays & - How to Put Them On.

SOOTIN, Harry
Teacher, author, native New Yorker. He received his B.S. degree from the College of the City of New York. Prior to entering the teaching profession, Mr.

Sootin was an industrial chemist. The Britannica Junior and many magazines have published his articles. Harry Sootin has been a member of the Authors League of America, the American Association for the Advancement of Science, and the Teachers Guild. For young people he wrote 12 Pioneers of Science.

SORENSEN, Virginia (Eggersten) 1912-
She was born in Provo, Utah, and graduated from Brigham Young University. She married Frederick Sorensen, and the Sorensens have lived and worked in several states. With the aid of Guggenheim Fellowships, she has studied in Denmark and Mexico. For children she has written: Curious Missie, Miracles on Maple Hill, the 1957 Newbery Medal winner. MJA.

SPEARE, Elizabeth George 1908-
Born in Melrose, Massachusetts, she studed at Boston University, and later, taught in high schools. She married Alden Speare. Her first book was Calico Captive. Mrs. Speare has been one of those rare authors who has been awarded a Medal twice. She was awarded the Newbery Medal in 1959 for The Witch of Blackbird Pond and again in 1962, for her book, The Bronze Bow. CA-2, MJA

SPERRY, Armstrong 1897-
Born in New Haven, Connecticut, he has attended Yale Art School, the Art Students League in New York, and continued his studies in Paris. He has always been interested in the sea since the time when he was a boy and listened to the exciting tales told by a great-grandfather. In 1941 his book, Call it Courage, was awarded the Newbery Medal. Juvenile titles include: All About the Arctic and Antarctic, All About the Jungle, The Amazon, River Sea of Brazil, Danger to Windward, Frozen Fire, Rain Forest. JBA-2

SPYRI, Johanna (Heusser) 1827-1901
Born in Hirzel, Switzerland. She lived near Zurich, Switzerland when she was a little girl, and

spent one summer high in the mountains for her health. This experience provided her with much of the background for her stories although she did not write until she was forty. She wrote: Heidi, The Pet Lamb, and Other Swiss Stories; Translated from the German by M. E. Calthrop and E. M. Popper. JBA-1, JBA-2

STEVENSON, Augusta
Author and teacher, born in Patriot, Indiana. When she first began to write, she selected plays as her subject. It was fitting that this author was born in the town of Patriot, because many of her stories have been about American patriots. Augusta Stevenson often obtained ideas for her books from visits to places where famous people had once lived. Included in her many children's books are: Andy Jackson, Boy Soldier, Anthony Wayne, Daring Boy, Ben Franklin, Printer's Boy, Clara Barton; Girl Nurse, Molly Pitcher; Girl Patriot, Myles Standish; Adventurous Boy, Sitting Bull, Dakota Boy (Childhood of Famous Americans series). CA-2, MJA

STEVENSON, Robert Louis 1850-1894
Born in Edinburgh, Scotland. He was often very ill, and died when he was only forty-four in Samoa in the South Pacific. He was married in the United States, and his story, Treasure Island, was created for his stepson. Juvenile titles include: The Black Arrow; A Tale of the Two Roses, A Child's Garden of Verses, Kidnapped, Prayers Written at Vailima, Strange Case of Dr. Jekyll and Mr. Hyde and Other Stories. JBA-1

STOLZ, Mary (Slattery) 1920-
She was born in Boston, Massachusetts, and attended the Birch Wathen School, Columbia University, and the Katharine Gibbs School in New York City. She has become well-known for her books for teen-agers. Mrs. Stolz has lived in Pelham, New York. Juvenile books include: And Love Replied, Because of Madeline, Belling the Tiger, The Day and the Way We Met, A Dog on Barkham Street,

Good-by My Shadow, Hospital Zone, Organdy Cupcakes, Rosemary. CA-5/6, MJA

STONG, Philip Duffield 1899-1957
Born in Iowa, he grew up on a farm there. Many of his stories have been based on animals and incidents which he encountered as a farm boy. Also, he remembered the stories which his grandfather had told to him about the Sauk Indian boys. Phil Stong later lived in Connecticut, but he enjoyed frequent visits to the family farm in Iowa. Juvenile titles include: Censored, the Goat, High Water, Honk: The Moose, No-Sitch: the Hound, Young Settler. MJA

STREATFEILD, Noel
Born in Sussex, England. Members of her family have lived in Chiddingstone, Kent, for four hundred years. Prior to her writing career, Noel Streatfeild was an actress. Her books have been published in England and the United States, and they have been translated into other languages. Juvenile titles include: Ballet Shoes, Circus Shoes, Family Shoes, First Book of England, First Book of the Ballet, Movie Shoes, Party Shoes, Queen Victoria, Traveling Shoes. JBA-2

SUTCLIFF, Rosemary 1920-
Painter and author, born in Surrey, England, daughter of a naval officer. When she was eighteen years old, the Royal Academy exhibited one of her miniatures and later, she became a member of the Royal Miniaturist Society. It was after World War II that Rosemary Sutcliff decided to write rather than paint. Juvenile titles include: Beowulf; retold by Rosemary Sutcliff, Dawn Wind, Knight's Fee, Lantern Bearers, Rudyard Kipling, Shield Ring, Silver Branch. CA-5/6, MJA

SWIFT, Hildegarde (Hoyt)
Author and teacher, born in Clinton, New York, the daughter of a college professor. She graduated from Smith College, and later attended the New York

School of Social Work. She married Arthur L. Swift, Jr., who has been Dean of the New School for Social Research in New York City. Also, Mrs. Swift has taught children's literature there. She has been a member of the Authors' League of America, the Pen and Brush Club of New York, and the Women's National Book Association. Included in her juvenile book titles are: Edge of April; a Biography of John Burroughs, Little Red Lighthouse and the Great Gray Bridge, North Star Shining; a Pictorial History of the American Negro. JBA-2

SZE, Mai-Mai
She was born in Tientsin, China. Her father was Chinese Ambassador in London and Washington. She studied at Wellesley College. Her paintings have been exhibited in Paris, the United States, and London. In 1937 she was instrumental in starting the first Chinese War Relief group in New York. She lectured on China, and wrote a column concerning it in the New York Post. She wrote Echo of a Cry; A Story Which Began in China.

T

TENSEN, Ruth Marjorie
Teacher and author, she received her Master's degree in Child Development from Columbia University. She has taught first grade in Rochester, New York. For boys and girls she has written: Come to See the Clowns, Come to the City, Come to the Farm, Come to the Pet Shop, Come to the Zoo.

TERHUNE, Albert Payson 1872-1942
He was born in Newark, New Jersey, the son of a clergyman, and graduated from Columbia University. Mr. Terhune bought his first dog at the age of thirteen, and since that time he has written many books about dogs which have been enjoyed and loved by countless boys and girls throughout the world. He has bred and raised collies including well-known prize winners. Also, he has been a newspaper reporter, short story writer, editor, and an extensive

traveler. Juvenile titles include: Collie to the Rescue, The Heart of a Dog, His Dog, Lad, A Dog. JBA-1

THURBER, James 1894-1961
Born in Columbus, Ohio, he attended Ohio State University. He has been a newspaperman, and a frequent contributor to the New Yorker magazine. His first book for boys and girls was Many Moons which was awarded the Caldecott Medal in 1944. Juvenile contributions include: Great Quillow, ... The White Deer. MJA

TODD, Mary Fidelis
Born in Detroit, Michigan, she majored in art and graduated from Stanford University. After graduation, she worked in her father's advertising agency (Michael Todd Advertising) in Hollywood. Her work has been shown in galleries, schools, and libraries in California. She wrote an illustrated ABC and 123, Juggler of Notre Dame; and old French tale retold and illustrated by Mary Fidelis Todd.

TODD, Ruthven 1914-
This science fiction (Space Cat books) writer has also been a poet. He was born in Scotland, and attended the Edinburgh College of Art. Mr. Todd became an American citizen, and has lived on Martha's Vineyard. Juvenile titles include: Space Cat and the Kittens, Space Cat Meets Mars, Space Cat Visits Venus. MJA

TOLKIEN, John R.R. 1892-
Born in South Africa, he graduated from Exeter College, Oxford University. During World War I, he served with the Lancashire Fusiliers. He has taught at the University of Leeds and at Oxford University. His imaginative books for boys and girls include: The Hobbit; or, There and Back Again, Farmer Giles of Ham. MJA

TOLSTOY, Serge, countess
She was born in France, and received her education

there and in England. Also, she attended the Sorbonne. She was married to a diplomat. She has written for The Social Spectator, and has had stories for children published in Canada and in France. She wrote The Gold Fairy Book.

TOMPKINS, Jane 1898-
Boys and girls have enjoyed reading her many stories about animals. She loved animals when she was a little girl in Westchester County, New York, and became interested in the animals of the Far North when she married Burt M. McConnell (a member of Stefansson's last Arctic expedition). For many years she provided scripts for Kate Smith on radio. Juvenile titles include: Beaver Twins, The Black Bear Twins, Moo-Wee, the Musk-Ox, The Otter Twins, Penguin Twins.

TOMPKINS, Walker Allison
Born in Washington, he grew up on a ranch there. During World War II, he was an army correspondent overseas. He married a writer, and they have lived in Santa Barbara, California. He has been very interested in ham radio, and has been president of the Santa Barbara Amateur Radio Club. He wrote: DX Brings Danger, SOS At Midnight (a Junior Literary Guild selection).

TOOZE, Ruth (Anderson) 1892-
The work which Ruth Tooze has done in books and music has become known through her Children's Book Caravan. The education division of the State Department asked her to go to Cambodia in order to help native writing. She found that music has been a universal language with children everywhere. She wrote: America, Cambodia: Land of Contrasts, Our Rice Village in Cambodia, Silver From the Sea, Your Children Want to Read: A Guide for Teachers and Parents. CA-5/6

TOR, Regina
She attended Skidmore College and studied art at the University of New Mexico, and at the Art Students

League. She has lived with her husband and two sons in Dutchess County, New York where she also has been a member of the Board of the Community Children's Theatre. Juvenile titles include: Getting to Know Canada, Getting to Know Greece, Getting to Know Korea, Getting to Know the Philippines. With Eleanor Roosevelt, she wrote Growing Toward Peace.

TOTTLE, John
Teacher, author. He has been editor of the weekly magazine, Young Citizens, published by the Civic Education Service in Washington, D.C. Also, Mr. Tottle has been a Lieutenant Colonel in the United States Army Reserves, and a member of the National Press Club. He wrote Benjamin Franklin: First Great American.

TOUSEY, Sanford
He was born in Clay Center, Kansas, and grew up on a ranch and has lived near an Indian reservation. He drew pictures when he was a boy, and later attended an art school in Chicago. Boys (and girls) who like to read about the West have enjoyed reading Mr. Tousey's books which include: Bill Clark, American Explorer, Cowboys of America, Davy Crockett; Hero of the Alamo, Fred and Brown Beaver Ride the River, Horseman Hal. JBA-2

TRACHSEL, Myrtle Jamison
Born in Missouri, she attended Hardin College and Oberlin College and Conservatory. She married Louis Trachsel, and has lived in St. Joseph, Missouri. She has been interested in history and nature. Her first book for children was Mistress Jennifer and Master Jeremiah. Also, she wrote Elizabeth of the Mayflower.

TRAVERS, Pamela L. 1906-
Born in Queensland, Australia, she lived in England where she wrote articles for The Irish Statesman and other publications. She has enjoyed gardening. Her delightful stories about "Mary Poppins" have

delighted boys and girls for many years. Juvenile contributions include: The Fox at the Manger, Mary Poppins, Mary Poppins Comes Back, Mary Poppins From A to Z. JBA-2

TREASE, Geoffrey 1909-
Born in Nottingham, England, and studied at Queen's College, Oxford. He has been a schoolmaster. During World War II, he served in the infantry and in the Army Educational Corps. He has lived in Herefordshire, England. Juvenile titles include: Escape to King Alfred, The Gates of Bannerdale, ...Message to Hadrian, Seven Kings of England, Young Traveler in Greece. MJA

TREAT, Roger L.
He has been a sports writer for the Chicago Herald American. In 1945 he was selected by the Army as one of five sports writers who were assigned to tour the service sport programs in the African, European and Mediterranean theatres. He wrote Walter Johnson: King of the Pitchers.

TREECE, Henry 1912-
He has lived in Barton-on-Humber, Lincolnshire, England. Mr. Treece has been a schoolmaster, has written adult novels and verse, and has been an editor of several anthologies. During World War II, he was a flight lieutenant in the R. A. F. Juvenile titles include: Castles and Kings, The Golden One, Viking's Sunset. CA-1, MJA

TREGASKIS, Richard William 1916-
He graduated from Harvard University. He was a war correspondent for the International News Service and has written several books about World War II. After the war, he traveled around the world and wrote Seven Leagues to Paradise. He wrote: John F. Kennedy and PT-109, Guadalcanal Diary. CA-3

TREICHLER, Jessie
She graduated from Montana State University, and has served many college presidents as a secretary

and assistant. She has been closely associated with Antioch College where she has been Director of Public Relations. Her husband Paul Treichler was Director of the Antioch Area Theatre, and their daughter Paula studied at Antioch. Her articles have appeared in the Yale Review, Mademoiselle, and in the Antioch Review. She wrote Educating for Democracy: Horace Mann.

TRENT, Robbie 1894-
She was born in Wolf Creek, Kentucky. She has served in an editorial and advisory capacity in the field of religious education. Also, she has been Elementary Editor for the Sunday School Board, Southern Baptist Convention. Juvenile titles include: In the Beginning, Jesus' First Trip, To Church We Go, What Is God Like?

TRESSELT, Alvin R. 1916-
He was born in Passaic, New Jersey. He has been Managing Editor of Humpty Dumpty magazine. His wife Blossom Budney also has written books for boys and girls (A Kiss Is Round). They have lived near Redding, Connecticut. In 1948 the book White Snow, Bright Snow (which was written by Mr. Tresselt and illustrated by Roger Duvoisin) was the winner of the Caldecott Medal. Juvenile titles include: Autumn Harvest, A Day With Daddy, Follow the Road, "Hi, Mister Robin!" The Rabbit Story, Sun Up. MJA

TRIMBLE, Joe
Born in Brooklyn, New York, he graduated from St. John's College. He has been a newspaperman on the New York Daily News. As a reporter, he has specified that his favorite assignments have been baseball and football as compared to hockey and basketball. He has been an officer of the Baseball Writers Association in New York, and was the official scorer in the 1950 World Series (Yankees-Phillies). Juvenile titles include: Phil Rizzuto; A Biography of the Scooter, Yogi Berra.

TROTTER, Grace

Her pseudonym is Nancy Paschal. Dallas, Texas was her home and where she attended public and private schools. She was of Welsh, Scots, Irish and French descent. Her first children's book, Clover Creek, appeared in serial form in the American Girl magazine; also, it was a Junior Literary Guild selection. She has been very fond of dogs, and this has been apparent in her books. Juvenile titles include: Make Way for Lauren, Name the Day, No More Good-Bys, Portrait by Sheryl, Spring in the Air. CA-1

TUCKER, Ernest Edward

Native of Chicago, he attended the University of Illinois. During World War II, he served with the Navy. He has traveled in Europe, Latin America, and the Far East on assignment as a reporter. He has been city editor of the Chicago American. He wrote The Story of Knights and Armor.

TUDOR, Tasha 1915-

Illustrator, author, born in Boston, Massachusetts, she attended the Boston Museum School of Art befor her marriage to Thomas L. McCready, Jr. The McCreadys have lived on a farm in New Hampshire in a house built in 1782. In an interview with a reporter on the Milwaukee Journal she once said: "All the animals, incidents, scenes, children, and grownups I use (for her books) are taken directly from our family and our farm and the surrounding country and people." Juvenile titles include: A Is For Annabelle, Alexander the Gander, Amanda and the Bear. Her husband wrote, and she illustrated: Adventures of a Beagle, Increase Rabbit. JBA-2

TUFTS, Anne

She was born in a suburb of Boston, Massachusetts, and attended Radcliffe College and did graduate work at Columbia University. She has lived at Gramercy Park, New York and has been a high school teacher in New York. She has spent summers in New Hampshire. She wrote about this part of the country (New

England) in her book, As the Wheel Turns.

TUFTS, Georgia
This author has enjoyed drawing pictures of cats since she was in the third grade. She has lived in Oberlin, Ohio. At the age of fifteen, she wrote and illustrated Catrina and the Cats.

TUNIS, John Roberts 1889-
Born in Boston, Massachusetts, he graduated from Harvard. He was on the staff of the Sports Department of the New York Evening Post, and was a broadcaster for the National Broadcasting Company from Paris and London. He was associated with the first sports broadcast, the Challenge Round of the Davis Cup in Paris, from Europe via short wave. Juvenile titles include: All-American, City for Lincoln, Schoolboy Johnson, Young Razzle. MJA

TURNBULL, Agnes (Sligh) 1888-
Born in New Alexandria, Pennsylvania. This well-known novelist wrote a children's story about a sheep dog in Scotland. It was not surprising that she selected this country since her father came from Berwick, Scotland, and her husband James Lyall Turnbull was from the "Border." She has lived in Maplewood, New Jersey, and the name of the book about a sheep dog was Jed, the Shepherd's Dog. CA-3

TURNGREN, Annette 1902-
She grew up in Minnesota, and attended the University of Minnesota. She has been a teacher, has written for teen-age magazines and has worked in a publishing house. Her sister was author Ellen Turngren. After listening to her mother tell about her childhood in Sweden, she decided to create a story, and this became her first book for young people, Flaxen Braids. Also, she wrote: Canyon of No Sunset, The Copper Kettle, Great Artists; 26 Master Painters, Mystery Clouds the Canyon, Steamboat's Coming. MJA

TURNGREN, Ellen

This author was from Minnesota, the daughter of Swedish immigrant parents. She has been a teacher and at one time was an editor of a country newspaper. She has lived near Minneapolis, Minnesota. Her sister was author Annette Turngren. She has been a member of the Minnesota Branch of the National League of American Pen Women and the Minneapolis Writers' Workshop. She wrote Shadows Into Mist.

U

UCHIDA, Yoshiko

Born in California, she attended the University of California, Smith College, and lived for two years on a fellowship in Japan. Her parents often entertained many of the Christian leaders of Japan when they visited the United States. She became acquainted with Dr. Toyohiko Kagawa and his daughter Umeko, and this led to her writing a story about the experiences of Umeko. It was called Full Circle. Other juvenile titles include: Dancing Kettle, and Other Japanese Folk Tales, The Forever Christmas Tree, Magic Listening Cap; More Folk Tales From Japan, Mik and the Prowler. MJA

UDRY, Janice (May) 1928-

She was born in Jacksonville, Illinois and graduated from Northwestern University. She has worked in a nursery school in Chicago, and later, moved to Garden Grove, California. In 1957 Marc Simont was awarded the Caldecott Medal for his illustrations in Miss Udry's book, A Tree Is Nice. Her other titles include: Alfred, Betsy-Back-In-Bed, Danny's Pig, End of the Line, Is Susan Here? Moon Jumpers. CA-5/6

ULLMAN, James Ramsey 1907-

Theatrical producer, dramatist, author. He has been interested in and written about mountain climbing and has been a member of the American Alpine Club. He was born in New York City and graduated from Princeton University. He has been a newspaperman and was co-producer of the play, Men In White (winner of a Pulitzer Prize). During World War II, he served with the American Field Service with the British 8th Army. He wrote Down the Colorado With Major Powell. CA-3

ULRICH, Homer 1906-
He studied at the Chicago Musical College and at the University of Chicago. Also, he attended the orchestral training school of the Chicago Civic Orchestra. He has played in the Chicago Symphony Orchestra and has been Professor of Music at the University of Texas. He wrote Famous Women Singers for young people.

UNDSET, Sigrid 1882-
She was born in Kallundborg, Denmark, the daughter of a Norwegian archaeologist. This outstanding novelist has been a recipient of the Nobel Prize. During the time that she lived in America, she wrote her first books for young people. One of these was Happy Times in Norway (tr. from the Norwegian by Joran Birkeland) which described Norwegian festivals as seen through the eyes of her own children. Also, American children have enjoyed her True and Untrue, and Other Norse Tales.

UNGERER, Tomi 1931-
He was born in Strasbourg. He has traveled extensively in Europe, and has worked in the graphic arts. He once said that traveling by foot and hitchhiking was "the best way to travel, meet people, and have adventure." His first book for boys and girls was The Mellops Go Flying. Also, he wrote: Adelaide, Christmas Eve at the Mellops', Crictor, Emile, The Mellops' Go Spelunking. With Miriam Ungerer, he wrote Come Into My Parlor...

UNNERSTAD, Edith (Totterman) 1900-
She was born in Finland, but has lived in Sweden most of her life. Edith Unnerstad enjoyed growing up as "next to the oldest" in a family of seven chil-

dren. She married an engineer and has lived in Djursholm, a Stockholm suburb. She once said: "Writing children's books is a responsibility, for any book that comes into the hands of a child may form his future attitude toward literature." Juvenile titles include: Journey to England, Little O, Pysen, Saucepan Journey. CA-5/6

UNWIN, David Starr 1918-
English author and traveler, son of publisher Sir Stanley Unwin. His pseudonym is David Severn. He has been both a printer and a bookseller. Later, he joined his father's firm and became an author. He has been interested in mountain climbing, winter sports, and the out-of-doors. For boys and girls he wrote Burglars and Bandicoots.

UNWIN, Nora Spicer 1907-
British artist. She studied at the Royal College of Art in London. She came to America in 1946 and has lived in Wellesley, Massachusetts. She has taught art to children in a private school and has illustrated many books for boys and girls. Also, she wrote: Joyful the Morning; the Story of an English Family Christmas, Poquito; the Little Mexican Duck (a Junior Literary Guild selection), Proud Pumpkin, Two Too Many. MJA

UPDIKE, John (Hoyer) 1932-
He attended Harvard College and the Ruskin School of Drawing and Fine Art in Oxford. He has been associated with The New Yorker magazine in which many of his stories and poems have appeared. Althought he has written many books for adults, his first book for children was The Magic Flute; music by Wolfgang Amadeus Mozart. Adapted and illustrated by John Updike and Warren Chappell. CA-4

V

VALENS, Evans G. Jr. 1920-
Born in State College, Pennsylvania, he received his B.A. degree from Amherst. He has been a reporter

on the Herald-Post in El Paso, Texas and has been a co-producer (with Dr. Glenn T. Seaborg of the University of California) of "The Elements," an educational film series. He has lived in Mill Valley, California. He wrote: Me and Frumpet; an Adventure With Size and Science, Wingfin and Topple. CA-5/6

VAN COEVERING, Jack 1900-
Attended Calvin College and graduated from the University of Michigan. He spent his youth in the Lake Michigan area. He has been editor of wildlife for the Detroit Free Press, and his stories and pictures have been published in many magazines, including Field and Stream, Outdoor Life, and Sports Afield. Mr. Van Coevering has been active in such groups as the Izaak Walton League, the National Wildlife Federation, and the Audubon Society. He has written A-Hiking We Will Go for young readers.

VAN DER VELDT, James A. 1893-
He was born in Amsterdam, Holland and did research work in psychology and philosophy at the Universities of Louvain (Belgium), Nimwegen (Holland), and Milan (Italy). He has taught in Holland, at the Pontifical University of the Propagation of the Faith in Rome and at St. Joseph's Seminary, Dunwoodie, Yonkers. His articles have appeared in many American magazines. He wrote The City Set On a Hill; the Story of the Vatican.

VAN HORN, Grace
She has been a librarian in Castle Rock, Washington. Also, Miss Van Horn has lived on a farm which provided her with a good background in order to write Little Red Rooster for boys and girls.

VAN LOON, Hendrik Willem 1882-1944
He was born in Rotterdam, The Netherlands, and arrived in the United States at the age of twenty. He graduated from Cornell University and also attended the University of Munich. He has been a newspaper correspondent in Russia, and also served

in that same capacity in Europe during World War I. He was the first recipient of the Newbery Medal in 1922 for his book, The Story of Mankind. Juvenile titles include: Around the World With the Alphabet and Hendrik Willem van Loon, Christmas Carols, Life and Times of Simon Bolivar, Thomas Jefferson. JBA-1

VAN STOCKUM, Hilda 1908-

She was born in Rotterdam and attended an art school in Dublin. While she lived in Dublin she did a great deal of work as a portrait painter. She married a man from New York City, Ervin Ross Marlin and they returned there to live. She has taught in the Child Education Foundation of New York. Mr. and Mrs. Marlin (and their six children) have lived in Washington, D. C. She based her story of The Mitchells on many of the happy experiences shared with her own children. Juvenile titles include: Andries, The Angels' Alphabet, Canadian Summer, Friendly Gables. Also, she illustrated Hans Brinker; Or, The Silver Skates by Mary Mapes Dodge. JBA-2

VANCE, Marguerite 1889-

Born in Chicago, Illinois, she received her education in private schools there and in Europe. She married William Little Vance (who died in 1931), and they lived in Cleveland, Ohio. Later, she moved to New York where she was director of the children's department of a bookstore and then an editor of children's books for a large publishing house. She has written many popular biographies for young people including: Ashes of Empire; Carlota and Maximilian of Mexico, Dark Eminence; Catherine de Medici and Her Children, Elizabeth Tudor, Sovereign Lady, Empress Josephine; From Martinique to Malmaison. MJA

VERMES, Hal G.

Journalist, author. During World War II, he was a public relations writer in the War Department. He has been a copy chief in advertising agencies, and has written many articles for magazines. Jean C. Vermes, his wife, has written The Girl's Book of Physical Fitness. He wrote The Boy's Book of Physical Fitness.

VERRAL, Charles Spain
Although he has been the author of many books, he has also written radio scripts and articles. He has organized model airplane meets and junior aviation clubs. Also, Mr. Verral has served as an advisor on several Chamber of Commerce aviation boards. The Verrals have lived in New York City. Juvenile titles include: Champion of the Court, Go! The Story of Outer Space, Jets, Wonderful World Series.

VIERECK, Phillip and Ellen
He attended Dartmouth, and Ellen Viereck studied at Vassar. After graduation, they served with the Alaska Native Service of the U.S. Bureau of Indian Affairs and spent two years with the King Islanders in Alaska. They have lived in North Bennington, Vermont where Mr. Viereck has taught history in the Bennington Junior High School, and Mrs. Viereck has been Acting-Director of the Nursery School of Bennington College. Their book for young people was Eskimo Island; A Story of the Bering Sea Hunters.

VIKSTEIN, Albert 1889-
Born in Sweden, he attended Norrland Folkschool and has received an honorary degree from the University of Upsala. He has been a newspaper editor and lecturer. At one time he traveled to Columbia in order to write articles on the wild life of the Andes for a Swedish magazine, Folket in Bild. In addition to novels, he has written verse, plays, and books on travel. He wrote Gunilla; An Arctic Adventure; translated by Gustaf Lannestock.

VILLIERS, Alan John 1903-
He was Captain of the 1957 "Mayflower" which came over to America from England. He has had experience sailing square-rigged sailing-ships because he

has sailed the "Joseph Conrad" on a trip around the world. This ship has been at Mystic Seaport, Connecticut, and the new "Mayflower" has been at Plymouth, Massachusetts. He wrote: The New Mayflower, Whalers of the Midnight Sun. CA-4

VINTON, Iris

She was born in West Point, Mississippi, but grew up in Texas. She has been a teacher in Texas in a small schoolhouse located near the beach. A student's father was an oyster fisherman and often he would bring a pail of oysters at noon for their lunch. Later, Iris Vinton lived in New York and has written for both magazines and newspapers. Juvenile titles include: Look Out For Pirates! Flying Ebony, The Story of Robert E. Lee, We Were There With Jean Lafitte at New Orleans.

VITTENGL, Morgan J.

He was born in Wilmington, Delaware, and received his A.B. and M.R.E. degrees from Maryknoll Seminary, and his M.S. degree from Columbia University. He has been Assistant Editor of Maryknoll magazine, and in Hong Kong was editor of Asia magazine. Also, Father Vittengl has taught journalism and English at the Maryknoll Seminary College in Glen Ellyn, Illinois. He wrote All Round Hong Kong.

VON HAGEN, Christine Sheilds

She has accompanied her husband, Victor von Hagen, on many trips of exploration. One trip was to the Amazon and the Galapagos Islands. Also, they have traveled to Panama, Honduras, and Guatemala. She wrote Pablo of Flower Mountain.

W

WABER, Bernard 1924-

He has been a layout artist for Life magazine. His first story was about a merry fish named Lorenzo. Mr. Waber and his family have lived in an apartment in Kew Gardens Hills, Long Island. He wrote: The House on East 88th Street, How to Go About

Laying an Egg. CA-3

WAGNER, Frederick
He was born in Philadelphia, and received his M.A. degree from Duke University. During the Korean conflict, he served in the Army. He has taught English at Duke and at the University of Oklahoma, and has been promotion manager for a publishing house. He and his wife Barbara Brady wrote Famous American Actors and Actresses. Also, he wrote: Famous Underwater Adventurers, Submarine Fighter of the American Revolution; The Story of David Bushnell.

WAGNER, Glenn A.
Writer, craftsman, lecturer, photographer, born in Buffalo, New York. He studied music at Fredonia State College, industrial arts at Oswego State Teachers College, and did graduate work at Harvard University. Mr. Wagner has been a teacher and a state supervisor of industrial arts. Also, he has written many articles on handicrafts for magazines. His hobbies have included model railroading, furniture building, and photography. He wrote: The Book of Hobby Craft, Things to Make Yourself.

WALDEN, Amelia Elizabeth 1909-
Born in New York City, she graduated from Columbia University and later studied at the American Academy of Dramatic Arts. She has taught dramatics in a high school in Connecticut. She married John William Harmon, and they lived in Westport, Connecticut. Her books for young people include: A Boy to Remember, Daystar, A Girl Called Hank, Victory for Jill, Where Is My Heart? CA-1, MJA

WALDMAN, Frank 1919-
Born in Chicago, Illinois, he attended Harvard University. He has been a screen writer in California, a sports writer on The Christian Science Monitor, and a sports director on a television station in North Carolina. Later, Mr. Waldman became a reporter on the Los Angeles Times. Juvenile titles include:

Bonus Pitcher, The Challenger, Delayed Steal, Lucky Bat Boy.

WALL, Gertrude Wallace
She spent part of her childhood on a farm in the state of New York, and later attended high school and college in California. She has been an elementary teacher in Los Angeles. She wrote: Gifts From the Forest, Gifts From the Grove.

WALLACE, John A. 1915-
He graduated from the University of Pennsylvania and has been associated with Beaver College (Economics Department) and Boston University (Director of Undergraduate Studies). Also, he has conducted programs of foreign study at Beaver College and Boston University. During World War II, Lieutenant Colonel "Jack" Wallace was a paratrooper. Mr. and Mrs. Wallace and their five daughters have lived in Putney, Vermont. He wrote: Getting to Know Egypt, U. A. R., Getting to Know the U. S. S. R.
CA-5/6

WALLACE, May Nickerson 1902-
Born in Willimantic, Connecticut and attended schools in Florida, Wisconsin, and Alberta, Canada. Later, she lived in Scarsdale, New York. Her stories have appeared in many magazines, but her first book for young people was the popular A Race for Bill. Also, she wrote: The Mystery of the Old House, The Plume Hunters Mystery.

WALLOWER, Lucille 1910-
Born in Waynesboro, Pennsylvania and attended the Philadelphia Museum Art School. She has been an art teacher and librarian. At one time, she was assistant children's librarian in the Harrisburg Public Library. In addition to writing books for children, she has compiled texts for use in the Pennsylvania schools. The Hippity Hopper, Or; Why There Are No Indians in Pennsylvania, The Morning Star, Old Satan; A Pennsylvania Folk Tale Retold and Pictured by Lucille Wallower.

WALSH, Frances

She was born and raised on a farm in Clark County, Missouri and graduated from Northeast Missouri State Teachers College. She has been a teacher both in Missouri and in Colorado. Also, she has taught children's literature at William Woods College, Northern Michigan College and at Northeast Missouri State Teachers College. She compiled That Eager Zest; First Discoveries in the Magic World of Books; An Anthology.

WALSH, Richard John 1886-1960

He was born in Kansas, and studied at Harvard University. He has been a reporter, a writer in the advertising field, and a magazine editor (including Collier's and Asia). Also, Mr. Walsh has been president of a publishing house, The John Day Company. He married the distinguished writer, Pearl S. Buck. He wrote Adventures and Discoveries of Marco Polo.

WALTERS, Marguerite

She was born in Bridgewater, Massachusetts, and graduated from Boston University. She has been associated with a Boston publishing company and has taught school. Marguerite Walters has been interested in painting, gardening, cooking and sewing. She and her husband have lived in New York City. She wrote Up and Down and All Around.

WALTNER, Willard and Elma

Brother and sister photographer and writer team. They have specialized in writing about handicrafts. They grew up on a farm in South Dakota where they received their early training in "making things." Mr. Waltner has taken the pictures which illustrated their craft articles, and Elma Waltner has often assisted him ("...holding parts of things at just the right angle..."). They wrote Wonders of Hobbycraft.

WARD, Lynd Kendall 1905-

Artist, author. He married author May McNeer

whom he met while attending Columbia University. When they were first married, they lived in Leipzig where Mr. Ward studied graphic arts. He has written many books with his wife, and he has been an outstanding illustrator. Mr. Ward has been equally proficient in water color, lithography, and oil. They have lived in Leonia, New Jersey. He illustrated May McNeer's The American Indian Story, Esther Forbes' America's Paul Revere. He was awarded the Caldecott Medal in 1953 for his book, The Biggest Bear. JBA-1, JBA-2

WARD, Nanda Weedon 1932-
Her parents were author May McNeer and illustrator-author Lynd Ward. She attended Colorado College where she met her husband Robert Haynes. While she was in college she wrote her first book, The Black Sombrero (with Lynd Ward). Mr. Haynes later did research work at London University. When they lived in London, Mrs. Haynes created the stories for Wellington and the Witch and Mister Mergatroid. They both wrote: Beau, Wellington and the Witch.

WARE, Leon 1909-
He graduated from Northwestern University. He has written for radio, magazines and motion pictures. Mr. Ware has served in the United States Navy. The Wares have lived in Arcadia, California. He wrote The Threatening Fog. CA-2

WARNER, Gertrude Chandler 1890-
She has been a teacher and a writer. In addition to creating books both for children and adults, she has written publicity for the National Cancer Society and the American Red Cross. Miss Warner has lived in Putnam, Connecticut. Her hobbies have included cooking, arranging flowers, and playing a pipe organ. Juvenile titles include: Blue Bay Mystery, The Boxcar Children, Mike's Mystery, Mystery Ranch. CA-4

WARREN, William Stephen 1882-
He attended the Academy of Fine Arts and the Art Institute in Chicago. He has enjoyed writing books about cowboys (he has been one in Colorado). Also, he has drawn cartoons for newspapers including the Chicago Tribune, Philadelphia Public Ledger, Buffalo Evening News, and the Cleveland News. Juvenile titles include: Golden Palomino, Headquarters Ranch, Ride West Into Danger.

WASHBURNE, Heluiz (Chandler) 1892-
This author has spent a great part of her life in child education and has become very familiar with the reading interests of boys and girls. She has been an extensive traveler and after a visit to the Vale of Kashmir in India, she wrote Rhamon, A Boy of Kashmir. Also, she has lived in Italy and Switzerland. She wrote: Children of the Blizzard (and Anauta), Little Elephant's Christmas, Little Elephant Visits the Farm.

WASSERSUG, Joseph D.
He graduated cum laude from Tufts Medical School. He has lived in Quincy, Massachusetts where he has practiced Internal Medicine. Also, he has been a teacher at the Quincy Hospital School of Nursing and at Tufts Medical School. He has written many articles for magazines, and has been a columnist for the New York Herald Tribune ("You're the Doctor"). He wrote Hospital With a Heart.

WATSON, Helen (Orr) 1892-
She was born in Minnesota and graduated from Carleton College. She married Colonel James T. Watson, Jr., and they have lived in Puerto Rico, South America, Japan, China, the Philippine Islands, and Europe. Later, she lived in Washington, D.C., where she has served as President of the Children's Book Guild. She wrote: Beano, Circus Dog, High Stepper, Trooper, U.S. Army Dog.

WATSON, Sara Ruth and Emily
Sisters, natives of Cleveland. Sara Ruth Watson

graduated from Flora Stone Mather College of Western Reserve University, and Emily graduated from the Cleveland Institute of Art. Emily Watson has worked in her late father's architectural and engineering firm, Wilbur Watson Associates. Sara Ruth Watson has been Associate Professor of English at Fenn College, Cleveland. They wrote Famous Engineers.

WEART, Edith Lucie
She studied chemistry at Oberlin College and has been a chemist at Mt. Sinai Hospital in Cleveland, Ohio. She has written many articles on medicine for the layman. She wrote: The Story of Your Brain and Nerves, The Story of Your Glands.

WEAVER, John D.
Born in Washington, D. C., he graduated from the College of William and Mary, and received his M. A. degree from George Washington University. He has been a newspaperman on the Kansas City Star, and married writer Harriett Sherwood. Mr. Weaver's first book for young people was Tad Lincoln: Mischief-Maker in the White House.

WEISGARD, Leonard 1916-
Born in New Haven, Connecticut, this illustrator-author attended Pratt Institute. Also, he felt that his work experience with many leading magazines provided him with a great deal of information. He has lived in Danbury, Connecticut. Numerous authors have had their books illustrated by Leonard Weisgard. His illustrations in The Little Island (written by Margaret Wise Brown), won the 1947 Caldecott Medal. Mr. Weisgard has written for children: Clean Pig, Mr. Peaceable Paints, Pelican Here, Pelican There, Silly Willy Nilly, Who Dreams of Cheese? JBA-2

WELLS, Robert L.
Native of Illinois, he has been a Lieutenant Colonel in the Army Signal Corps reserve. As he was collecting material for his book, Navigation in the Jet

Age, he was aboard a flight to the South Pole and made a close study of the work of the navigator during the trip. He has been an associate member of the American Rocket Society and has lived in New York City. Also, he wrote Early Warning; Electronic Guardians of Our Country by Robert Wells and C.R. Whiting.

WENNING, Elisabeth
Librarian-author. During the time that this author lived in Bavaria, Germany, and Austria she decided to write The Christmas Mouse. Also, she has written historical fiction for young people. She wrote The Christmas Mouse.

WERSTEIN, Irving
Born in Brooklyn, New York and attended New York University. During World War II, he served in the infantry and was field correspondent in Panama for Yank magazine. He has written radio and television scripts and has had articles published in magazines. A great deal of his writing has been about the Civil War. His titles for young people include: The Battle of Aachen, The Battle of Midway, Civil War Sailor, The Many Faces of the Civil War, A Nation Fights Back; The Depression and Its Aftermath.

WHEELER, Post 1869-
Diplomat-author. As one of America's first "career diplomats," he was assigned to Tokyo where he met and married author Hallie Erminie Rives. Also, he has been Minister to Albania, Special Ambassador to Paraguay, and editor of the New York Press. Juvenile titles include: Albanian Wonder Tales, Hathoo of the Elephants, Russian Wonder Tales.

WHITE, Anne Terry 1896-
She graduated from Brown University and received her Master's degree from Stanford. She has been both a teacher and social worker. She wrote Lost Worlds, an outstanding book on archaeology which has been translated into eight languages. For young

people she wrote: *All About Archaeology*, *All About Great Rivers of the World*, *First Men in the World*, *Prehistoric America*. MJA

WHITE, Bessie (Felstiner) 1892-
She has lived in Washington, D. C., and Brookline, Massachusetts. *A Bear Named Grumms* was her first book for boys and girls. Both the New York *Herald Tribune* and the *New York Times* included it in their lists of outstanding books. Also, she wrote *Carry On, Grumms!*

WHITE, Elwyn Brooks 1899-
Born in Mount Vernon, New York, he studied at Cornell University. He has been associated with the *New Yorker* magazine. E. B. White has written several books for adults and has contributed these titles for boys and girls: *Charlotte's Web*, *Stuart Little*. MJA

WHITE, Percival 1887- and Pauline (Arnold)
Husband-wife team, market researchers, authors. Mr. White received his M. A. degree from Harvard, and has done further study at M. I. T. Prior to her marriage, Pauline Arnold was head of Arnold Research Service which made surveys throughout the nation for manufacturers. In 1934 Mr. and Mrs. White started Market Research Corporation of America. In 1951 they sold their interests in the company and have devoted a lot of their time to writing. They wrote *Clothes and Cloth; America's Apparel Business*. CA-1

WHITE, Robb 1909-
Born in the Philippine Islands, the son of a missionary. He attended the Naval Academy at Annapolis. During World War II, he served in the Navy assigned to the Pacific fleet. He has lived in Malibu, California. His books of adventure include: *Deep Danger*, *Flight Deck*, *Secret Sea*, *Up Periscope* (which was made into a movie). CA-2, JBA-2

WHITNEY, Leon Fradley 1894-
Veterinarian, author. His father was Dr. George D. Whitney, also a veterinarian. His personal bloodhounds, raccoons, and coonhounds have been kept at the Whitney Veterinary Clinic in Orange, Connecticut. His chief interest has been breeding bloodhounds. He wrote That Useless Hound.

WHITNEY, Phyllis Ayame 1903-
Librarian, instructor, author. Her books have been very popular with young people. She once said: "Some grownups can't remember what it was like to be young. But for me the problems of my growing up years are as vivid as ever in my mind." She was born in Yokohama, Japan, and came to the United States when she was fifteen. She has been a prize winner in the Youth Today Contests (for her book, Willow Hill,) a book reviewer, and has taught a class in writing for young people at New York University. Her many titles include: Creole Holiday, The Fire and the Gold, The Highest Dream, Mystery of the Hidden Hand. CA-4, JBA-2

WIBBERLEY, Leonard Patrick O'Connor 1915-
Newspaperman-author. His pseudonym is Patrick O'Connor. This Irish author started his career as a newspaper reporter in London, became an editor in Trinidad, foreign correspondent in New York, and columnist on the Los Angeles Times. Juvenile titles include: The Ballad of the Pilgrim Cat, Black Tiger at Indianapolis, Coronation Book; The Dramatic Story in History and Legend, The Epics of Everest, Five-Dollar Watch Mystery. MJA

WIER, Ester
She was born in Seattle, Washington, and attended schools in Oklahoma and California. She married an American naval officer Henry Robert Wier in Hankow, China. After his retirement from the Navy, they lived in Virginia where he taught at the Virginia Military Institute. Mrs. Wier has conducted a radio program for women, has worked with children and teen-agers, and has been active in women's

clubs. She wrote Gift of the Mountains, Loner.

WIESE, Kurt 1887-
Illustrator, author, born in Minden, Germany. He has lived in China, Australia, and South America. In 1927 he made his home in the United States. Mr. Wiese has worked and lived in a house near the Delaware River in New Jersey. Boys and girls have often visited his studio in order to watch him work. He has illustrated many books, but he wrote and illustrated: Cunning Turtle, The Dog, the Fox, and the Fleas, Groundhog and His Shadow, Happy Easter. JBA-1, JBA-2

WILBER, Donald N. 1907-
Artist, architect, author. He obtained his Ph.D. degree from Princeton University, and has traveled throughout the Arab countries, Iran, Afghanistan, Pakistan, India, and Ceylon. He has been an artist associated with the University of Chicago at Luxor, Egypt, an architect on archaeological explorations at Olynthus, Corinth, and Antioch. Also, he has been on the staff of the Asia Institute, New York City, as an Associate Professor. He wrote Land and People of Ceylon. CA-5/6

WILCOX, Don
Born in Lucas, Kansas, and graduated from the University of Kansas. He has taught in high schools, at the Chicago campus of Northwestern University, and at the University of Kansas. Also, he has written scripts for television and articles for Argosy and Jack and Jill. He based his portrayal of the coach in Basketball Star on the great Kansas coach, Phog Allen. Also, he wrote Joe Sunpool.

WILDER, Laura (Ingalls) 1867-1957
She wrote the story of her own life in her popular "Little House" books. She was born in a log cabin on the edge of the Big Woods of Wisconsin and traveled West by covered wagon with her family. She married Almanzo Wilder, and they had a daughter Rose, who became a novelist (Rose Wilder Lane).

Mrs. Wilder lived on a farm in Missouri until her death at the age of ninety. In 1954 the Children's Library Association established the "Laura Ingalls Wilder Award" to be given for "a lasting contribution to literature for children..." Titles in the "Little House" series include: By the Shores of Silver Lake, Little House in the Big Woods, Little Town on the Prairie, These Happy Golden Years. JBA-2

WILKIE, Katharine Elliott 1904-
She was born in Lexington, Kentucky and attended the University of Kentucky where she met her husband Raymond. She has been a seventh grade teacher at Lafayette Junior High School. Her first book for teen-agers was John Sevier: Son of Tennessee. Juvenile titles include: Daniel Boone: Taming the Wilds, Mary Todd Lincoln, Girl of the Bluegrass. With Elizabeth R. Moseley, she wrote Father of the Constitution: James Madison.

WILKINS, Hugh Percival 1896-
Engineer, civil servant, author, born in Carmarthen, South Wales. He has been a recipient of an honorary Ph. D. degree, and a Fellow of the Royal Astronomical Society. He has lectured in adult education sponsored by Oxford University, and has been Director of the Lunar Section of the British Astronomical Association. He wrote Clouds, Rings and Crocodiles; By Spaceship Round the Planets.

WILLIAMS, Edgar
A native of Lansdale, Pennsylvania, he graduated from West Chester State Teachers College. Newspapers, radio, and sports, have claimed much of his time. Edgar Williams has been a feature writer on the Sunday magazine, Today, of the Philadelphia Inquirer. His stories have been published in The Saturday Evening Post, Coronet, Boys' Life, and other leading magazines. Also, he has been a member of the Philadelphia Basketball Writers Association. He collaborated with Dave Zinkoff to write Around the World With the Harlem Globetrotters.

WILLIAMS, Eric Ernest 1911-
Born in London. During World War II, he served in a Bomber Squadron of the Royal Air Force. After being shot down over Germany, he was taken prisoner. Later, he escaped and was assigned to the American Forces in the Philippines. It was during his voyage home that he wrote a great deal of his book, The Wooden Horse. He has lived in South Devon, England. He wrote The Tunnel.

WILLIAMS, Garth Montgomery 1912-
Artist-author, born in New York, the son of artists. He attended the City of London School, Westminster Art School and the Royal College of Art. The first children's (adults also have enjoyed it) book which he illustrated was E.B. White's Stuart Little. An unusually distinguished combination was Mr. Williams' illustrations for Laura Ingalls Wilder's books (the "Little House" series). He wrote and illustrated: The Adventures of Benjamin Pink, Rabbits' Wedding. MJA

WILLIAMS, Jay 1914-
Born in Buffalo, New York and attended the University of Pennsylvania. During World War II, he served in the Infantry. In addition to writing books for young people, he has had poems and articles published in magazines. His hobby has been building ship models. The Williams family (a wife and two children) have lived in Redding, Connecticut where Mr. Williams has participated in many civic activities. Juvenile titles include: Battle for the Atlantic, Caesar Augustus, Danny Dunn and the Anti-Gravity Paint (with Raymond Abrashkin), Danny Dunn, Time Traveler (with Raymond Abrashkin). CA-2

WILLIAMS, Lou
She has been on the staff of the Geology Department of Stephens College and on the Physical Sciences Staff of the College of the University of Chicago. Also, she was managing editor of the Journal of Geology. Lou Williams has been very active in the

Girl Scouts as she was Girl Scout National Camp Counselor on Nature Study for many years. She wrote *Weather Handbook*.

WILLIAMSON, Margaret 1924-
She spent her childhood on a farm in Quebec and later graduated from McGill University. She majored in zoology, and then studied art following graduation from college. She has lived in a suburb of Detroit, Michigan. Juvenile titles include: *First Book of Birds*, *First Book of Bugs*, *First Book of Mammals*.

WILLIS, Priscilla D.
She has lived near Chicago, Illinois, but has spent part of her time on a plantation in Georgia and on a farm in Indiana. The Willis family have been proud owners of horses (including a thoroughbred colt from Ireland), and have enjoyed all events concerning horses. She wrote: *Alfred and the Saint*, *The Race Between the Flags*.

WILLIS, Robert J.
As a boy in upstate New York, one of the most exciting experiences of his life was visiting a harness-race track near his home. His favorite horse was a black one, and he helped the trainer care for him. Later, he studied art at Pratt Institute, but he interrupted his studies to join the Army. He served with the Tenth Mountain Infantry Division in Italy. He has lived with his wife and four children in Woodland Hills, California. He wrote: *Caesar's Blue Ribbon*, *Model A Mule*.

WILLSON, Dixie
She was born in Mason City, Iowa. Following graduation from college, she joined a touring theatrical company. She enjoyed traveling, but writing became her main interest. Many of her stories were included in O'Brien's "best of the year." One story was *God Gave Me Twenty Cents* which opened at the Paramount Theater in New York. She married Charles Hayden. Her brothers were Cedric Willson,

a research engineer, and Meredith Willson, a composer-conductor. She wrote Mystery in Spangles.

WILSON, Eleanore (Hubbard)
Born in Baltimore, Maryland, and studied at the Chicago Art Institute and the Art Students League. Also, she attended an art school in Michigan where she met her husband Ronald Lee Wilson. The Wilsons have lived in New York City. She wrote: The Secret Three, Treasures Three.

WILSON, Hazel (Hutchins) 1898-
Native of Maine, librarian, author, teacher. She attended Bates College in Maine. In 1956 Bates awarded her an honorary degree of Master of Arts. Several of her stories have a Maine background including The Owen Boys and His Indian Brother. Juvenile titles include: Herbert, Herbert Again, Jerry's Charge Account, The Seine, River of Paris. CA-4

WILSON, Holly
She was born in Duluth, Minnesota, and studied at the University of Michigan. When she was in college, her novel, The King Pin, received an award in the Avery and Julie Hopwoods Awards Contest. Also, while she was a student at the University, she married Dr. Frederic W. Wilson. Due to Dr. Wilson's work with the Veterans Administration, they have lived in Kansas and Pennsylvania. Juvenile titles include: Always Anne, Maggie of Barnaby Bay, Snowbound in Hidden Valley.

WILSON, Ruth
Resident of Philadelphia, Pennsylvania. She has written books and articles for magazines, but her favorite literary contribution was a poem written to her husband ("The Quiet Man") and purchased by the New York Times. She has been interested in cooking (her recipes have won prizes), music (Mozart), and painting (her work has been exhibited at the Philadelphia Art Alliance). She wrote Outdoor Wonderland.

WINTER, Ginny Linville 1925-
Commercial artist, author. She grew up in Indiana, and has worked in a Chicago advertising agency. She has attended the Art Institute, the American Academy, and the Institute of Design. Mrs. Winter has been very interested in the ballet, and has attended many performances in Chicago. She wrote The Ballet Book. CA-4

WINTER, William
He has been very interested in the construction of model airplanes, and at one time, he had his own model airplane hobby shop. He has written articles about model airplanes for many magazines. Also, Mr. Winter has been associate editor of Air Trails magazine. He wrote Model Aircraft Handbook.

WINWAR, Frances 1900-
Her name was Francesca Vinciguerra in the town of Taormina, Sicily, where she was born. She attended Hunter College, City College of New York, and Columbia University. She has had her poems published in magazines, and she has been a book reviewer for the New York World. One of her biographies was awarded the Atlantic Monthly Non-fiction Prize. Juvenile titles include: Elizabeth; the Romantic Story of Elizabeth Barrett Browning, Land of the Italian people, Napoleon and the Battle of Waterloo.

WIRT, Mildred (Augustine) 1905-
She has always enjoyed writing, and at the age of twelve, she won a silver medal from St. Nicholas. Mildred Wirt has been a courthouse reporter for the Toledo Times. Also, she has written serials and mystery stories for magazines. She wrote Pirate Brig.

WISE, William
He was born in New York and attended Yale University. During the war, he was in the military police, and assisted in the operation of prisoner of war camps. After the war, he returned to Yale where

he was an editor of the Yale Literary Magazine. He has written short stories and a volume of children's poems. Juvenile titles include: Alexander Hamilton, The Cowboy Surprise, Silversmith of Old New York: Myer Myers.

WISE, Winifred E.
She graduated cum laude from the University of Wisconsin. She has been a staff editor of Compton's Pictured Encyclopedia, and an advertising executive. She married mystery writer Stuart Palmer and they have lived in Laguna Beach, California. She wrote Lincoln's Secret Weapon.

WISSMANN, Ruth H.
She was born in Lima, Ohio. As she was growing up, her family began moving west. They lived in Colorado, Arizona, and settled in Los Angeles, California. She interrupted college in order to dance in motion picture musicals. After her marriage, she painted and began writing. She was awarded the Calling All Girls - Dodd, Mead Prize Competition for her novel, The Summer Ballet Mystery.

WITHERS, Carl
Born in the Ozark country, in similar surroundings to those described in his book, Plainville, U.S.A. He has been interested in folklore and social anthropology for many years, and has done research work on these subjects in Cuba, the United States, Venezuela, and Brazil. He has been a Fellow of the American Anthropological Association and has held membership in the American Folklore Society. He compiled: A Rocket in My Pocket, the Rhymes and Chants of Young Americans. With Benjamin A. Botkin he wrote Illustrated Book of American Folklore; Stories, Legends, Tall Tales, Riddles, and Rhymes.

WITTON, Dorothy
Born in Michigan, the daughter of a minister. She attended the University of Michigan, and the New School for Social Research in New York. She married a Mexican forestry engineer, Luis Romero, and

became a naturalized Mexican citizen. She has particularly enjoyed writing Mexican stories for teenagers because "she hopes that in those she may have contributed a little to the understanding between young people of two nations who have so much to offer each other." She wrote: Crossroads for Chela, Treasure of Acapulco.

WITTY, Paul Andrew 1898-
Professor, author, born in Terre Haute, Indiana. He graduated from Indiana State Teachers' College, and received his M.A. degree from Columbia University. He has been a Professor on the staff of the University of Kansas, and Professor of Education and Director of the Psycho-Educational Clinic at Northwestern University. During World War II, he served in the United States Army. He has been a member of the board of directors of the National Society for the Study of Education and has been President of the International Council for the Improvement of Reading. In addition to writing many readers, including the "Reading for Interest" series, he wrote True Book of Freedom and Our U.S. Family.

WOHLRABE, Raymond A. 1900-
Native of Wisconsin, he graduated from the University of Washington, and continued his education at the University of Southern California and Purdue University. He has been a teacher on the staff of the West Seattle High School in Seattle, Washington. During his summer vacations, he has traveled extensively throughout the world. With Werner E. Krusch, he wrote: The Key to Vienna, Land and People of Austria, The Land and People of Denmark. CA-4

WOLCOTT, Carolyn Muller
Prior to her marriage, she was a director of children's work in churches in Pennsylvania. After her marriage to Dr. Leonard T. Wolcott, she lived in England. He served a church in Oxford, and she continued her work in the children's program there.

Later, the Wolcotts lived in Nashville, Tennessee, where Dr. Wolcott has been head of the Department of Missions at Scarritt College. As Carolyn E. Muller, she wrote God Cares For Me, God Planned It That Way. Jesus Goes to the Market Place can be found in libraries under the name, Carolyn Muller Wolcott.

WOLFE, Louis 1905-
He was born in Bound Brook, New Jersey, and graduated from Rutgers University. He did graduate work in history at New York University, College of the City of New York, New School for Social Research, and Columbia University. He taught for many years in the New York City public schools, and has served with the Bureau of Curriculum Research of the Board of Education in New York City. He wrote: Indians Courageous, Let's Go To a Weather Station, Let's Go To the Louisiana Purchase. CA-5/6

WOLFERT, Jerry
Newspaperman and author. During World War II, he served as an army combat correspondent in Europe. He has been a newspaperman in Buffalo, New York, a seaman, and a wild animal collector in West Africa. After collecting information and doing research at the Buffalo Historical Society, Old Fort Erie, Ontario, Fort Niagara, and Quebec, he wrote: Brother of the Wind; A Story of the Niagara Frontier.

WOLLHEIM, Donald A. 1914-
Science fiction writer. In this space age boys and girls have been fortunate to find this author who has endeavored to fulfil their requests for science fiction. He has lived in New York City all of his life, and has been an editor since 1940. In 1952 he became an editor of paperbacks (Ace Books). He wrote: One Against the Moon, Secret of the Ninth Planet (Cecil Matschat, ed.; Carl Carmer, Consulting ed.). CA-4

WOOD, Laura Newbold 1911-
Born in St. Louis, Missouri, and educated in a private school there. She has been a free-lance writer, and has done editorial work. She married a lawyer and has lived in Washington. She wrote: Raymond L. Ditmars; His Exciting Career With Reptiles, Animals and Insects, Walter Reed; Doctor in Uniform.

WOODWARD, Hildegard 1898-
Born in Worcester, Massachusetts. She studied at the School of Museum of Fine Arts in Boston. She has painted in Mexico, Europe, and Haiti, and many of her paintings have been exhibited throughout the United States. After observing the construction of a house near her home in Connecticut, she wrote the charming and informative book, The House on Grandfather's Hill. Also, she wrote Time Was. CA-5/6

WOODY, Regina Llewellyn (Jones) 1894-
She was born in Chestnut Hill, Massachusetts. When she was a little girl, she used to ride and train horses. Later, she rode cross-country in England. Since she once danced professionally, she has been very interested in the dance, an art which Mrs. Woody described as one which knows no race, creed, or language barrier. She has contributed articles to many magazines including Reader's Digest, Parents' Magazine, and Harper's Bazaar. Also, she has been editor of the "Young Dancer" section of Dance Magazine. She married a physician, Dr. McIver Woody. She wrote: Dancing for Joy, Starlight, Young Dancer's Career Book. CA-5/6, MJA

WOOLLEY, Catherine 1904-
Born in Chicago, Illinois, she has lived in Passaic, New Jersey. This author's pseudonym is Jane Thayer (her grandmother's name). She attended Barnard College and graduated from the University of California at Los Angeles. She has worked in the advertising field, and has done sales promotion and editorial work. Also, she has written articles for magazines. Included in her many children's books are: Andy and His Fine Friends, The Blue-

berry Pie-Elf, Catherine Leonard Calling, The Chicken in the Tunnel, David's Hundred Dollars, Ginnie and Geneva. CA-2, MJA

WOOLSEY, Janette 1904-
Librarian, author. She graduated from Middlebury College, Pratt Institute, and Columbia University. She has been a children's librarian at Ohio University, and later, at the Martin Memorial Library in York, Pennsylvania. With Elizabeth Hough Sechrist, she wrote: It's Time for Brotherhood, It's Time for Christmas, It's Time for Easter, It's Time for Thanksgiving, It's Time to Give a Play; New Plays For All Occasions. CA-4

WORCESTER, Donald Emmet 1915-
He was born in Tempe, Arizona, and grew up on ranches there and in California. At the age of twelve, he and his brother captured their first wild horse. He studied at the University of Arizona, Bard College, Annandale-on-Hudson, New York, and the University of California. He has been head of the History Department at the University of Florida. His books include: John Paul Jones: Soldier of the Sea, Lone Hunter's First Buffalo Hunt, War Pony. CA-2

WORLINE, Bonnie Bess
Teacher, author, born in El Dorado, Kansas. She graduated from the University of Chicago. She married a minister, Irvill Courtner King, and has been a Director of Religious Education. Also, she has been a teacher at Endicott College in Beverly, Massachusetts, at Gorham State Teachers College in Gorham, Maine, and at the University of Kansas. She wrote Sod House Adventure for boys and girls.

WRIGHT, Dare
Photographer, author, born in Canada. She began her career as a photographer's fashion model, and later became a well-known free-lance photographer. Her photographs have appeared in Vogue and Harper's Bazaar. Also, editorial photography by Miss Wright

has been seen in Town and Country and Good Housekeeping. Her books include: The Doll and the Kitten, Date With London, The Little One, Lonely Doll.

WYATT, Edgar
This author has lived in Tucson, Arizona, and has made a thorough study of the Apache country. His biographies for young people have been based on intensive research into old records and obscure sources. He wrote: Cochise, Apache Warrior and Statesman, Geronimo, the Last Apache War Chief.

WYATT, Geraldine (Tolman) 1907-
She was born at Hope, Kansas. At sixteen, she was left on her own, but she finished high school, attended a business college, and studied music. Also, she has taken extension courses on creative writing from the University of Missouri. She married a lawyer, Roy A. Wyatt, who encouraged her to write. She wrote: Sun Eagle, Wronghand.

WYATT, Isabel
She was born in South Staffordshire, England. During World War II, she served as a volunteer caseworker with child refugees in southwest England. Miss Waytt has been Co-Director of Studies at Hawkwood College in Gloucestershire. She wrote The Golden Stag, and Other Folk Tales From India; Selected and Retold by Isabel Wyatt.

WYLER, Rose
She has been a science teacher, and has written for films, radio, and magazines. She married Gerald Ames who has written in collaboration with her. They have lived in New York City where Rose Wyler claimed that the roof of their apartment house has been used by her family as both a weather station and an astronomy observatory. Juvenile titles include: Electricity Comes to Us, The First Book of Science Experiments, First Book of Weather, Golden Picture Book of Science.

WYMER, Norman 1911-
He was born in England and received his education at Charterhouse. During the war, the British Ministry of Information asked him to write articles on the British way of life for newspapers in America. Also, he has written for radio and television. The Wymers have lived in Sussex near South Downs. He wrote Gilbert and Sullivan.

WYNDHAM, Lee 1912-
In the words of Lee Wyndham: "there's no business like book business for me." She was educated here and abroad, and has studied oil painting and music. She has reviewed books and written columns for newspapers, and has lectured on books for young people. Also, she has worked in a book shop in Morristown, New Jersey, which has afforded her the opportunity to meet "the final judges of books - the folks who buy and read them." She wrote Thanksgiving. MJA

Y

YATES, Brock Wendel
Sports-car enthusiast, reporter, author, born in Buffalo, New York. He graduated from Hobart College in Geneva, New York. He has served in the Navy as communications officer aboard a destroyer escort. As the driver of a Sadler Formula Junior racing car, he has driven in races at Watkins Glen and Dunkirk, New York, and at Harwood Acres in Ontario, Canada. Mr. Yates, in collaboration with his father, Raymond F. Yates, wrote Sport and Racing Cars. Also, he wrote: Destroyers and Destroyermen; the Story of Our "Tin-Can" Navy, Famous Indianapolis Cars and Drivers, The Indianapolis 500; the Story of the Motor Speedway.

YATES, Elizabeth 1905-
Born in Buffalo, New York, she won the Newbery Award in 1951 for her book, Amos Fortune, Free Man. She married William McGreal and has lived in Peterborough, New Hampshire. She has listed

her interests as: gardening, cooking, hooking rugs, raising Scotties, and climbing mountains. She has taught at the Writers Conference of the University of New Hampshire in the summers. She wrote: Around the Year in Iceland, Children of the Bible, Patterns On the Wall. CA-2, JBA-2

YATES, Raymond Francis 1895-
Editor, prolific writer, born in Lockport, New York. As a student at Niagara Falls High School, he wrote articles for technical and scientific journals. He has been managing editor of Popular Science Monthly, and editor of Popular Radio and Everyday Mechanics. Also, he has been on the staff of the New York Herald Tribune. His son Brock also became an author. He wrote: Atomic Experiments for Boys, Boy and a Battery, Boys' Book of Magnetism, Boys' Book of Model Railroading. MJA

YOST, Edna 1889-
She received her A.B. and Litt.D. degrees from Allegheny College. Miss Yost has contributed to the Dictionary of American Biography, Encyclopaedia Brittanica, and World Book Encyclopedia. Also, she has written articles for Scribners, Harpers, Forum, Century, and North American Review. She has lived in New York City. Juvenile titles include: Famous American Pioneering Women, Modern American Engineers, Modern Americans in Science and Technology. CA-2

YOUNG, Bob 1916- and Jan 1919-
California husband-wife team. He was born in Chico, and she was born in Lancaster, California. They found that they both enjoyed writing while they were students at the University of California at Los Angeles. Later, Mr. Young transferred and graduated from the University of Nevada. Their marriage followed his graduation. During World War II, Bob Young served in the Army. They have farmed in the Coachella Valley, and Bob has published and edited his own paper, the San Gabriel Sun. They wrote: Across the Tracks, One Small Voice. CA-5/6

YOUNG, Ella 1867-1956
Born in Ireland, she graduated from the Royal University (now part of the National University). She came to the United States to live, and lectured on folklore and became known as a "master storyteller." Later, she held the Phelan Memorial Lectureship of Celtic Mythology at the University of California at Berkeley. She wrote: The Tangle-Coated Horse and Other Tales, Episodes From the Fionn Saga, The Unicorn With Silver Shoes. JBA-1, JBA-2

YOUNG, John Richard
He graduated from Marquette University, and has lived in Milwaukee, Wisconsin. His father was a rancher in Wisconsin, and the author grew up loving horses. He once said that his "earliest memory is of trying to ride the family Irish terrier." He has been particularly interested in the Arabian horse. He wrote: Arizona Cutting Horse, Olympic Horseman.

YOUNG, Miriam
She has been a fashion artist, and has written articles for Story Parade, Better Homes and Gardens, Humpty Dumpty, and Mademoiselle. She married a commercial artist, Walter Young, and they have lived in Goldensbridge, New York. Mrs. Young has been interested in reading, swimming, writing, and amateur dramatics. She wrote Please Don't Feed Horace.

YOUNG, Stanley 1906-
Playwright, publisher, author. He has written plays which have been produced on Broadway. Mr. Young married an author, Nancy Wilson Ross, and they have lived in Old Westbury, Long Island. He wrote Tippecanoe and Tyler, Too!

Z

ZAFFO, George J.
Born in Bridgeport, Connecticut. He attended Pratt

Institute, and once worked as an apprentice to Norman Rockwell. During the war, he served in the Signal Corps. George and Dorothy Zaffo have four children, and they have lived in Tuckahoe, New York. He has said that he has often tried out his ideas on his family first. He has been interested in hunting and model railroads. Juvenile titles include: Big Book of Real Trains, Big Book of Real Trucks, Building Your Super Highways, Your Police.

ZAIDENBERG, Arthur 1903-
Artist-author. He has taught drawing at New York University. His work has been on exhitition at the Metropolitan Museum of Art in New York. His illustrations in books have received praise and acclaim. Juvenile titles include: Drawing the Human Figure in Action, How to Draw Dogs, Cats and Horses, How to Draw Farm Animals, Your Child is an Artist.

ZARCHY, Harry 1912-
His pseudonym is Roger Lewis. Author, illustrator, New Yorker. He studied at New York University and Pratt Institute. He grew up in a family that was usually making something. "There was always something going on - being built, or repaired, or just plain investigated." He taught fine arts in a high school at Brooklyn, New York. In addition to his work in crafts, he has enjoyed taking hunting and fishing trips. Harry Zarchy has combined these interests as he has often served as a camp counselor of arts and crafts. Juvenile titles include: Ceramics, Creative Hobbies, Let's Fish; a Guide to Fresh and Salt Water, Let's Go Boating. CA-4, MJA.

ZAREM, Lewis
He received his B.A. degree from the University of Wisconsin. During World War II, he served in the Air Force. He has worked at the Wright-Patterson Air Force Base, Ohio, and during his free time (nights and weekends) has written books and articles on science. He has lived in Dayton, Ohio. He

wrote: New Dimensions of Flight, New Era of Flight; Aeronautics Simplified (with Robert H. Maltby).

ZIM, Herbert Spencer 1909-
Born in New York City. He received his B.S., M.A., and Ph.D. degrees from Columbia University. He has been head of the Science Department at the Ethical Culture Schools in New York, and a professor at the University of Illinois. His books on science, including the renowned Golden Nature Guides, have proven to be invaluable aids for boys and girls working on school assignments and hobbies. He has been Editor of Our Wonderful World, Educational Director at Artists and Writers Press, and Educational Consultant for the United States Fish and Wildlife Service. He married Sonia Bleeker who has written many books on the American Indian. Juvenile titles include: Alligators and Crocodiles, Big Cats, Codes and Secret Writing, Comets, Dinosaurs, Your Food and You. JBA-2

ZINER, Feenie 1921-
She was instrumental in organizing the "Trick or Treat for UNICEF" program in Evanston, Illinois. Her book was the result of these efforts. She has felt that children of all races "can play happily together." Feenie Ziner and her family have lived in Dobbs Ferry, New York. Juvenile titles include: Counting Carnival by Feenie Ziner and Paul Galdone, True Book of Time by Feenie Ziner and Elizabeth Thompson. CA-3

ZINKOFF, Dave
Sports announcer, author, he graduated from Temple University. While he was a student there, he received his start as a sports announcer by broadcasting the first Sugar Bowl Game. Later, as a sports announcer, Dave Zinkoff was known as the "Voice of Philadelphia." He has been tour secretary of the famous Harlem Globetrotters and has organized shows for Army hospitals. During World War II, he was with the Special Services, and was decorated for a

Icelandic youth sports program. Mr. Zinkoff collaborated with Edgar Williams to write Around the World With the Harlem Globetrotters.

ZION, Gene 1913-
Author, free-lance art director, born in New York City. He graduated from Pratt Institute, and studied at the New School in New York. While he was working for the Conde Nast Publications, he met his wife, illustrator Margaret Bloy Graham. They have collaborated on many picture books for boys and girls, including: All Falling Down, Dear Garbage Man, Harry and the Lady Next Door, Harry the Dirty Dog, Plant Sitter. MJA.

ZIRBES, Laura
Educator, author. She has been a university professor for many years, and was the Ohio State Consultant in Elementary Education. Also, the National Woman's Press Club bestowed on Dr. Zirbes the National Award as Woman of the Year (1948) in Education. She has written many articles for educational journals, and has lived in Columbus, Ohio. She wrote How Many Bears?

ZOLOTOW, Charlotte (Shapiro) 1915-
Born in Norfolk, Virginia. She attended the University of Wisconsin where she met her husband, writer Maurice Zolotow. She has lived in Detroit, Boston, and California; however, after her marriage, she lived in New York City. She has been a reader and editorial assistant in the Children's Book Department of a publishing house in New York City. Juvenile titles include: Big Brother, Mr. Rabbit and the Lovely Present, Over and Over, The White Marble. CA-5/6, MJA